NEW
ESSAYS
ON
Performance
Practice

This work first appeared as part of the
UMI Research Press series **Studies in Musicology**
George J. Buelow, Editor

NEW
ESSAYS
ON
Performance
Practice

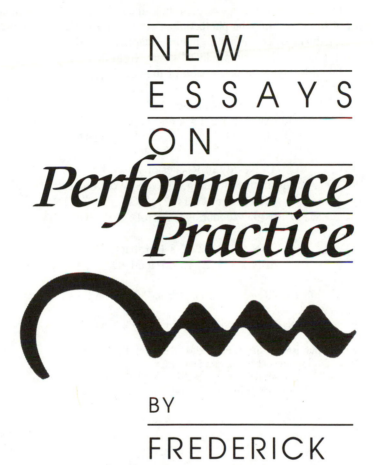

BY
FREDERICK
NEUMANN

UNIVERSITY OF ROCHESTER PRESS

First published 1989
Reissued in hardback and paperback
by the University of Rochester Press 1992

University of Rochester Press
200 Administration Building, University of Rochester
Rochester NY 14627, USA
and at PO Box 9, Woodbridge, Suffolk IP12 3DF, UK

ISBN 1 878822 12 8 Hardback
ISBN 1 878822 13 6 Paperback

Library of Congress Cataloging-in-Publication Data
Neumann, Frederick.
New essays on performance practice / by Frederick Neuman.
    p.   cm.
Originally published: Ann Arbor : UMI Research Press, 1989.
Includes bibliographical references and index.
ISBN 1–878822–12–8 (HBK) : — ISBN 1–878822–13–6 (PBK) :
1. Performance practice (Music)   2. Embellishment (Music)
I. Title.
[ML457.N45   1992]
781.46 — dc20   92-4081

British Library Cataloguing in Publication Data
Neumann, Frederick
    New Essays on Performance Practice.
    I. Title
    781.247
    ISBN 1–878822–12–8
    ISBN 1–878822–13–6 pbk

This publication is printed on acid-free paper
Printed in the United States of America

For
George J. Buelow
in friendship and gratitude

Contents

Preface

The gratifying reception accorded my *Essays in Performance Practice* published in 1982 by the UMI Research Press, prompted George J. Buelow, the editor of the Music series, and the acquisitions editor to suggest that I prepare these *New Essays on Performance Practice*.

The present volume contains major *new* essays specifically written for the occasion, along with reprints of articles, most of them revised, that have appeared in various publications since 1982. The two introductory essays dealing with the early music movement are new, as are the second of the two essays on Haydn's ornaments, and the essay (no. 10) on some problems of Mozart interpretation (written in answer to Robert Levin's criticism). The first of the Haydn essays will also be new to practically all readers for it is my English translation of a paper presented in German at the International Haydn Conference in Vienna in 1982.

Readers familiar with some of my work will not be surprised to find that these new essays also question many orthodox beliefs of the performance practice tradition. They also take a critical view of some exaggerations of the early music movement.

To give a few examples, I contend that in the case of binary-ternary conflicts there are contexts where assimilation is in order, and others where conflict was intended; that a recent attempt to reclaim international validity for the French *notes inégales* was not successful, and that the same holds true for an effort to salvage a small fraction of the French overture style; that many a Haydn ornament preceded the beat and that his trills started preferably on the main note; that the idea of nonvibrato singing and playing is historically unfounded; that the widely advocated and widely practiced literal interpretation of ornament symbols subverts the very function of ornaments. And as to the authenticists, I question their dogma that early music performed on period instruments, nonvibrato, in lower pitch and in would-be original *Besetzung* is, *ipso facto,* musically superior to a modern performance, however true the latter may be to the style and spirit of the work. I know such doubts are unfashionable today and in the eyes of the authenticists tantamount to heresy. But they need to be expressed because the credo of the authenticists may be an article of faith to them, but a self-evident truth it is not and therefore it is permissible, indeed necessary, to test its validity by probing questions.

Only one essay in the volume does not deal with performance practice: chapter 14 on Bach. It was included because it too has a background of controversy: at issue here are the two important subjects of Bach's style during the years 1730–45 and the doubtful authorship of the Goldberg Variations Aria.

Here I wish to express my warmest thanks to George J. Buelow for valuable editorial help and for his gratifying initiative, to Barbara Anderson for the splendid preparation of the index, and finally to all the publishers or editors who so kindly gave permission to reprint essays that had come out under their copyright.

Part One

Introduction

1

The Rise of the Early Music Movement

What is now commonly known as the "early music movement" has become a powerful presence on our musical scene. It is visible—and audible—in a multitude of forms. One is the large and ever-growing number of organizations devoted exclusively to the performance of music of the more or less distant past. These groups vary in character and in their focus on specific time spans and musical forms, but they generally aim at "authenticity" of performance, use historical instruments, either antiques or reproductions, and apply what they consider to be historically correct techniques.

Other than these professional groups, there are organizations devoted to the same goal in numerous universities, colleges, schools of music, and conservatories in the United States, England, Germany, Holland, and Belgium. By now, at least in this country, the resident string quartet, for long a status symbol at many a university, has been overshadowed by groups with a name of antique flair such as *collegium musicum* that, like the professional groups, are devoted to "authentic" performance of "early music." As a further sign of the powerful presence of the movement we find that of new recordings of pre-1800 music, as many as maybe three-fourths originate from the "authentic" organizations.

The movement moreover reveals its dynamism by its quasi-imperialistic expansion into ever new eras of musical history, which raises the question: how early is "early music"? Some twenty years ago, or thereabouts, the term referred to music before 1750. Since then the movement has reached out to the end of the eighteenth century to encompass Mozart and Haydn; and soon after this conquest, it invaded the nineteenth century, first Beethoven, Schubert, Schumann, Chopin, Berlioz, and the end of this expansion is not yet in sight.

Only persons old enough to have lived through both World Wars can fully appreciate the enormity of the upheaval that the early music movement has brought about, an upheaval that can truly be called a revolution in the history of musical performance. We have to do here with a sociological and cultural phenomenon of great complexity, and what I am trying to offer in this first introductory chapter is only a rough sketch of the various elements that contributed to the movement, and a summary chronicle of its major landmarks.[1] In the second chapter I shall deal with the movement's search for authenticity, and the problems and controversies it encountered in pursuit of its goal.

At the root of the early music movement are the vast changes over the last few centuries in the attitude towards the music of the past with, overall, a striking shift of preference from the new to the old. This shift is a complex phenomenon whose various aspects need to be viewed separately.

First is the purely scholarly interest in history, where music is considered along with world events, with literature, architecture, and the figurative arts. When music of the past is viewed within such a frame, hardly ever is any thought given to its performance. Second is the case of sacred music, where the link to liturgy confers a special status to the music. Third are secular songs or dances that became and remained popular for a long time. Fourth is the performance of music of the past for the pleasure in its beauty, where the "past" may be thirty to forty years or centuries old. Fifth is an added dimension to the performance of "early music": the striving for historical authenticity. This fifth point is, of course, the focus of the early music movement and as such will need to be discussed in detail. But to set it in proper perspective, we need to consider first the other listed aspects of the early music complex.

Scholarly Interest

Scholarly interest in the music of antiquity produced whole libraries of books from the fifteenth century on. Though the great majority deal with the music of the Greeks and Romans, a surprising number of books, written mostly by theologians, treat Hebrew music and its instruments. In addition there were studies on old Egyptian, Abyssinian, and Chinese music. In Carl Ferdinand Becker's *Darstellung der musikalischen Literatur* (Leipzig, 1836), close to fifty columns list books between the fifteenth and eighteenth centuries on such scholarly works, and many more columns in the Supplement of 1839. In addition, eight columns list works on the music of the Middle Ages.

Among well-known composers and theorists, Michael Praetorius, in his three-volume *Syntagma musicum* (Wolfenbüttel, 1614–19), devoted the first volume to a history of music, the second to the description of instruments old and new, among them, old organs. Wolfgang Caspar Printz offers in his *Historische Beschreibung der edelen Sing- und Klingkunst . . .* (Dresden, 1690), a history of music that starts with musicians before the great flood and ends in the seventeenth century. Jacob Adlung, in his *Anleitung zu der musikalischen Gelahrtheit* (Erfurt, 1758), devotes the second chapter to a survey of the literature on the history of music. Padre Martini, the eminent composer-scholar and the first musicologist in a modern sense, embarked on a monumental project of a multivolume history of music, of which the first three volumes were published in 1757, 1770, and 1781 without reaching beyond the music of the Greeks. A fourth volume, dealing with the early Middle Ages, remained unfinished in manuscript.

All the books mentioned so far were scholarly works of pure theoretical inquiry about the nature of old music. In contrast, a remarkable development in sixteenth-century Italy had to do with an inquiry into the past that would serve as guide for the present, therewith *de facto* anticipating by 300 years today's striving for historically authentic performances. Girolamo Mei (1519–1594), a philologist, was inspired by a group of humanists of the Italian Renaissance to explore Greek drama and its music. He arrived at the conclusion that Greek drama was sung throughout, not spoken. He sent letters describing his findings and ideas to Vincenzo Galilei in Florence (father of Galileo), and thereby started a chain of events that was to lead to the birth of recitative and opera. Galilei, a scholar and composer, wrote the influential book *Dialogo della musica antica et della moderna* that adopted Mei's ideas and proposed to rediscover the Greek musical style. From discussions in a learned circle of Florentine noblemen interested in the arts, of philosophers and musicians (the Camerata), emerged the speculative consensus that Greek drama was realized in a declamatory manner that lay halfway between speech and song. From experiments aimed at recreating Greek musical style emerged, mainly at the hands of Galilei, Cavalieri, Caccini, and Peri, recitative, monody, and opera. Historically it was wrong, since Greek music knew no harmony, but the outgrowth of this mistaken reconstruction—in an epic attempt at "authenticity"—was a momentous event in musical history.

Sacred Music

Sacred music has often enjoyed a longer life than its secular counterparts, because a link with a liturgy that remained unaltered for centuries is apt to form a firm association with certain musical works. The link is strongest with music that is hallowed by an age-old tradition. The most obvious case is that of the medieval chants that remained alive in some churches and monasteries for a millenium and a half.

Secular Songs and Dances

Over the last centuries certain folk songs and dances have had an appeal so strong that they outlasted many generations. They were truly in the modern sense popular "hits," and because of their appeal were used by eminent composers either as *cantus firmi* for masses or other polyphonic works, or as themes for variations. A famous example of the first type is the song "L'Homme armé" from the early fifteenth century that was used by many composers (among them Dufay, Obrecht, Josquin, Palestrina, Carissimi) over the span of two centuries, and would hardly have been, had it not still been a living presence. An example for the second type is the "Folia," a dance and song also from the fifteenth century with an equally impressive list of master composers who used it well into the eighteenth century.

The Changing Attitude towards Old Music

It has been said that up to the year 1800 listeners were not interested in old music and wanted to hear only the latest and newest, that the nineteenth century liked the old along with the new, and that the twentieth century far prefers the old to the new. This is obviously a crass oversimplification, but as such it contains more than a kernel of truth.

During the patronage system of the feudal-aristocratic era that came to an end around 1800, the demands of the royal courts, the aristocrats, the opera houses, and even the church were for a steady stream of freshly composed music. The patrons who gave their musicians full-time employment as quasi servants expected new music from their house composer as they expected fresh rolls from their house baker. The opera impresarios needed new operas for every season, in Italy especially for carnival. This accounts for the colossal output of most seventeenth- and eighteenth-century composers whose work was comparable to that of today's journalists or of the writers and composers of the daily television shows. They wrote for the day, having little or no expectation of future glory; by and large, music had a short life expectancy.

There were exceptions. The French were generally more conservative in cultivating the music of yesteryear. Lully's operas, for example, remained in the Paris repertory until the mid-eighteenth century, some seventy years after his death. Handel's music remained alive in England, though performances were limited to several oratorios, while his operas and his instrumental works went into a long hibernation. There were also in all countries individuals who had access to older sources and appreciated their importance. For example, Gottfried Bernhard van Swieten (1733–1803), who collected scores of older music, became in Vienna in the 1780s a champion for Handel and Bach. It was he who introduced Mozart to *The Well-Tempered Clavier* that left a strong mark on the latter's style. Howard M. Brown, in a paper on the history of authenticity in performance, lists several cases, beginning with the Middle Ages, of music that remained alive for fifty and more years after the composer's death.[2] These cases were rather exceptional and far from the norm. The norm was the vast preponderance of new over old music.

Towards the end of the eighteenth century the patronage system that had lasted for well over a thousand years started to fade away, first in England, and then on the continent; by 1800 it had practically come to an end. The French Revolution and the end of feudalism, the Industrial Revolution with its spectacular ascent of industry and commerce, and the concomitant rise of a prosperous large bourgeoisie, dramatically changed the sociological structure of Europe. The nineteenth century that roughly coincides with the Romantic era marked also a new stage for the role of "early music." The rising bourgeoisie, as the music-cultivating and concert-going public, replaced the former patrons as the chief economic support of composers, who were now dependent on the marketplace for their livelihood.

The new customers on the music market had no proprietary interest in the newness of the music they paid to hear or to play. Moreover, Romanticism's concern with the national heritage favored a retrospective attitude that benefited "early" composers. Gluck, Haydn, and Mozart were perhaps among the first masters to profit from this changed attitude, and at least some small fractions of their creative output were carried over alive into the nineteenth century. It was in keeping with this frame of mind that Bach was rediscovered after seventy-five years of near-total neglect. The revival was helped by certain aspects of Bach's affective style that struck a responsive chord in the romantic soul. A few adventurous choral directors went further back to the great masters of the Renaissance, among them to Palestrina, Victoria, and Marenzio.

This incipient interest in old music, which at first reached only infrequently beyond Bach, was not yet accompanied by a concern for stylistic consistency, for "authentic" performance. Instead, the Romantics without hesitation or self-consciousness instilled their own spirit into both their performances and their editions of old music. Typical of the nineteenth-century mentality is Carl Czerny's edition of *The Well-Tempered Clavier* that aimed to show how Beethoven played it. Interesting as this may be, today we wish we had a comparable earwitness to tell us how Bach played it. Other editors had a less illustrious model and followed their own feelings and ideas. As a consequence the resulting text differed, often widely, from the original. Yet among the mass of such adulterated editions, many of which are still in wide circulation today, there were some shining exceptions. The second half of the nineteenth century witnessed the birth of a scholarly method in musical publication that a few eminent editors had adopted from the methods developed earlier by classical scholars. It involved a "diplomatic" reproduction of the best available source(s) and a critical apparatus that reported on, and evaluated, the sources, variants, revisions, questionable readings, etc., with a view to arriving at the most authoritative text possible under the circumstances. The first great monument to these endeavours was the "old" Bach *Gesamtausgabe* published by the Bach Gesellschaft between 1851 and 1899. Wilhelm Rust was an editor from 1853 on, and chief editor from 1858 to 1881. The twenty-six volumes he supervised are a model of editorial excellence. Hardly less admirable is Friedrich Chrysander's *Gesamtausgabe* of Handel's works in ninety-three volumes (1853–94). The "old" Mozart *Gesamtausgabe* (1876–1907) had a variety of editors and the result was mixed: some of the volumes are fairly reliable; others are not. Philipp Spitta's edition of Heinrich Schütz in sixteen volumes (1885–94) is more faithful to the original than is the new Bärenreiter edition.

The second half of the nineteenth century also saw the beginnings of the publication of musical "Monuments" in careful scholarly editions, complete with prefaces and critical commentaries. The indefatigable Chrysander was one of the pioneers with his *Denkmäler der Tonkunst* (1869–71), containing in six volumes works of Palestrina, Carissimi, Corelli, François Couperin, and Urio. By the end of the century many publications of such monuments or *Denkmäler* were in progress in many European countries. Many came out organized by nations, i.e., of music composed, not necessarily by natives of that particular country; others were organized by time periods, by media, or by forms.

All these scholarly editions were not yet a manifestation of a search for authenticity in performance, but they were its precondition. Authenticity of performance is beset by a multitude of problems, but without a reliable text, the attempts at reaching such a goal would have been stopped at the very first hurdle.

The Striving for "Authenticity"

Concern with historical correctness or "authenticity" of musical performance is a surprisingly recent phenomenon that was practically unknown before the end of the nineteenth century.[3] When the Baron van Swieten, the above-mentioned avant-garde apostle of early music, performed Handel's *Messiah, Alexander's Feast,* and the *Ode to St. Cecilia* in the 1780s, he commissioned Mozart to modernize the works by reorchestrating them. We can be certain that at the time not a single eyebrow was raised at what in the eyes of today's authenticists would be a musical crime.

The idea of authenticity was foreign not only to musical performance; artists in other fields could think and feel and create only in the style of their own time. The builder who, in the sixteenth century, designed the second spire for Chartres cathedral, never gave even a passing thought to matching the austere and simple first spire built almost three hundred years earlier in the style of the early Gothic. Instead, without regard to either authenticity or symmetry, he built a spire in the flamboyant style of the late Gothic, one that is taller, heavier, and far more ornate. The same attitude animated all builders through the ages until modern times, when what could be called the "age of authenticity" began to dawn. Thus many of the great churches in Europe, which required many hundreds and more years to complete, are a conglomerate of many styles. The record is presumably held by the cathedral in Syracuse, whose structures represent styles over 2000 years apart, from a Doric colonnade of the sixth century B.C. to a Baroque facade of the seventeenth century.

The nineteenth century, which lacked a powerful autochthonous style of its own, became the age of revival architecture with its many "neo-" styles: Neo-Classic, Neo-Gothic, Neo-Baroque, etc. The concomitant preoccupation with historical styles was a fertile ground for an emerging concern with authenticity in both the restoration or completion of monuments of the past. In the mid-nineteenth century the leading exponent of this movement was the French architect-scholar Eugène Emmanuel Viollet-le-Duc, who restored on the basis of thorough research many historic buildings, among them several famous cathedrals, châteaux, and the city of Carcassonne. What were then pioneering deeds became in the twentieth century matters of course, as witnessed by the faithful restorations of historic buildings destroyed in both World Wars. This new orientation towards the art of bygone ages is truly a counterpart to the search for authenticity in music.

In music, too, the recent striving for authenticity was foreshadowed in the nineteenth century, when here and there sporadic historical concerts were given on antique instruments and when in various countries interest deepened in unearthing and reviving music that had lain buried for generations.

The famous pianist Ignaz Moscheles was well ahead of his time when he gave in the 1830s a series of historical recitals on an eighteenth-century harpsichord, albeit one that he had equipped with a swell mechanism.[4] It was not, however, until the end of the century that the movement began to gather momentum. In 1894 Charles Bordes and the composer Vincent d'Indy founded the Schola Cantorum in Paris, with an original focus on the revival of old church music. Several years later the school branched out into the field of opera and other secular forms. In 1901 Henri Casadesus, supported by Camille Saint-Saëns, founded the Société des Instruments Anciens that organized periodic concerts on old instruments. In 1903 Wanda Landowska, who was a teacher at the Schola Cantorum, gave her first recital on the harpsichord. A year later, in 1904, she published her book *Musique ancienne* (6th ed., Paris, 1921) in which she pleads for the use of the harpsichord where it is historically called for. In the interest of textual fidelity—the *sine qua non* of authenticity—she excoriates editors and transcribers who deviate from the original score; among others she names Hans von Buelow, who added measures to Bach's *Chromatic Fantasia,* and Hummel, who bowdlerized Mozart concertos. But when she had the piano firm Pleyel build a harpsichord to her specifications, she added to the historical model a sixteen-foot stop and an iron frame. By so doing she departed too, albeit in a less objectionable way, from the ideal of authenticity. As a famous performer and sought-after teacher, Landowska was a powerful propagandist for the harpsichord and, indirectly, for the use of other historical instruments. She was certainly one of the seminal figures of the authenticity movement.

Important as was Landowska's role, the towering figure in the nascent search for authenticity was Arnold Dolmetsch (1858–1940). Born in France, he studied in Belgium where he became fascinated with Renaissance and Baroque music and above all with antique instruments. Clever with his hands, he built his first clavichord in 1894 and two years later his first harpsichord. After moving to England he also built lutes and was the first to reconstruct the recorder. His intimate involvement with instruments led him to explore the original ways of playing them, their "authentic" techniques. He organized many concerts of old music on old instruments and thus played a part in fanning the interest in these endeavors. But he made the strongest impact with his book *The Interpretation of the Music of the 17th and 18th Centuries* (London, 1915), which casts his shadow to the present day. As far as research in the performance of old music is concerned, the book was preceded by several studies on ornamentation that were needed because the knowledge of the many old ornament symbols had faded, and their understanding was indispensable for the performance of many masters the nineteenth century had revived. But Dolmetsch's book was a pioneering work because it dealt for the first time with problems of tempo, rhythm, expression, and instruments and their technique. He studied old tracts on performance and related documents such as ornament tables and prefaces to compositions; and from a combination of old texts and his own musical instincts, he set out to formulate rules for interpretation that have exerted a lasting influence. Later, in the second essay, I shall try to show why this influence was not thoroughly beneficial. But there is no denying that with his book more than with his activities as performer and instrument builder, he became the true founder of the authenticity movement.

At first this movement was slow in getting off the ground, but in the first three decades of the century encouraging symptoms of the growing interest in the performance of pre-repertoire music appeared in many places and countries.

In Germany Bernhard Stavenhagen and Christoph Döbereiner founded in 1905 Die deutsche Vereinigung für alte Musik, playing with old instruments (but modern techniques) baroque and early classical music.[5] In 1908 Hugo Riemann founded at the University of Leipzig the first German musicological institute and called it Collegium Musicum. The name came from the seventeenth- and eighteenth-century German organizations that, composed mainly of students and amateurs, played or sang publicly, in order to share their own enjoyment with an audience. The most famous was the Collegium Musicum that Telemann had founded in Leipzig, which Bach took over in 1729 and directed until 1739. By contrast, Riemann's Collegium was primarily an academic seminar, and performances by his students were strictly an internal affair serving the purpose of illustrating his scholarly program. He emphasized the Mannheim school along with other Pre-Classical masters, and from these endeavors sprang a publication series that also was called "Collegium Musicum."

The name caught on, and with the proliferation of musicological chairs at German universities there sprang up many Collegia Musica that combined scholarly pursuits with public performances of old music.

Wilibald Gurlitt founded one such organization at the University of Freiburg, with which he gave concerts of medieval music in 1922 and 1924. And as another milestone in the history of the early music movement, Gurlitt, whose dissertation had dealt with Praetorius, built an organ in 1921, the "Praetorius Organ," according to the specifications in the latter's *Organographia* of 1619. His example found a ready response and "Baroque" organs began to proliferate in Germany.

What Howard Brown in the paper mentioned above considers "perhaps the most important event in the history of early music in the 1930s," was the founding in 1933 of the Schola Cantorum in Basel. Among the founding musicians was August Wenzinger, eminent viola da gamba player, who was one of the leading proponents of the use of authentic techniques as well as instruments.

Also in 1933, the American Safford Cape founded the group Pro Musica Antiqua in Brussels, devoted to the performance, on historical instruments, mainly of music of the thirteenth to sixteenth centuries. He also established a European Seminar on Early Music in the ancient Belgian city of Bruges.

World War II enforced a practical cessation of these endeavors. But soon after its end, the slow-burning fuse initially lit by Dolmetsch and Landowska and kept alive by their students and admirers exploded in an outburst of enthusiasm that grew in intensity during the following decades and at this time shows no signs of abating. England was and still is the leader, but Holland, Belgium, and Germany followed closely behind, later joined by the United States. In recent years France, which in the nineteenth century was the leader in the revival of forgotten music without, however, a focus on authenticity, has shown signs of following the new trend.

Dolmetsch died in 1940, and after the war the mantle of spiritual leader of the early music movement fell on the shoulders of Thurston Dart, a young harpsichordist, self-taught in musicology, who became a professor at Cambridge. He was the first editor of the *Galpin Society Journal,* which dealt with the history and the uses of European instruments. Close to a hundred articles in various musicological journals came from his pen, and for five years he directed the Philomusica of London that performed mainly Baroque music on modern instruments. But his greatest influence was due to a small book, *The Interpretation of Music* (London, 1954), that went through many editions and was translated into numerous languages. (A paperback edition came out in New York in 1963.) He supplemented Dolmetsch's teachings, dealt in an easy-going way with the interpretation of the music from the Middle Ages to the eighteenth century, and issued capsule directives that were accepted as authoritative by the new seekers of authenticity.

Next to Dart, who, as a father figure, strongly influenced the practicing performers, Dolmetsch's student Robert Donington may have carried more weight in academia with a voluminous book, *The Interpretation of Early Music* (London, 1963; "new version," 1975). After Dart's premature death in 1971, Donington became the undisputed theoretical leader in the quest for historical correctness.

In the field of performance of early music, the English musical scene saw the emergence of many individual artists, instrumentalists, singers, and directors, and of organizations devoted uniquely to that purpose. Already starting between the world wars, but most dramatically after World War II, recordings and radio broadcasts played a huge role in spreading the gospel in England as well as in other countries. The "Third Programme" of the BBC, established in 1946, became a potent force in promoting the cause.

Three years earlier, in 1943, Karl Haas, a refugee from Nazism, founded the London Baroque Ensemble that remained active until 1966. (Haas is now a regular commentator on the American National Public Radio.) Charles Farncomb founded the Handel Opera Society in 1955 with the aim of reviving interest in Handel's dramatic works, and in the following years performed, with modern instruments, around twenty operas and oratorios. In the 1960s, Raymond Leppard directed Monteverdi's *Orfeo* and *Poppea* at Glyndebourne in his own modernized arrangement and performed many works of Bach, Handel, and other Baroque composers, and did so, almost militantly, on modern instruments. Colin Davis, a Dart student, similarly directed many pre-1750 works with modern instruments while striving for historical correctness as did Neville Marriner in the 1970s with the Academy of St.-Martin-in-the-Fields.

Gradually the attitude of the early music specialists became more strict about the original sound, and today the use of historical instruments and techniques has become a near-absolute requirement. Among those who abide by it are Trevor Pinnock, harpsichordist and leader of the English Concert that performs choral and instrumental music; John Eliot Gardiner, conductor of the English Baroque Soloists, with many performances of Handel and other Baroque operas to his credit; Christopher Hogwood and his Academy of Ancient Music that extended their reach from the Baroque masters to include all of the Mozart symphonies and most recently all of Beethoven's piano concertos; Derek Solomons with L'Estro Armonico that likewise moved into the Classical era and is recording the whole set of Haydn symphonies; the Hanover Band under Roy Goodman with its focus on Haydn and Beethoven; Roger Norrington with his London Classical Players who, in addition to a cycle of Beethoven symphonies have been doing "authentic" Berlioz, whose works have thereby been officially elevated to the status of "early music."

The sheer number of these London organizations is astonishing and becomes only slightly less so when we realize how much their personnel overlaps.

This is unavoidable since all these groups work on a free-lance basis, and none can offer its members full-time employment. To give just one prominent example: Roy Goodman, concertmaster of the Hanover Band, is today also concertmaster of the Academy of Ancient Music, of L'Estro Armonico, of the Orchestra of the Age of Enlightenment, and principal second violin of the London Classical Players. The overlapping has recently taken on an international dimension when members of early music organizations, like opera stars, are in demand in several countries.

The Dutch have been particularly active in the field of authenticity, where they tend to be very orthodox in the pursuit of their goal and in their insistence on period instruments. For that small country the sheer number of groups striving for authenticity is remarkable. Among the leading artists involved in this pursuit are Gustav Leonhardt, the well-known harpsichordist, who directs the Leonhardt Consort for works of an intimate character, and Concerto Amsterdam for larger-scale works; Frans Brüggen, eminent recorder and flute player who organized the Orchestra of the Eighteenth Century, with a repertoire that ranges from Rameau to early Beethoven. Often associated with these two artists are the three Kuijken brothers on violin, gamba, and flute, of whom Sigiswald organized La Petite Bande that performs the Baroque masters, especially Bach, Handel, and Vivaldi, on period instruments (in the Netherlands a matter of course). The organist and harpsichordist Ton Koopman formed the Amsterdam Baroque Orchestra that extended its repertoire to include the Classical masters. All these artists collaborated with one another and with the Hague Conservatory, which has established an early music program. The Dutch activities may not match in numbers those of England, but relative to the size of the population, they easily outstrip what is being done in any other country today.

In Belgium the Pro Musica Antiqua of Brussels, founded before World War II, was mentioned above. Today's leading artist is Philipp Herreweghe, a choral director who organized and directs La Chapelle Royale, teamed with the Collegium Vocale of Ghent for the performance of major early choral works.

Germany witnessed in the 1920s a remarkable revival of Handel's operas. Launched by Oskar Hagen in Göttingen, the move proved contagious and spread to many other German cities. In Germany, as in England, a few radio stations were powerful factors in the popularization of much hitherto unknown early music. The first important postwar performing organization was Konrad Ruhland's Capella Antiqua in Munich, followed in 1954 by the Capella Coloniensis under August Wenzinger. In 1960, the American lutenist Thomas Binkley, together with the German singer Andrea von Ramm organized, in Munich, the Studio der Frühen Musik, which was unusual in being devoted chiefly to medieval music. (Binkley is now the director of the Early Music Institute at Indiana University, Bloomington.) Today the leading groups are the Collegium Aureum, directed by Franzjoseph Maier, with a repertory from Vivaldi and

Bach to Beethoven, and the Musica Antiqua in Cologne, directed by Reinhard Göbel in predominantly Baroque chamber works. Göbel is an avid reader of the scholarly literature; and it is a tribute to his open mind that, after reading my articles on the illusory nature of the so-called French overture style, he was the first to discard this still widely practiced manner.

In Austria, in the 1950s, Nikolaus Harnoncourt founded the Concentus Musicus, which has won international renown through its travels and its wealth of recordings. Harnoncourt also directs many other groups in western European countries, among them some mainstream organizations such as the Zurich Opera and some symphony orchestras. This activity is symptomatic of a recent—so far only sporadic—crosscurrent of rapprochement between the two rival performing media. Harnoncourt's case is paralleled by that of Christopher Hogwood, who works with a modern orchestra as the recently appointed director of the Boston Handel and Haydn Society.

In the United States both the early music movement and its offshoot, the authenticity cult, were slower in taking hold. Professional organizations involved in these pursuits were for a long time limited to a few Eastern cities: New York, Philadelphia, and Boston (a wit referred to them as "Baroque ghettos"). Outside of these centers it was the universities, colleges, and a few conservatories that spread the gospel of authenticity and kept doing so in ever-increasing numbers.

These developments were foreshadowed by a relatively early interest in and involvement with historical instruments. In 1925 the American Society of Ancient Instruments was founded in Philadelphia, patterned on the model of the Casadesus Society in Paris. The Boston Society of Ancient Instruments followed in 1938 along the same lines: antique instruments and periodic concerts. In the same year, at the University of Chicago, Siegmund Levarie organized the first American Collegium Musicum, a group that remained active until 1952. More influential was the Collegium Musicum that Paul Hindemith organized at Yale in 1945 and directed until his return to Europe in 1953. This group covered a wide range of music from the Middle Ages to the Baroque and gave concerts both in New Haven and in New York. It became a model for many other universities and from that time on the collegium idea spread around campuses all over the country.

In the 1950s one of the key figures of the authenticity movement was Noah Greenberg, who founded the New York Pro Musica, an ensemble of soloists and singers that performed medieval and Renaissance music. The group won its widest acclaim with the staging of medieval liturgical dramas. The *Play of Daniel,* done in the genuinely authentic setting of the Cloisters (a medieval monastery, dismantled in Europe and reassembled stone by stone north of New York on the Hudson river), became a great popular success. Greenberg had studied the available sources carefully and tried to be faithful to them, but he was also eager to appeal to the public at large. He filled the huge gaps in our knowledge about the historical facts with his vivid imagination and keen theatrical flair. He enchanted the audiences with an opulent musical arrangement, a striking visual display, and the evocation of a medieval atmosphere. The result was quite certainly far from authentic, but the success of his colorful products and concerts made many converts to the cause of early music. The organization survived by only a few years Greenberg's premature death in 1966 at the age of forty-seven.

Besides New York, Boston was an important center of early music activity and had probably the earliest concentration in this country of musicians dedicated to this repertory and its associated performance practices. Erwin Bodky, author of a book on the interpretation of Bach's clavier works, and Frank Hubbard, who aimed at purging harpsichord building from modern accretions, were among the early pioneers. The Boston Society for Ancient Instruments was mentioned earlier. Martin Perlman's orchestra Banchetto Musicale may have been the first permanent ensemble of this sort in this country. In the 1950s the Boston Camerata was founded in association with the Boston Museum of Fine Arts and later became an independent organization. Twenty years later, also in Massachusetts, the Aston Magna Foundation under the direction of Albert Fuller organized concerts mostly of Baroque masters.

Residing in Boston, though active mostly in New York and England, Joshua Rifkin, musician-musicologist, produced a number of recordings of Renaissance and Baroque music with various ensembles in the 1960s and 1970s. In 1978 he founded the Bach Ensemble and created a stir in the musical community when he performed and recorded a number of Bach's vocal works with soloists singing the choral parts. He argued skillfully for the authenticity of this arrangement, but so far the jury is still out on the controversy he created.

Of late the authenticity movement has, outside of the collegium musicum circuit, gained a professional foothold on the West coast with the founding, in San Francisco, of the Philharmonic Baroque Orchestra, which performs on period instruments under the direction of Nicholas McGegan.

As a further sign of the continuing growth of the authenticity movement in the United States, the year 1988 witnessed the birth of two semiannual journals devoted primarily to questions of performance practice: *Historical Performance,* the journal of Early Music America, an organization founded in 1986; and *Performance Practice Review,* published by the Claremont Graduate School in California.

As can be gathered from this very brief report, the authenticity movement, internationally carried forward by an ever-growing momentum, continues by all outward signs in its victorious march to further conquests. There is, however, as so often, another side to the coin. Questions can be raised about the basic propositions, procedures, and priorities of the movement, and about some of its attendant phenomena, such as some excesses of zealotry. The next chapter will discuss some of these questions and the shadows they might cast on the brightness of this extraordinary success story.

Notes

1. Readers who wish to explore the subject in greater depth will find a rewarding source in Harry Haskell's thoroughly researched book, *The Early Music Revival: A History* (New York and London, 1988).

2. "Pedantry or Liberation? Notes towards a History of Authenticity in the Performance of Early Music," in *Authenticity and Early Music*, ed. Nicholas Kenyon (Oxford, 1988), p. 47.

3. In addition to Harry Haskell's book and Howard M. Brown's article, I am indebted for some of the factual information in this section to Clarke Bustard, music critic of the *Richmond Times-Dispatch*, who kindly gave me the benefit of his comprehensive knowledge of recordings by the "authentic" organizations; also to Joshua Rifkin who graciously answered in a personal letter a few questions I had asked him.

4. Haskell, p. 20.

5. Ibid., p. 55.

2

Some Controversial Aspects of the
Authenticity School

The preceding chapter ended its chronicle signaling the triumphant march of the early music movement. There is, however, as was briefly hinted at, another side to the story that needs to be told in order to round out the picture: we need to balance the achievements of the movement against some areas of uncertainty, doubt, and controversy. These areas can perhaps best be circumscribed by the following questions: (1) What is authenticity? (2) How sound is the scholarship that endeavors to fill the lacunae in our knowledge? (3) How do the authenticists justify their claim to historical correctness? and (4) What is and what should be the role of the past and the present in performing early music for modern audiences? The questions are difficult and some of the answers attempted in the course of this chapter can only be tentative.

The Nature of Authenticity

When we speak of an authentic Rembrandt or of an authentic work by Bach, the meaning of the adjective is clear. But what is an authentic performance? A solo performance by a composer who is also a virtuoso player might deserve this designation: Bach at the organ, Couperin at the harpsichord, Mozart at the fortepiano. A cantata directed by Bach or an opera directed by Mozart could be described as an authentic performance, but it would not necessarily provide a desirable model to emulate: incompetent performers or lack of rehearsal time may have left the composer dissatisfied. A contemporary performance without the composer's participation is certainly "historical" but not "authentic" and may have missed the composer's intentions by a wide mark. In fact the likelihood of such misses is very great since masters like Bach or Mozart were not nearly as much appreciated and as well understood by their contemporaries as they are by today's musicians. (See also chapter 11 of this volume for a further discussion of authenticity.)

Here we need no semantic hairsplitting, but we do need a bearing on what today's authenticists are trying to accomplish, so that we may judge how their efforts measure up to their aims. Whether or not they believe or claim to offer "authentic" performances in the sense of matching an ideal historical model, they will probably all agree that they aim at bringing to life a work true to the spirit in which it was conceived.[1]

The Challenge to Scholarship

The aim of being true to the creative will of an old master is the focus of the young discipline of "performance practice" that set out to find out how composers wished their music to be rendered, and therewith to provide advice and direction to today's performers.

The goal of the search is ultimately unreachable and the best we can hope for is to approach it as closely as is feasible. The problems besetting the search have their principal root in the inadequacy of musical notation, which is eloquent on many matters but silent on many others. Even today's sophisticated scores have their silences: they are far removed from the precision of an architect's blueprint. The farther back we go in time, the greater are the silences that form gaps between what the composer wrote down and how he meant it to sound. It is the role of the performer to fill these gaps with his "interpretation" which, in contrast to the builder's execution of a blueprint, is an act of autonomous artistry. Ideally, the performer will have, in Marpurg's sense, the greatest sensitivity and most auspicious gift of divination; one, we might add, that is informed by an imaginative artistry. For the interpretation of a work from the distant past we should add, as a further desideratum, a keen sense of style. But the key word here, too, is "divination": the need to fill with guesswork the gray areas of uncertainty that for "early music" are very large indeed. The scholars of performance practice have been laboring to shed light on this gray area, but they have been meeting with formidable difficulties in these endeavors.

We can perhaps best illustrate these difficulties if we take a look at a Bach score. There we find the notes with their exact pitches and their mostly exact rhythms, i.e., the relative distances between their starting points, and often nothing more. I said "mostly exact rhythms" because the notation ⌐ ♪ for a 2:1 ratio in a binary meter was not yet available, and either the dotted note or two evenly written notes had to serve as makeshift. As a consequence both the meaning of dotted notes and (more rarely) of even binary notes became ambiguous. Moreover, there were other situations apart from these where the dotted note did not have its literal meaning.

Tempo indications, largely absent in keyboard works, are reasonably frequent in chamber music and vocal works. But they are mostly limited to six basic speeds: largo, adagio, andante, allegro, vivace, and presto; they give us a certain rough range, but they still leave considerable leeway in the selection of the tempo. There were no signs for slowing down or speeding up.

For expression, a vital element in performance, there were no indications at all, nor were there any for phrasing.

Dynamic markings were rare; practically absent in keyboard works, elsewhere they are mostly limited to "forte" and "piano." There were no signs for accents, for swelling or tapering.

Articulation signs too were, with few exceptions, absent in keyboard works; elsewhere slurs were frequent, but staccato marks rare, while the way a note is started, whether gently or sharply, and the length a note is to be held, were entirely at the discretion of the performer.

The whole field of ornamentation is a problem area because the meaning of the symbols was far more flexible and varied than is commonly assumed to be the case. It was, in fact, the beauty of the symbols that they did admit a flexible reading that also taxed the interpreter's acumen. Then there was the free ornamentation that did not appear in the score. For most of Bach's Italian, German, and English contemporaries the need to add ornamental figurations to an austerely written slow melody adds another considerable difficulty to the many others already listed.

A further gray area is accompaniment, where the realization of the thorough bass, and occasionally the choice of instruments, was left to the discretion of the player(s).

We are reasonably well informed about the old instruments, but our knowledge is spotty about playing techniques, tone production instrumental and vocal, vibrato, and related matters.

Finally, there is the question of pitch that looms large in the authenticists' arsenal. It is complicated and not amenable to unqualified solutions.

This long list of areas in all shades of gray is far from complete, but it should suffice to illuminate the magnitude of the problem we face in our search. Let us next review the means that are available for the task and see how the young discipline of performance practice has fared in its attempts to meet the challenge.

Except for two major books on ornamentation[2] the research in this field was set on its present course by Arnold Dolmetsch, whose achievements in the revival of old music and old instruments were described in chapter 1. He was a true pioneer and visionary but wielded his greatest influence with his book of 1915, *The Intepretation of the Music of the 17th and 18th Centuries*. In this book he tried to answer some of the hardest questions we face in interpreting old texts. His enterprise was noble but his research was flawed. That this should have been the case is understandable: as a frontiersman in uncharted territory he had no precedent on which to build. He had to shape his own tools, and we must not be surprised if they turned out to be somewhat crude. Dolmetsch studied old treatises, extracted from them rules about performance, and then applied these rules in summary fashion to the great masters of the period. He thus became the originator of what could be called the "cite-and-apply" method. In principle there is nothing wrong with the method, but it can produce wrong leads when carelessly and mechanically applied.

As to treatises, they are indispensable sources for our research, but we must properly screen them: we must examine the probable relevance of a quoted sentence or paragraph to the work of a given composer. While stylistic congruence is the basic prerequisite for such relevance, the latter needs to be further tested for the demands of musical logic, musical common sense, and any musical evidence that can be extracted from the music in question. Treatises can mislead when their relevance is taken for granted. Often they are automatically applied across lines of stylistic upheaval and across lengthy periods of time. Thus we find scholars covering a whole century by citing the writings of C. P. E. Bach and applying them to the music of his father, Haydn, and Mozart. They justify such massive extrapolation by their belief in a "common practice" of the age. The assumption of such a common practice is convenient but illusory: while a few performance conventions were widely used, they focused on specific points, such as bass figuring, whereas a general across-the-board common practice has never existed in the past and does not exist today. This concept is based on what E. D. Hirsch called the "fallacy of the homogeneous past."[3]

Even Dolmetsch was more subtle. He at least realized that not every treatise is pertinent to every master within an extended period. He illustrates this point in a formal exposition of his method that, alas, points up other weaknesses of argument. He writes:

> Quantz, although twelve years younger than Johann Sebastian Bach, belonged to his school. Agricola, although very much younger, was a direct pupil of Bach and followed his master's ideas for a long time. But C. P. E. Bach was the leader of a new school; it is he that Türk calls "Bach." . . . Therefore Türk's interpretation applies to the C. P. E. Bach–Haydn–Mozart period. Quantz and Agricola should be followed for the works of the preceding generation, which includes d'Anglebert, Couperin, Rameau, Handel, J. S. Bach.

In this manifesto of the cite-and-apply method, all too peremptorily applied, we have in a nutshell the cause of many of the troubles that beset the field of performance practice: "Quantz belonged to Bach's school" and Agricola, his pupil, followed him for a long time. Therefore these two writers can be cited and safely applied to Bach, and not only to Bach, but also to Handel and the three listed French masters. As matters were, Quantz did not at all belong to Bach's school, nor did Agricola follow him for any length of time. Both of these men embraced the aesthetic of the *galant* style, and this fact alone makes their testimony on behalf of the five older masters highly suspect. We encounter similar difficulties when we "apply" Türk to the Classical masters. While Türk's ideas are reasonably congenial to C. P. E. Bach (who spoke eloquently for himself), in many important matters they are not at all congenial to Mozart and Haydn in spite of their being contemporaries.

The cite-and-apply method harbors other dangers besides the risk of picking the wrong expert, and Dolmetsch did not escape several of its pitfalls. One is misinterpretation of a text. Dolmetsch found a citation in Quantz about over-dotting in very specific circumstances: limited to soloists, and to dotted eighth or shorter, but not longer notes, in order to increase their liveliness. By linking the quote to a misinterpreted single sentence referring to French orchestral dances, he turned what was a spotty North German—and mainly Berlin—*galant,* soloistic mannerism into a global law of drastic rhythmic contractions that, he posited, applied to "all old music" from the sixteenth to the eighteenth centuries.[4] Here we see the idea of a "common practice" getting out of control: a local fashion that was disavowed by other North German *galant* masters was blown up into an all-embracing principle lasting for three centuries! Though in this extreme formulation the doctrine did not take hold, a nucleus of it, which became known as the French overture style has found a solid place in the canon of Baroque performance practice. Adopted as dogma by practically all authenticists and by many mainstream artists as well, the doctrine is responsible for some severe rhythmic distortions, mainly of overtures, but of a few other works of different forms as well.[5]

Another passage in Quantz in which he endorsed the French convention of the *notes inégales* led Dolmetsch to declare the convention as internationally valid and to show how to apply it to various numbers of *Messiah* and to some works of Bach.[6] This conclusion, too, is unjustified, yet it has made a strong impact on the performances of some authenticists.[7]

One of the major dangers of the cite-and-apply method is the citing of certain theoretical statements that, while valid in principle, become misleading when taken too literally. The classical case is found in ornament tables. The designs shown in these tables are pure abstractions that have to be adjusted with sensitivity and imagination in a thousand different ways to the demands of specific musical situations. Yet the scholars of performance practice—following here too the lead of Dolmetsch—mistake the abstract design for a model to be used literally whenever the respective symbol appears. Such mechanical application subverts the very function of ornaments: instead of loosening the musical texture by a touch of improvisatory flexibility, grace, and elegance, they become agents of rigorism.[8] This procedure has produced the almost universally accepted, misleading, and rigidifying rule that all ornaments have to start on the beat and that all trills have to start with the auxiliary—on the beat, of course.

It is painful to be so critical of Dolmetsch to whose vision we owe so much. But to do so is necessary, because his ideas continue to wield an enormous influence, both directly, owing to the prestige of his name, and indirectly, through his students, followers, and successors who have continued using the same procedures.

Dolmetsch's immediate follower, Thurston Dart, codified the French overture style according to Dolmetsch's illustrations and declared that its rhythmic contractions are to be applied to music from Monteverdi to Beethoven.[9] For the same period, as mentioned before, he had stipulated a basic pitch level slightly more than a half tone below today's standard.

The true heir to Dolmetsch is his student Robert Donington, a thorough and painstaking scholar. He carried the cite-and-apply method to its ultimate limit by quoting in his large book, *The Interpretation of Early Music,* a huge number of excerpts from old theorists and transforming them into instant prescriptions. His belief in a "common practice" is evident in the way his quotes often leap from one country to another, from one era to the next. He endorses the French overture style, the international validity of the *notes inégales* and, by taking ornament tables at their face value, has been and continues to be (in his article on ornaments for *The New Grove*) a potent force in the rigidification of ornaments.

These three men, Dolmetsch, Dart, and Donington, a true triumvirate, are to this day the most influential voices in matters of performance practice. They form the chief pillars of what could be called the performance practice establishment. Other scholars have gathered as supporting actors under the roof of this establishment, strengthening and supplementing it with kindred methods and principles. Among them one could name Putnam Aldrich and his student Michael Collins in America, Jean-Claude Veilhan and Antoine Geoffroy-Dechaume in France, and Karl Hochreiter and Hans Klotz in Germany.[10] Eva and Paul Badura-Skoda stand outside of the establishment: they are far more flexible, do not mechanically cite and apply, and see the music first, the rules later. They are playing a major role in the urgently needed re-examination of many principles of performance practice. In the fields of ornamentation and rhythm I myself have attempted to take a new look at the well-established ideas and have, I hope, succeeded in showing that they are in need of revision. Here it is important to realize that it is by and large the doctrines of the establishment that the authenticists followed in order to fill the many gaps in our knowledge, though in many instances these doctrines are unhistorical and occasionally unmusical. Most faulty procedures can be reduced to one single cause: the mechanical cite-and-apply method and the ensuing fact that scholars go by the book instead of by the music. By that I mean that they obediently follow rules without considering in each case whether the result is musically logical and sensible.

In addition to precepts they derived from the establishment scholars, the authenticists have formed an at least partial consensus on some other principles that they follow in their performances. One is the lowering of the pitch up to a half-tone and more, on which the consensus is practically total. This procedure may be establishment-based if it followed Dart's above-mentioned statement about the general pitch level from 1600 to ca. 1820 having been more than a half-tone lower than today's level. Yet the idea of such general and long-lasting lower pitch is mistaken. There was no single pitch that was widely used in those times: the pitch varied from region to region, from city to city, from church to church, from one recorder, or oboe, etc., to another. Arthur Mendel reports that three recorders made around 1700 by the famous Denners from Nuremberg are at a' = 410, 450 and 465—that is from more than a semitone lower to a semitone higher than our present pitch of 440.[11] Flutes had interchangeable second joints so that they could be played in different pitches. Mendel also points out that there was no such thing as a "Mozart pitch" and that a tuning fork of the Augsburg pianoforte maker J. A. Stein at a' = 421.6 (slightly less than a half-tone lower than modern pitch) has no provable connection with Mozart.[12] At such pitch level, Osmin's eight-measure-long low D (below the staff) in his aria "Ha! wie will ich triumphieren" would be unsingable: it is at extreme basso range in modern pitch.

Another practice of the authenticists is singing and playing with no vibrato or only a minimal one. The consensus here is very large. Yet the nonvibrato theory has no solid grounding. Historically, the use of the vibrato has had its ups and downs between greater and lesser use. A nonvibrato for singers was probably never the norm, not even for boys.[13] Strings use it more today, and more pervasively, also in a presumably wider form than in the eighteenth century, but it was used.[14] The same seems to be the case with singers. Generally, a vibrato that is so heavy and obtrusive as to blur the musical line is as objectionable today for modern music as it would have been in centuries past.

The nonvibrato principle is not an establishment idea. Dolmetsch and Dart do not mention it, and Robert Donington rejects it. He writes, very convincingly, "Totally vibrato-less string tone sounds dead in any music. It is just as much an illusion to think that early performers preferred it as to think that early singers preferred a 'white' tone. Sensitive vibrato not only can but should be a normal ingredient in performing early music."[15]

Then there are questions of articulation where some fashionable theories are followed by some but not by other authenticists. One is the principle of short detachment as allegedly basic articulation of the seventeenth and eighteenth centuries. Here we encounter again the "fallacy of the homogeneous past." Wide varieties of articulation were practiced. French violinists from Lully on used a sharply articulated bowstroke that was fitting for dances. The Italians, who always had the voice in the back of their minds, preferred a long, sustained one. Saint Lambert, Couperin, and Rameau aimed at a perfect legato; some later French keyboardists preferred sharp detachment. Bach's organ playing was praised for its legato style. He used of course on other occasions the detached and the staccato mode, but none of these could be sensibly called "basic." If there was a "basic" articulation, it varied from nation to nation, from individual to individual.

Another of the practices of at least some authenticists is the *messa di voce* on every note of a certain length. Occasionally these procedures are appropriate; often they are not, and an unremitting series of *messe di voce* can be disconcerting. If those who follow this practice believe to have found the justification in a passage where Leopold Mozart explains the bow stroke, as I suspect they do, they are mistaken: the passage in question, as Mozart makes clear in the further course of the chapter, describes not a *messa di voce,* but gives a singularly clear and perceptive directive for connecting two bowstrokes as smoothly as possible.[16]

Considering the great lacunae of our knowledge about composers' preferences for such matters as tempo, expression, articulation, phrasing, rhythmic freedoms, etc.; considering furthermore the many false leads that scholarship has offered performers on such matters as ornamentation and rhythm, as well as the many questionable principles the authenticists adopted from various sources on such matters as articulation, dynamic nuances, pitch, vibrato, etc., the claim of an "authentic" performance assumes a mythical quality.

Some of the early music performers are aware of these problems. Harnoncourt, for instance, acknowledges the chimerical nature of authenticity and is consequently more flexible and much less doctrinaire than most of his colleagues who do believe that their performances come close to a reconstruction of the composer's concepts. How do these true believers go about achieving their aim? Their first and most stringent principle is the use of the period instruments with lower pitch. This requirement is to the authenticists beyond debate, self-evident, a true article of faith because they fervently believe that the spirit of a work is indissolubly linked with its original sound. Is this dogma incontestable? Must a timeless masterwork forever be tied to a time-bound medium? Must it forever be frozen and crystallized in an immutable shape, impervious to changing conditions, attitudes and sensibilities? Or, as Robert P. Morgan put it, do we have to bring old masterworks back as fossils rather "than trying to revive them, to give them new life through an infusion of new ideas, lending them the sort of richness and flexibility characteristic of a living tradition"?[17] For addressing this question we have to consider the role of the past and the present in the performance of early music.

The Role of the Past and the Present in the Performance of Early Music

May reason, which sometimes weakens in old age, protect me from the common mistake of exalting the past at the expense of the present.

—Voltaire

If we accept the proposition that the role of the interpreter is to convey to the listener the true spirit of the work at hand, the principle that it must be rendered with the original tone color is not an *a priori* truth. If it were, then would it not also be self-evident that Shakespeare be performed only with sixteenth-century pronunciation and his women's parts played only by boys and men; or that Chaucer be read only in the original, never in the modernized version? These questions alone show that the axiom about the original sound is vulnerable and an axiom that is vulnerable ceases to be one.

Forty years ago, in the early stages of the authenticity movement Jacques Handschin, the eminent Swiss musicologist, put it succinctly when he wrote about the performance of early music (my translation): "An exact reproduction of the acoustical phenomenon—supposing that science were capable of realizing it—does not match the reconstruction of the musical phenomenon as long as one does not also reconstruct the contemporary listener with his exact musical perceptions and habits. . . . One must not proclaim as a dogma the idea that a musical work must necessarily be played in the manner in which it was played originally."[18]

For another, recent view, Richard Taruskin writes: "The claim of self-evidence for the value of old instruments, like the claim of self-evidence for the virtue of adhering to a composer's 'intentions,' is really nothing but a mystique, and more often than one can tell, that is the only justification offered."[19]

Handschin certainly has a strong argument with the need to reconstruct the listener in order to justify the reconstruction of the—would-be—authentic sound. Of course we cannot transform ourselves into eighteenth-century listeners just by an act of will, when our ears have absorbed the music from Wagner to Stravinsky and beyond. No mental effort can undo this conditioning. Our ears are further conditioned to the pitch of $a' = 440$ and to the more brilliant sound of our violins, to the richness of resonance of modern pianos, to the range of sound of our woodwinds and to the technical nimbleness of our valve horns and trumpets, etc.

The spirit of a composition was equated in Baroque aesthetics with its "affection," i.e., the impression it made on the listener's mind and soul. Yet with our conditioning our aural perceptions have changed, and the message transmitted by period sonorities has changed with it because the "authentic" sound has lost some of its communicative power. A strong case could then be made to adjust the sound to modern sensibilities so that the impression on today's listener is equivalent to that made on the eighteenth-century listener.

Here the question comes to mind: how important are tone color and pitch for an artistically convincing, authoritative performance, and how does their importance compare with that of the other elements of interpretation?

I don't believe I risk controversy when I say that expression, melody, harmony, rhythm, and tempo are at the core of a musical work. And ornamentation as part of the melody belongs here too. Dynamics, articulation, and phrasing may share in a similar eminence but only to the extent to which they are essential to melody or rhythm or both. All the first-named factors are, and the second-named ones may be, basic to the spirit of a composition. Ideally we would like to render them in a way that would have satisfied the composer. A possible reservation might be in order for the tempo. Just as with sonority and pitch, it is conceivable that over the time gap that separates us from early music, our sensation of the passage of time may have changed; that, say, given the faster metabolism of the twentieth century, the tempo may need to be accelerated for today's audiences in order to match the musical effect on eighteenth-century listeners. This is possible but not too likely, inasmuch as we have documents about surprisingly fast tempos in the seventeenth and eighteenth centuries.

What about pitch and sonorities? A case can be made for some of the lower pitches used by the authenticists when genuine antique instruments are involved—instruments that either cannot be tuned higher or that produce the best sonorities at a lower pitch level. Thus we can justify a lower pitch as an adjustment to circumstances, but it is hard to justify it where such circumstances do not obtain and the selection of the pitch is arbitrary. A historical rationale is hardly ever available since we rarely know the historical pitch for a certain work on a certain occasion. And where neither a musical nor a historical rationale favors a lower pitch we have to consider its drawbacks. First, such lowering confuses our sense of tonality. We have been conditioned to perceive tonalities in relation to modern pitch. If, as often done, the pitch is lowered by a half-tone (a′ = 414), all our tonalities are playing musical chairs: the B-Minor Mass turns to B♭ minor, and the whole *Well-Tempered Clavier* has a whole set of new keys. And even where the pitch is lowered less, the tonality is altered to some musical no man's land that can be unsettling to listeners, and most of all to those who have the precious gift of absolute pitch.

Furthermore, a lower pitch dims the luster of a piece, and intensifies the loss of brilliance due to non-vibrato playing or singing and the generally lesser brightness of the period instruments. Now an argument can be and has been made that brightness as such is not an asset. Certainly there are types of music that do not call for brilliance, but there is a huge body of music that to many, perhaps to most perceptive listeners, will gain by a brighter sound in the way pictures will gain by better lighting.

As to the role of tone color, it will vary from case to case. Its importance, great for the colorist masters of the nineteenth century, diminishes as we recede in time. For pre-1750 music it is mostly small and few would rank tone color along with those elements that were listed above as shaping the core of a musical work and determining its nature, its aesthetic message. There are, it is true, some compositions of that period that are thoroughly idiomatic for a certain instrument, perhaps the clavecin pieces of d'Anglebert, Couperin, and Rameau, which might lose some of their character by transfer to the modern piano. For still earlier music, for works of medieval and Renaissance masters, a use of modern istruments would be incongruous, and here authentic instruments or their replicas would seem to be indispensable to safeguard the archaic flavor and aura of that music.

The case is different for Bach. The essence of his music lies in its line, not in its color. For this reason he never hesitated to transcribe his works from any medium to just about any other one. His frequent indifference to color shows also in his persistent failure to indicate registrations for his organ works. Their sound can vary radically dependent on the registration the player chooses. Clearly, color combinations of the organ must have ranked near the bottom of Bach's musical priorities.

Certainly we would not want to miss the brilliance of Bach's (or Handel's) high trumpet-cum-timpani sound. Nor do we want to miss the harpsichord as continuo instrument, because its fine blending with strings makes up for its inability to balance properly with the soloist(s). But regarding works for the solo clavier, a strong case can be made for the proposition that they gain musically and do not lose their soul by being transferred to the modern piano. In view of the supremacy of line and indifference to color, the spirit of Bach's music stands to be enhanced, not denatured, by the modern piano's potential of giving his phrases plasticity in three-dimensional space.

The case is strengthened by Eva Badura-Skoda's stunning discovery that Bach, as early as 1733, played some, maybe all, of his clavier concertos with his Leipzig Collegium Musicum on the fortepiano! These concertos, all of which were transcribed from works for the violin and other instruments in one sequence in Leipzig were then most likely destined for similar performances with the Collegium. They were, consequently, piano, not harpsichord, concertos.[20] This finding clearly punctures the harpsichord-only principle of the authenticists.

Mozart's fortepiano offers different problems. The "Viennese" piano of Mozart's time had a delicate but dry sound that decayed quickly, and a light touch that permitted clear and brilliant passage work. Its small range reached upwards only to the f'''. When we hear Mozart played on such an instrument we realize that he exploited its resources to the fullest, as Liszt did with the Erard. In passionate or dramatic sections we can get a sense of power pushing forcefully against the instrument's limits, a sense that escapes us if we hear the same on a modern concert grand piano with its reserves of unused tonal resources. That does not mean that the fortepiano is necessarily the most desirable instrument for all Mozart performances. A fine specimen does have greater transparency in the low register, where chords that sound muddy on the modern piano can be clearly discerned on the older instrument. But the low notes have a buzz-like rattle that to many ears is disturbing. The modern piano has more brilliance, power, and resonance; and these assets, I believe, more than outweigh its lesser transparency in the bass register.

To give just one illustration from a famous authentic organization: Mozart's C-Minor Concerto played by John Gibbons on the fortepiano with Frans Brüggen directing the Orchestra of the Eighteenth Century (in a 1986 recording). This grandiose concerto simply does not make the effect it ought to make. The dry sound of the fortepiano and the quick decay of its tone are drawbacks that are further accentuated by the very low pitch (practically a half-tone lower). The drawbacks are perhaps most noticeable in the slow movement where the empty spaces between notes often threaten to disrupt the line, and where the unquestionable loveliness of the woodwinds cannot make up for the unsatisfactory sound of the piano. At the very slow tempo taken, too slow in my opinion, the movement needs more added ornamentation than would be proper for a modern piano or for a faster tempo.

True, there are other recordings where the sound of the fortepiano is less disturbing but never fully satisfying. By and large, a Mozart concerto played by a fine artist on a modern piano offers an artistic experience that to a listener with an open mind will convey the spirit of the work with greater immediacy, power, and intensity than could be had from a performance by an artistically equivalent authenticist. "Immediacy" is the key word, because the listener does not have to go through the mental effort of putting himself or herself into a historic frame of mind, of adjusting to a seemingly wrong pitch, and of trying to impersonate an eighteenth-century listener. For much of the music of that era only an unbalanced sense of proportions can assign such commanding priority to exact tone color and would-be historical pitch in view of the essential elements listed previously that combine to form the core of a work's nature.

It is sometimes a similar lack of proportion that informs the obsession with the exact number of performers where we believe we know it. Only if the numbers had been the composer's free artistic choice would their integrity be of musical significance, but such was rarely the case. Mostly the numbers were dictated not by musical but by economic reasons; if such was the case, then there is little reason for aiming at literalness, as long as a larger complement of players or singers does not upset the balance or blur the sonorities.

If we are to orient ourselves in the controversial territory of how to perform early music for today's audiences, we must realize that two factors are involved and that the two should be kept apart. One is historical; the other, musical, and the two can be at odds. A replica of an authoritative old performance would be of great *historical* interest as an exhibit of musical archeology: the unearthing of an old monument in its original shape. But to do so is clearly beyond our grasp. Still, even if the attempt at reconstruction cannot help falling short of its aim, it is fascinating to hear the sound of the period instruments. And that sound can be enlightening too: it can sometimes reveal facets of a composition that the modern instrument could not communicate. The greater clarity of the bass register of the fortepiano has been mentioned. Old playing techniques can reveal characteristics of articulation. Or, for another example, the density of *agréments* in Couperin is closely linked to the quickly decaying, inflexible sound of the harpsichord, while their quantity is redundant on the modern piano. Similarly, with regard to *Besetzung*, a small chorus with its greater transparency can bring a polyphonic texture into clearer focus than some of today's huge choral organizations.

As to the musical factor, performance has to be above all *musically* satisfying; it is not sufficient that it is historically interesting. The authenticists will not admit that the historical and the musical factors can be in conflict. In their conviction, what they claim to be historically correct, like the period instruments and the lower pitch, is *ipso facto* also musically superior. Now the question of whether the old instruments have a more beautiful and expressive sound than their modern counterparts is of course a matter of taste, and taste, as the old saying goes, is not open to debate. Hence, they are entitled to their belief, but so are others, including myself, entitled to disagree. But I am not alone even among my peers and I quote again from Taruskin's essay on authenticity: "The common claim . . . that 'Baroque instruments, played in an appropriate manner, have a greater expressive range than their modern equivalents' is the purest gabble."[21]

The meaning of a composition can be revealed only in *musical* terms and most effectively in the musical language that is most familiar, hence most readily understood and assimilated by today's listener. What matters in a performance above all is that it gives for the work in question a compelling account that is in rapport with its style and spirit. Questions of sonorities will enter into the equation but for most works only superficially. And whatever importance one might assign to them, they must not be subjected to a moral judgment of right and wrong, only to the aesthetic one of adding to or subtracting from the effectiveness with which the message of a work is conveyed. The way the authenticists make the use of period instruments the object of a categorical imperative, hence an issue of morality, reveals a cultist trait of their movement;

and this in turn explains the zealotry with which some of their followers demand conformance and condemn any questioning of their dogmas.

In expressing my personal opinion I know that I speak for a small outspoken minority, but also, I believe, for a large silent majority. I feel that, apart from concerts devoted to historical demonstration, we would do well to use the period instruments for standard performances whenever their sound will yield musical benefits; or where, like for music of the Middle Ages and the Renaissance, they are well-nigh indispensable; we should feel free to use modern instruments where the latter will offer musical results that to modern ears have a superior sound and can therefore, in terms of eighteenth-century aesthetics, more powerfully arouse our emotions.

We must credit the early music movement for two important benefits to our musical life. It has substantially enriched the living repertory through the revival of numerous works that hitherto had been unjustly neglected. And it has given us new insights into familiar works when, for instance, a greater transparency allowed inner voices to be heard that had often been obscured, or when the different sonorities revealed new kinds of balance between the parts.

On the other hand, the movement has had a certain stultifying effect through the dogmatic insistence of its practitioners on freezing old masterworks in the form of their alleged original sound, then hermetically sealing them as a protection against any harm from exposure to twentieth-century fresh air. In so doing, the authenticists behave like custodians of museum exhibits, when they ought to behave like wardens of living organisms whose souls are capable of constant renewal in adjusting to changing conditions.

In the aesthetic pleasure we derive from listening to old masterworks, both the past and the present are involved. Try as we might, we cannot disown our ears, accustomed as they are to modern pitch and modern instrumental and vocal sounds. Of course we should never cease trying to find out all we can about the past and about the composer's presumable concepts. And we must study and explore the spirit of a work so that we can communicate our understanding of it to our listeners in the most effective way possible. Often, perhaps mostly, the most effective medium of communication will be the musical vernacular of our time, not the pronunciations and dialects of centuries past. In following this path we have a good chance of successfully merging the past with the present while neither betraying the past nor shortchanging the present.

Notes

1. Friedrich Wilhelm Marpurg had in the mid-eighteenth century already implied this aim when he wrote that a musician "has to have the greatest sensitivity and most auspicious gift of divination" ("die grösste Empfindlichkeit und die glücklichste Errathungskraft") if he is to interpret properly somebody else's work. *Des critischen Musicus an der Spree*, vol. 1 (Berlin, 1750), p. 216.

2. Edward Dannreuther, *Musical Ornamentation*, 2 vols. (London, 1889–90); Adolf Beyschlag, *Die Ornamentik der Musik* (Leipzig, 1908).

3. Richard Taruskin in *Early Music* 12 (February 1984): 12.

4. Arnold Dolmetsch, *The Interpretation of the Music of the 17th and 18th Centuries* (London, 1915), p. 62.

5. On this point see my *Essays in Performance Practice* (Ann Arbor, 1982), chaps. 5–9.

6. Dolmetsch, pp. 78–87.

7. On this point see chap. 4 of this volume and chap. 3 of my *Essays* (1982).

8. See also chap. 7 of this volume.

9. Thurston Dart, *The Interpretation of Music* (American edition, New York, 1963), pp. 81–82.

10. Regarding H. Klotz, see chap. 9 of this volume.

11. Arthur Mendel, "Pitch in Western Music since 1500: A Re-examination," *Acta Musicologica* 50 (1978): 19–20.

12. Ibid., p. 82.

13. On this point see chap. 11 of this volume.

14. Ibid.

15. Donington, *The Interpretation of Early Music*, new version (London, 1974), p. 235.

16. *Versuch einer gründlichen Violinschule* (Augsburg, 1756), chap. 5, par. 3. On this point see also chap. 8 of this volume.

17. "Tradition, Anxiety, and the Current Musical Scene," in *Authenticity and Early Music*, ed. Nicholas Kenyon (Oxford, 1988), p. 70.

18. *Musica aeterna* (Zurich, 1950), p. 126.

19. "The Limits of Authenticity," *Early Music* 12 (February 1984): 7.

20. Eva Badura-Skoda will publish her convincing evidence in the *Bach Jahrbuch* of 1990.

21. Taruskin, p. 11.

Part Two

Problems of Rhythm

3

Conflicting Binary and Ternary Rhythms:
From the Theory of Mensural Notation
to the Music of J. S. Bach

From the sixteenth through the nineteenth centuries, the question of simultaneous binary and ternary rhythms has been a controversial issue of performance practice. For any composer and any era the problem focuses on two alternatives: literalness (and the ensuing rhythmic clash) or assimilation (of one rhythmic mode with the other). The issue is complex, and it would be well to start with basic principles. Later, I shall discuss Bach's usage, but not before taking a look at the antecedents present in mensural notation.

The Nature of the Problem

Binary rhythms such as c ♩ ♫ ♫. ♫ and ternary rhythms such as c ♩ ♪ ♫ ♫ or ⁹₈ ♩ ♪♫ ♫ are defined by clear mathematical ratios. Problems arise whenever the execution deviates more than marginally from these relationships. There are two main reasons for such deviations: deficiencies in the notation, in which case the deviations were intended; or deficiencies in the performer's skill, in which case the deviations were not intended.

The notational deficiency with the most serious consequences for our problem is the absence—from the post-mensural era until the mid-nineteenth century—of the 2:1 symbol ♩♪ within binary meter. To compensate for its absence, composers used as substitutes either the 3:1 dotted-note symbol ♫ (. ♩♪) or, much less frequently, the 1:1 symbol of two equal notes, ♫ (. ♩♪). As a result, both of these binary symbols have become ambiguous and their intended meaning must be inferred from the context.

Deficiencies in a performer's skill do not normally enter into a discussion of a desired performance, but certain deficiencies deserve mention because they

This article originally appeared in *The Music Forum* 6, no. 1 (New York, 1987). Reprinted by permission of the publisher.

gave rise to questionable theories of interpretation. In considering such technical shortcomings, we find that some rhythmic formulas are troublesome in themselves, whereas others become troublesome because of what precedes them or occurs simultaneously. Both the dotted note and the triplet can be troublesome in themselves. The dotted-note figure, when rendered literally, expresses a 3:1 ratio. As the tempo increases, however, this ratio becomes more and more difficult to execute and tends to move toward a 2:1 or even a 3:2 proportion:

♩♪ becomes ♩♪ and may become ♩♪ .

While triplets are generally easy to render when strung out in a row (e.g., c♩ ♪♪♪ ♪♪♪ ♪♪♪), they can be difficult when they occur alone. Here we find a tendency (still operative today among performers at all levels of accomplishment) to execute them as binary anapests; thus c♩. ♪♪♪ | ♩. becomes ♩. ♪♪♪ | ♩. . This tendency is strengthened when a triplet is preceded by binary rhythms (e.g., c♩ ♪♪ ♪♪ ♪♪♪). Conversely, even binary notes can be troublesome when they follow a series of triplets. Here the binary notes often tend to adjust to the ternary swing, and c♪♪♪ ♪♪♪ ♪♪♩ becomes ♪♪♪ ♪♪♪ ♩ ♪♪ .

These tendencies are intensified when the conflicting rhythms occur simultaneously in two voices. When one of these rhythmic modes is dominant, it tends to pull the other into its orbit; thus a dominant binary rhythm can easily cause triplets to become binary:[1]

Similarly, a dominant ternary rhythm might cause duplets to become ternary:

The weaker the skills of the performer in mastering complex rhythms, the stronger the tendency toward assimilation.

The Two-against-Three Polarity in the Era of Mensural Notation

In the course of the sixteenth century, singers' skills in handling polyrhythms may have gradually declined as the rhythmic complexities in the age of Obrecht and Isaac gave way to the simpler rhythms of the age of Palestrina and Lasso.

At the end of the century, extended polyrhythms in the form of different mensuration for simultaneous voices became rather rare; more common were short passages, typically written in blackened notation, indicating ternary (3:2) hemiolia proportion within an otherwise binary setting. The most frequent two-against-three rhythmic clashes were now occasioned by single triplets, sometimes written as blackened breves or semibreves, but most characteristically notated as blackened minims together with the numeral 3 (the predecessor of the modern triplet: ♩♩♩). Even the mild difficulty of singing three against two in such settings obviously prompted some singers to take the path of least resistance and to give the triplets a binary performance, mainly transforming them into anapests, though sometimes rendering them as dactyls.

In the seventeenth century, when mensural notation was in dissolution, a further decline of vocal skills may have prompted Rudolph Lasso, in his posthumous edition of his father's works, to change Orlando's blackened triplets into anapests.[2] In keeping with such practices, or in an effort to facilitate performance, a few seventeenth-century theorists, mainly those writing in Germany, formally authorized this kind of simplification. Such authorization is analogous to the inclusion in a dictionary of a popular usage heretofore considered illiterate. However, as will be shown presently, the great majority of writers, among them such eminent sixteenth-century theorists as Zarlino and Zacconi, as well as Banchieri, Praetorius, Friderici, Carissimi, Crüger, Mylius, and other theorists of the seventeenth century, insisted on literalness for single triplets for the very sake of the rhythmic conflict that occasionally ensued.

Yet the existence of a few permissive theorists has caused some modern writers, such as Ernst Praetorius and Michael Collins, to mistake their license for a binding law. Collins even goes so far as to outlaw all rhythmic conflict: he asserts that, from the fifteenth to the eighteenth century, any rhythmic clash of two against three is a musical chimera, existing only on paper, since it is always assimilated in performance. In his effort to achieve complete consistency he insists on assimilation even when the two rhythmic modes follow one another in a single voice, with no clashes in sight. To illustrate this principle, he purges Prelude XIV of *The Well-Tempered Clavier,* Book II, of all its many triplets by "resolving" them into binary figures. The patent inappropriateness of such radical surgery is hardly in need of a critical probe. We have every reason to assume that when Bach wrote a triplet he intended it to be just that: the little numeral 3 he invariably used signaled a ternary rhythm—it was not written for the purpose of deceiving the performer into reading the figure as binary.[3]

In his essay on mensural notation, Arthur Mendel comments briefly on the work of Collins, Ernst Praetorius, and several other writers.[4] He characterizes as "Eier des Columbus" (i.e., as simplistic solutions to complex problems) their attempts to elevate into law a practice occasionally engaged in by singers—the practice of avoiding a hurdle of notation by taking the easiest way out.[5] Mendel's criticism goes to the heart of the matter, yet several factors prompt me to present a brief reply to Collins's thesis: First, his study, undertaken with an impressive scholarly apparatus, is the most ambitious of all modern attempts to ban two-against-three discrepancies. Second, Collins claims that this taboo lasted for three hundred years, from 1450 to 1750, hence encompassing all of Bach's works.[6] Third, the many scholars, editors, and performers who share the belief in obligatory synchronization for the works of Bach and his contemporaries add credibility to Collins's thesis, even if he was not the source of their opinions.

Collins's ideas are expounded in two articles, one devoted to the sesquialtera proportion in the sixteenth century, and the other to the triplet in the seventeenth and eighteenth centuries.[7] I shall discuss mainly the first of these articles, which provides the foundation for his entire thesis, inasmuch as Collins assumes that the interpretation of triplets in the seventeenth and eighteenth centuries was still rooted in sixteenth-century rules.

In the sixteenth century, the application of the sesquialtera proportion was signaled by $\frac{3}{2}$, which indicated that three notes would thereafter have the same combined duration as that previously given two notes of the same nominal value. It could apply to all note values, but most commonly referred to the minim (half note) whereby $c\downarrow\downarrow$ or $\mathcal{C}\downarrow\downarrow$ would equal $\frac{3}{2}\downarrow\downarrow\downarrow$. Each new half note would lose one-third of its former value and so would all of its subdivisions and aggregates. The effect is a speeding up of the tempo and the establishment of a ternary meter in the modern sense. We have here the exact equivalent of the modern indication used at a change of meter as when, for example, the composer writes the equation $\downarrow\downarrow = \downarrow\downarrow\downarrow$ above the staff at a change from $\frac{4}{4}$ to $\frac{6}{4}$. The hemiolia has the same rhythmic effect as the sesquialtera but is indicated by blackened notes instead of by a proportional fraction.

There are numerous flaws in Collins's arguments, of which inner contradictions may be the most striking. For instance, concerning the sesquialtera (and hemiolia) Collins presents three conflicting theories:

1. He states that these proportions "do not exist at all in performance"[8] and "have no audible effect in sixteenth-century music";[9] hence they are only a "chimera."[10]

2. He contends that they *do* exist when they appear in all voices of a composition, in which case "a triple measure results."[11] Yet he affirms that they cease to exist when set against a binary measure in another voice. In other words, they are part "chimera," part reality.

3. For Collins, the sesquialtera is not *one* proportion, but a mixture of several: only perfect (i.e., ternary) breves and semibreves can lose one-third of their value, but all imperfect (i.e., binary) values, including all minims and smaller denominations (which are imperfect under any circumstances), can lose only one-fourth, one-half, or nothing at all. Collins argues: "To the sixteenth-century theorists it would be unthinkable for a minim to lose one-third, for minims . . . were always imperfect and therefore not divisible by three. In sesquialtera, therefore, either the first or the third of three minims retains its value, while the remaining two lose half their value. . . . Thus the sesquialtera proportion . . . is changed by the equal tactus into a binary measure."[12]

A binary sesquialtera—a contradiction in terms, like a binary triangle—could never assume the part-time ternary role Collins assigns it in what I list above as his second theory. The conflict between the three theories cannot be resolved.

The third theory given above is the centerpiece of Collins's thesis and needs a closer look. Why should a minim, or an imperfect breve or semibreve, not be divisible by three? Or by five, by nine, or by any random number? Is not the very essence of the system of proportions its capacity to reduce or expand *any* note value by *any* ratio indicated in the multitude of fractions we find in the proportional tables formulated by theorists from Gaffurius to Morley? If the simple proportion 3:2 is incapable of reducing a minim by one-third of its value, then the whole system of proportions becomes meaningless.

What is the basis for such ideas? They seem to originate in two misconceptions. First, Collins equates, and thereby confuses, coloration with sesquialtera. Now it is true that blackened notes occurring in groups generally signify hemiolia proportion; they lose one-third of their individual value, exactly as in sesquialtera. But coloration—an issue beset with controversy and ambiguity—can have different functions and effects. It can signify syncopation, whereby no value is lost, or in other situations it can variously mean the loss of one-fourth, one-third, or even one-half of the value of the notes. Sesquialtera, on the other hand, by definition always—and unambiguously—subtracts one-third of the value of the notes in a simple and straightforward process of diminution. Second, Collins subscribes to the mistaken notion that equal tactus enforces binary rhythm. This is comparable to the erroneous idea that a modern binary meter such as $\frac{2}{4}$, with its two equal beats, can tolerate only binary rhythms, and that in this environment triplets are inconsistent elements which must be reshaped into dactyls or anapests.[13]

Collins is further led astray by his injudicious use of the numerous sources he cites. He summons many important theorists—Tigrini, Glareanus, Vanneo, Zarlino, Zacconi, Banchieri, and others—as witnesses in defense of his theories, yet in fact they contradict his ideas, as we shall see. (For reasons of space, I shall limit my discussion to only a few of Collins's many quotations.)

The pitfalls of translation are made apparent in Collins's quotation from Stefano Vanneo's *Recanetum de musica aurea* of 1533. Vanneo explains that the proportion 3:2 results in the reduction of *every* note by one-third, with three notes becoming equal in both measure and length to what were formerly two: "ideo quaelibet notula, diminuetur in tertia, itaque tres notulae aequivalebunt metro & quantitate duarum."[14] Collins translates: "whatever note [exceeds another by the third part of three] is to be diminished by a third."[15] Now the word *quaelibet* (the feminine form of *quilibet*) signifies "any one without distinction," "no matter who," "any," or "all."[16] Collins's insertion of the bracketed phrase limits the reduction by one-third to specific notes instead of applying it to *all* of them, thus contradicting the meaning of the original text. By his arbitrary insert Collins tries to stave off Vanneo's clear inference of a ternary measure.

Collins's basic premise that only a perfect note—never an imperfect one—can be shortened by one-third through blackening, is contradicted by a number of theorists. I shall cite two among many. Gregorius Faber writes: "How does color affect imperfect notes? If blackness appears in single notes, then one-fourth is taken away, except where the blackening of a series of notes indicates hemiolia proportion."[17] Since hemiolia proportion is 3:2, the imperfect notes involved do in fact lose one-third of their value. Martin Agricola, speaking of sesquialtera, says that every note governed by the sign $\frac{3}{2}$ is deprived of one-third of its value. He goes on to say that "this proportion will (as Franchinus [Gaffurius] says) on occasion be expressed and recognized without such a sign, alone through the blackening of the *imperfect* notes."[18]

For an example of how Collins misinterprets his sources, let us turn to Gioseffo Zarlino. Zarlino gives the standard explanation for the meaning of the sesquialtera proportion. He tells us that when the $\frac{3}{2}$ sign occurs in all the parts it is conducted with unequal beat ("si usa . . . la Battuta inequale"),[19] but when it is opposed in one or more voices by a binary meter, equal beat should be used.[20] This is plain common sense. One cannot beat two different meters at the same time, and this is just as true today as it was four hundred years ago. When there is polymeter, the conductor beats the simpler of the two meters (here the equal beat); the other meter with its contrasting rhythms must simply fit in—to use Zarlino's expression, "accomodarsi" (or, as Zacconi has it, "adattarsi"). Collins's inference that a sesquialtera cannot clash with an equal beat and that its first two notes must fall on the downstroke and the third on the upstroke of the equal beat is an arbitrary interpretation that finds no support in Zarlino's text.

Collins also quotes several passages by Ludovico Zacconi. Speaking only of the single triplet, Zacconi declares that it is not to be sung "in proportion."[21]

He speaks of "Proportione" here only in the sense of ternary meter (indicated by such signs as $\frac{3}{2}$ or $\frac{3}{1}$). By contrast, individual triplets (to which he refers as "Sesquialtere ò Emiolie") occur in binary meter, hence under equal tactus. To fit such triplets into equal tactus is difficult, he admits, since it involves a conflict between tactus and notes. And because of this difficulty, he continues, the older masters took the precaution of using these figures sparingly ("gli antichi ... hanno anco havuto quest' avertenza d'introducrene poche per la difficultà che seco portano, convenendosi fare due attioni contrarie, una del tatto, & l'altra delle figure"). He goes on to tell us that when they were indeed used, such figures enriched compositions with "not unpleasant" effects ("non sono disdicevoli").[22] The three points Zacconi makes about individual triplets—the difficulty of execution, the conflict with the tactus, and the "not unpleasant" effect—confirm that the triplet is rendered in its literal ternary rhythm; this description would not make sense if the triplet were to be squared in assimilation. It is difficult to see how Collins could have hoped to extract from these quotations a confirmation of his theories.

Even more pertinent to the central issue of Collins's thesis is Zacconi's devotion of an entire chapter to the legality of two against three. He writes in chapter 73 of book 3: "If we consider the great potentialities of music and the vast jurisdiction of the composers in arranging and using the musical materials, ... everybody can judge for himself, if he is not out of his mind ['se non è privo di mente'] that ... in particular, hemiolia, sesquialtera, and tripla within a binary melody make no unpleasant effect, but a very satisfying one that gives great delight ['non fanno effetto difforme; ma effetto competente, che rende assai dilettatione']."[23] The whole chapter is in effect a eulogy of such polyrhythm. As an illustration, he presents an example by Senfl in which all parts are in ternary rhythm except the tenor, which is written from beginning to end in a binary measure ("secondo la misura binaria sino al fine").[24] The implication of rhythmic clashes that give "great delight" is inescapable and, of course, so is the inference that a "chimerical" sesquialtera proportion could not produce such pleasurable results.

The rhythmic conflict of two against three is suggestively evoked by several eminent theorists who emphasize the rhythmic clashes by their use of the word "contra." For instance, Hermann Finck explains the sesquialtera thus: "quando tres notulae *contra* dues (natura & specie sibi similes) locantur."[25] Specifying that the three notes of the sesquialtera are of the same kind, as are the two notes of the binary meter, he excludes any rhythmic assimilation. Lucas Lossius echoes Finck's definition of the sesquialtera: "Est, in qua tres notae *contra* duas sibi specie similes proferuntur." Again, three notes of equal character set against two notes of equal character.[26] For Michael Praetorius, singing "against the beat" is characteristic of the sesquialtera: "in Sesquialtera proportione si quando *contra* tactum cantatur."[27] Adriano Banchieri describes the sesquialtera as three minims sung against two: "quand' una ò più voci cantano tre minime *contra* altri che ne cantano dui."[28]

As mentioned above, there were a few German theorists who legitimized the "path of least resistance" by sanctioning the binary performance of single triplets. With one exception, they all date from the early seventeenth century, a time when the mensural system was in decline. It is important to note that they all limit such squaring to the *single triplet;* they do not apply it to the sesquialtera proportion as the prevailing mensuration (meter). Thus one should guard against confusing a triplet with ternary meter and avoid generalizations about the sesquialtera based on procedures intended for a single triplet. Finck, who predates the other theorists, squares the single triplet into the unusual form of a

dactyl (♩♪♪) rather than the far more common anapest. He explains that this reflects the verbal rhythm of the German word *sech-ze-hen.* We have already seen that he spoke of a rhythmic clash when the sesquialtera, as opposed to the single triplet, is set against a binary rhythm.

Collins cites seven theorists of the seventeenth century: Elsmann, Gengenbach, Hase, Trümper, Quitschreiber, Vulpius, and Beringer.[29] All seven speak only of the single triplet, not of the sesquialtera proportion, and most of them, as Collins admits, mistake the blackened minims of the triplet for regular semiminims. When viewed as semiminims, the three notes of the triplet leave a metrical void, which these theorists then fill by extending one of the "semiminims" to a minim. Yet if correctly viewed as blackened minims, each shortened by one-third through the color, the three notes fit perfectly into the measure. It is unwise to accept the testimony of men on a matter they do not understand. And these theorists are unreliable for other reasons. Beringer was a self-confessed plagiarist whose writings are hardly useful as a primary source. The same is true of Vulpius, whose work is a paraphrase of Heinrich Faber's treatise. Elsmann's treatise is so primitive that it does not include a single word on proportions. Quitschreiber, in what is basically an elementary textbook, deals with proportions in only one brief sentence. As for the rest, Hase and Trümper make it clear that the squaring does not apply to sesquialtera. Nicolaus Gengenbach, the most substantial writer of the group, illustrates the integrity of the sesquialtera proportion:

He writes: "When in tripla proportion three black breves, or in sesquialtera three [black] semibreves follow one another they have the value of only two beats, hence the middle note is divided in half."[30] This is, of course, the equivalent of the present-day "hemiola," where a triplet crosses a beat or the measure line.

Other theorists confirm this explanation. Daniel Friderici formulates his "third rule" in nearly identical terms: "When three blackened breves follow one another, they are not perfected, but the three fit into two beats ["sie gehen alle 3 auf 2 Schläge"] and the one in the middle is halved."[31] The same applies, he continues, to minims and semibreves in sesquialtera:

[musical notation example]

Johann Crüger says exactly the same thing about three successive blackened breves in tripla: they fit into two beats whereby the middle one is split in two ("omnes ad duos solummodo tactus exprimuntur, una media tactus separatur").[32] He graphically illustrates the split:

[musical notation example]

Crüger adds that the same applies to the three blackened semibreves of *hemiolia major* (which he says is the same as tripla) and to the three blackened minims of *hemiolia minor,* which he equates with sesquialtera. In *Ars cantandi,* a treatise presumed to be written in the mid-seventeenth century and attributed to Giacomo Carissimi, the author explains that the blackened breves and semibreves have the same value as the white ones, and are used when the middle note in a succession of three is to be divided:[33]

[musical notation example]

In very much the same way, Wolfgang Michael Mylius, writing in 1685, illustrates the identical value of blackened and white breves, and demonstrates the use of the blackened breves for straddling the beat:[34]

[musical notation example]

As late as 1707, Franz Xaver Anton Murschhauser shows the *hemiolia major* with the second of three blackened breves split by the measure line:[35]

[musical notation example]

None of these quotations and illustrations—and more could be given from such authors as Calvisius, Walliser, Gesius, Crappius, and Crusius (who make not a single mention of squaring)—support the patterns of resolution (i.e., binary interpretation) of the hemiolia given by Collins:[36]

Though single triplets may often have been squared by unskilled singers, the sesquialtera proportion as such was neither affected by such practices nor included in the theoretical descriptions of rhythmic alterations. And, as we have seen, many substantial writers of the seventeenth century affirm the integrity of even the single triplet in their explanation and depiction of the straddling middle note. Set against a binary rhythm in another voice, such a triplet is bound to produce a rhythmic clash.

The sesquialtera itself was thus neither inaudible nor chimeric; it was very audible and real. Its occurrence against binary mensuration in other voices became less frequent as the sixteenth century progressed, but it did not by any means vanish from the musical scene. Zacconi, as we have seen, praised the pleasurable effect of its rhythmic conflicts, and Palestrina used the device from time to time, e.g. in the Kyrie of his *Missa L'Homme armé*.

There are still later examples of binary-ternary confrontations. In the preface to Frescobaldi's *Primo libro delle canzoni* . . . (1628), the publisher, Bartolomeo Grassi, discusses the unusual time symbols ("qualche tempo non solito"). He tells us that these symbols, with one part in ternary measure ("tempo di proportione") and the other in common time ("tempo ordinario"), are not mistakes, but have been carefully thought out, and that the exquisite care with which he has printed the notes in the exact disposition of their values ("che ogni una delle note porta il suo valore al debito luogo") has made them easy to play.[37] The ninth Toccata in Frescobaldi's *Secondo libreto di toccate* . . . (1637) contains fascinating binary-ternary cross-rhythms in several episodes; the sesquialtera, expressed respectively as $\frac{6}{4}$ and $\frac{12}{8}$, is set against ₵ in the other hand. Frescobaldi comments on the problem of execution: "Non senza fatiga si giunge al fine" (it takes trouble to reach the end).[38] If he had intended assimilation rather than conflict, the performance of the piece would not have been troublesome. We find similar cross-rhythms in some works of Johann Kaspar Kerll, Frescobaldi's student.[39]

A few striking cases of binary-ternary conflict occur in the *Fitzwilliam Virginal Book,* dating from the early years of the seventeenth century. Perhaps the most remarkable passage is to be found in Variation 14 of John Bull's *Gloria tibi trinitas*.[40]

The documentation that supports the existence of two-against-three rhythmic conflicts is abundant and impressive. Thus we do not have to worry about would-be "sixteenth-century rules" that prohibited such conflicts, let alone about the possibility that they could have remained in force for over one-and-a-half centuries beyond their time—thus well into Bach's era. The attempt to establish the existence of such a long-lasting ban deserves more commendation for single-minded courage than for persuasiveness.

The Performance of Bach's Binary-Ternary Rhythms

Turning now to Bach—and implicitly to many of his contemporaries—we find that a belief in the obligatory assimilation of simultaneous (not successive) rhythmic discrepancies is widespread among modern performers and editors. There are indeed many cases where such assimilation was intended, but many others where it was not, and still others where the answer is uncertain. In the following pages I shall attempt to sort out these alternatives.

At the outset, it would be well to show that binary-ternary rhythmic clashes, far from being outlawed, are an important ingredient of Bach's musical idiom. We can draw upon a reliable testimonial by Johann Friedrich Agricola who, as a young man, had studied with Bach. In 1769, reviewing a clavier treatise by Löhlein that advocated the synchronization of triplets with dotted notes, Agricola writes: "Such synchronization takes place only in extreme speed. Barring this, the note after the dot must be played not with, but *after* the last note of the triplet. Otherwise the difference between the binary measure, where such notes occur, and the $\frac{3}{8}$, $\frac{6}{8}$, $\frac{9}{8}$, or $\frac{12}{8}$ meter would be obliterated. This is what J. S. Bach taught all his students and this too is what Quantz teaches in his treatise. Surely no one will have reservations about the performing skill and artistic sensitivity of these two men."[41] With its allusions to such high authority, this statement would seem to call for literalness in most binary-ternary clashes. Yet we shall presently see that this theoretical rule, like most others, is subject to qualifications.

One of the most striking passages in Bach's works where clashes were obviously intended is found in the Chorale from Cantata No. 105 (ex. 3.1). Here the clashes are made explicit beyond any possible doubt. Against a steady $\frac{4}{4}$ meter for voices and continuo, the initial sixteenth notes of the strings change to even eighth notes in $\frac{12}{8}$ meter halfway through the sixth measure, becoming *de facto* triplets in genuine sesquialtera proportion. In measure 12 they slow down even further to regular eighth notes in $\frac{4}{4}$. Then, in order to clarify the return to ternary rhythm in measure 18, Bach (in one of only two cases known to me) wrote the numeral 3 over four of the quarter plus eighth note figures—a notation that, strangely enough, was to elude composers for more than a century.[42] The autograph score is a document impervious to any rhythmic manipulation, and is indeed a manifesto for the eloquence of binary-ternary clashes.[43] The gradual slowing of the agitated orchestral rhythm is a poignant musical description of faith calming a troubled conscience.

Example 3.1.   J. S. Bach, Cantata No. 105, Chorale

Example 3.1.   (continued)

Equally clear are the clashes shown in example 3.2: between the binary timpani figures and the oboe triplets in a passage from the Easter Oratorio (ex. 3.2a); between trumpet and strings in Cantata No. 75 (ex. 3.2b); and between binary string patterns and clavier triplets in the Clavier Concerto in E Major (ex. 3.2c). In the opening of the Brandenburg Concerto No. 1 (ex. 3.2d), the horn triplets must be given a literal reading that clashes with the binary patterns played by the rest of the orchestra; this is confirmed by the alternation of triplets and anapest figures.

Example 3.2a.   J. S. Bach, Easter Oratorio

Example 3.2b.   J. S. Bach, Cantata No. 75

Example 3.2c.   J. S. Bach, Harpsichord Concerto in E Major

Example 3.2d. J. S. Bach, Brandenburg Concerto No. 1, first movement

Less explicit notationally but just as convincing musically is the situation in the Sonata for Violin and Harpsichord in E Major (ex. 3.3). The first thirty-four measures are strictly binary (see the opening given in ex. 3.3a). Note that

the rhythmic motive ♩♪♪♩│♩ in measures 23–25 is of thematic importance (see ex. 3.3b). Then measure 35 initiates a long section with triplet figuration (see ex. 3.3c). The triplets are interspersed with a series of quotations from the binary section and in addition are consistently set against the thematically significant binary rhythmic motive. This motive has a claim to rhythmic integrity: a literal reading is not only more logical but also adds a new dimension to the contrapuntal interweaving of the voices.

Example 3.3. J. S. Bach, Sonata for Violin and Harpsichord in E Major,
                 final movement

Example 3.3.   (continued)

The claim of a motive to rhythmic integrity will often tip the scales in favor of literalness whenever there could be a reasonable doubt. I shall give two illustrations out of many. In the Organ Sonata in D Minor the motive ♫ ♫ starts and ends the movement and recurs many times, thus establishing its identity as a leading thematic idea. As such it must not be tampered with, specifically in measure 57 (ex. 3.4) and in measure 85, where it is set against a triplet figure in the left-hand part.

Example 3.4.   J. S. Bach, Organ Sonata in D Minor, first movement

Especially interesting is a passage from the three-voice Ricercar of *The Musical Offering* (ex. 3.5a). At first glance we would be inclined to synchronize the iambic beats in the lower voice with the third note of the triplet figure in the upper voice because of the simple motion of the two voices in parallel thirds. But if we look at an earlier passage in the same piece (ex. 3.5b), we see that the iambic figure has motivic importance. Hence the lower voice in example 3.5 is not a harmonic filler, but is the inversion of the earlier statement of the motive. Its motivic nature should therefore be emphasized through rhythmic independence.

Example 3.5a.   J. S. Bach, *The Musical Offering*, Ricercar

Example 3.5b.   J. S. Bach, *The Musical Offering*, Ricercar, earlier
             passage

It is instructive to compare this example with the passage from the early Organ Chorale, *Christ lag in Todes Banden,* given in example 3.6. Here, within the framework of a completely ternary passage, where the harmony often changes on the third note of the triplet figure, the eighth-note iambic upbeats in the left hand have no motivic significance. They serve a purely harmonic function and were presumably meant to be synchronized with the third note of the triplet.

Example 3.6.   J. S. Bach, Organ Chorale, *Christ lag in Todes Banden*

Another case of evenly written notes that are given a ternary interpretation is shown in example 3.7, which presents passages from *Herr Gott, nun schleuss den Himmel auf* found in the *Orgelbüchlein.* Here internal factors suggest synchronization through a 2:1 adaptation of the eighth notes in the right hand, which results in a superior polyphonic combination with the running sixteenth notes of the left hand. This is seen most convincingly in measure 19: the eighth notes B♮–B♭ in the right hand, if played with rhythmic literalness, would clash intolerably with the left hand's sixteenth notes C♯–B♮. External evidence—the vertical alignment found in the autograph—provides a measure of confirmation (see the dotted lines in ex. 3.7).[44] Not all of these alignments are conclusive, but in two cases, the B♭ in measure 19 just mentioned, and the F♯ in measure 22, are clearly placed directly about the fifth sixteenth note of the left hand, and in two other cases the second eighth is definitely written to the right of the fourth sixteenth note. The strange alignment in the last measure was caused by great crowding.

Example 3.7.   J. S. Bach, *Orgelbüchlein: Herr Gott, nun schleuss den Himmel auf*

The *Orgelbüchlein* provides another example: the controversial passage from *In dulci jubilo*. Example 3.8 shows the two pages of the autograph.[45] Beginning in measure 3 (see ex. 3.8a), quarter notes are set against eighth-note triplets that fill the space of a half note. This autograph, like that of *Herr Gott, nun schleuss den Himmel auf* (ex. 3.7), is not a calligraphic score, and the vertical alignments are on the whole inconclusive. But it was Bach's practice to space his notes horizontally according to their value; here we invariably find the repeated quarter notes written with great regularity, lined up like soldiers in a row. He surely would not have done this, not even in a sketch, if he had had a rhythmic 2:1:2:1 spacing in mind. Moreover, it is probable that the quarter notes on the repeated pitch are an imitative reflection of the chorale's opening

Example 3.8. J. S. Bach, *Orgelbüchlein: In dulci jubilo*, autograph

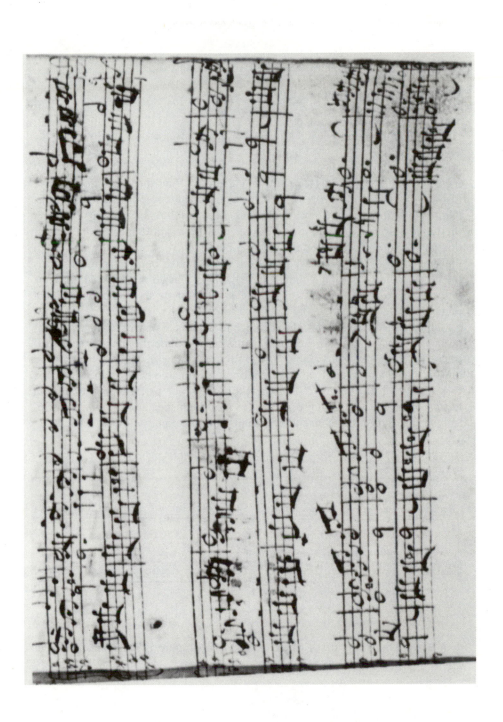

Example 3.9.   J. S. Bach, *Orgelbüchlein: Herr Gott, nun schleuss den Himmel auf*

with its three half-note A's and their canonic answer an octave lower in the second measure, as sketched in example 3.9. Thus the evenness of the quarter notes would be thematically essential. In addition, there is the evidence of measures 25, 26, and 28 (see ex. 3.8b). Here we find the second of the two instances known to me where Bach wrote a quarter plus eighth note with a triplet symbol in order to ensure synchronization. Measure 28 is particularly eloquent: the ternary figure on the first beat is preceded by a whole measure of regular quarter notes. The contrast in the notation between measures 25, 26, and 28 on the one hand and measure 27 on the other must have been intentional and is therefore indicative of a contrast in meaning. I need hardly add that the polyrhythms enrich the piece by adding a sense of depth to the intertwining parts.

In examining Bach's vocal music, we find many instances of binary versus ternary rhythms; typically, the vocal part is binary while the more agile instruments are given ternary rhythms. The ensuing rhythmic disparities were almost always intentional. Here I shall present only one notable case. In the tenor aria from Cantata No. 147 (ex. 3.10), dactyls in the voice part are contrasted with triplets in the cello. It would seem that this very sophisticated notational discrepancy was designed to produce a delicate rhythmic interplay.

Example 3.10.   J. S. Bach, Cantata No. 147, *Herz und Mund und Tat und Leben*, No. 7, Aria

But it is in those cases where a dotted-note figure is set against a triplet that we most acutely miss the 2:1 symbol ♩³♪. Whenever Bach wanted to

express the 2:1 ratio in combination with eighth-note triplets, he used the makeshift dotted eighth plus sixteenth. The problem here is to know whether the dotted note has ternary or binary meaning, i.e., whether assimilation or rhythmic contrast was intended.

A good example of a case where rhythmic contrast was presumably intended is the Adagio from the Sonata for Violin and Harpsichord in C Minor (ex. 3.11). Here the violin part and the left hand of the cembalo part are in binary rhythm throughout, in contrast to the flowing triplet motion of the right-hand cembalo part. If Bach's teaching (as reported by Agricola) were ever to apply, it would be here, where the tempo is slow enough for the rhythmic contrast to be clearly perceived as intentional. Both the violin and the bass part reinforce each other in their binary integrity.

Example 3.11.   J. S. Bach, Sonata for Violin and Harpsichord in C
Minor, Adagio

In a lively tempo, however, Bach could intend synchronization: this is clearly evident in the Brandenburg Concerto No. 5. In the third movement, there are several places in the harpsichord part where the sixteenth note of the dotted figure meets the third eighth of the triplet at the interval of one step (see ex. 3.12). With its careful calligraphy, the autograph of the harpsichord part twice places the sixteenth note inside the triplet figure;[46] this would be unthinkable if it were meant to be played after the third note of the triplet. In the rest of the movement, whenever the sixteenth meets the eighth at an interval larger than a second, the two notes are lined up in perfect verticality with unfailing consistency.

Example 3.12.   J. S. Bach, Brandenburg Concerto No. 5,
            third movement

Indeed, Bach so frequently gave the dotted note ternary meaning that it became second nature to him, and every so often he even used the dotted eighth note within a ternary context (such as $\frac{6}{8}$ or $\frac{9}{8}$ meter). Here it makes no notational sense: he should logically have written a quarter note and an eighth. A passage from *Jesus Christus, unser Heiland* provides a telling illustration (see ex. 3.13, transcribed from the autograph of the *Orgelbüchlein*).[47] The meter signatures C and $\frac{12}{8}$ appear together at the start of the piece, yet the dotted eighth-note figure in the upper voice is flanked by two ternary dotted quarter notes and is exactly lined up with the ternary 2:1 rhythm of the lower voice.

Example 3.13.   J. S. Bach, *Orgelbüchlein: Jesus Christus, unser Heiland*

Similarly, in Cantata No. 110 (see ex. 3.14, transcribed from the autograph score),[48] within $\frac{9}{8}$ meter we find an incongruous dotted eighth note in the third oboe part lined up with the logical notation of the second violin; the alto part, after a correct dotted quarter rest, has two illogical dotted eighth notes (a). This suggests that Bach was often forgetful of the exact meter signature, otherwise he would not have indiscriminately used binary-rhythm figures in ternary settings. This indifference is evident in the further course of this movement, where, still in $\frac{9}{8}$ meter, he writes the "wrong" dotted eighth notes at the end of measure 63, and then continues with the correct dotted quarter notes. A page turn interrupts the measure; in starting the new page Bach resumes as if writing in $\frac{3}{4}$ meter (b). In his mind the two meters were interchangeable; the autograph parts to this cantata, where $\frac{9}{8}$ changes to $\frac{3}{4}$, serve as direct proof.[49] But what emerges clearly from these carefree substitutions is the routine way in which Bach used the dotted eighth note with ternary meaning. From this we can conclude that whenever the tempo is not slow enough to make a rhythmic clash sound intentional, a dotted note that is set against a triplet will tend to be assimilated.

Example 3.14. J. S. Bach, Cantata No. 110

a

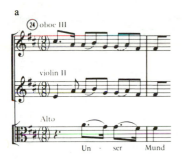

b

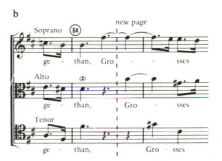

Unavoidably, an area of ambivalence will remain in cases where the tempo is not fast enough to call clearly for assimilation, nor slow enough to call clearly for rhythmic independence. The choice of tempo will understandably have a strong bearing on the performer's judgment regarding the rhythmic alternatives. The Tempo di Gavotta from the Partita in E Minor will serve as an illustration of such ambiguity (ex. 3.15). It starts with a purely binary theme (a) where the dotted notes would normally have literal meaning. In the middle of the third measure, a seemingly endless row of triplets begins in the upper voice; the dotted notes in the lower voice seem to be derived, at least in part, from the initial binary theme. A few times the theme actually opposes the triplets, as do occasional figures of four sixteenth notes that cannot be assimilated (b and c). Thus it would seem that the binary rhythm—and this includes the dotted notes—ought to affirm its independence throughout. Yet both the autograph of the early version of the piece in the *Clavierbüchlein* for Anna Magdalena and the original print of the final version show the sixteenth note of the dotted pattern consistently aligned with the third eighth of the triplet.[50] Thus it seems that passages of rhythmic conflict were meant to alternate with passages of assimilation.

Example 3.15. J. S. Bach, Partita in E Minor, Tempo di Gavotta

a

Example 3.15.   (continued)

In attempting to sum up, we may draw the following conclusions:

1. There is no basis for the idea that binary-ternary clashes were illegal—not in the sixteenth century, not in the senveteenth century, and certainly not in Bach's time.

2. For Bach and his contemporaries, the problem of synchronization versus polyrhythm derives chiefly from the failure to provide the notation $\srcnote$ for a 2:1 ratio in a binary meter.

3. Dotted notes set against triplets are generally synchronized in a lively tempo; they tend to be differentiated in a slow tempo. In a moderate tempo much depends on whether a dotted-note pattern partakes of a characteristic binary theme or has other musical claims to independence.

4. When two even binary notes are set against a triplet, there is reason to synchronize when the binary notes are only harmonic fillers; when they have polyphonic independence, notably when they are of motivic importance, they should be differentiated by rhythmic clash.

5. In the works of Bach, the triplet is always meant to remain a triplet, because its notation, in contrast to the binary rhythms, was unambiguous. *Any assimilation occurs only from binary to ternary, not from ternary to binary rhythms*.

6. Generally, literalness is desirable when the resultant rhythmic clash sounds purposeful in clarifying thematic, rhythmic, or contrapuntal relationships; it is not desirable when it does none of these things and sounds like unintentional imprecision.

There is no magic formula for solving all the problems we encounter. There are instances that clearly call for rhythmic independence; there are others that clearly call for synchronization; and there are others yet where, after careful study of the context, either option seems to make sense. In such ambivalent cases it usually does not matter very much which alternative we select.

APPENDIX

In the preceding essay I discussed a few of the arguments that Michael Collins set forth in support of his daring thesis that sesquialtera and hemiolia "do not exist at all in performance." In order to show further weaknesses of this theory I shall deal here briefly with three more witnesses whom Collins summoned in the hope of buttressing his case.

One such witness is Tigrini, who in 1588 called the sesquialtera a "proportion of inequality" when it is set against other voices in binary measures. In such a case "when one or more parts sing two semibreves, or two minims in one tactus, the other parts sing in contrast ("all'incontro") three semibreves, or three minims.[51] With no word about rhythmic alteration, adjustment or binarization, literalness of the note values is implied and further confirmed by the wording "in contrast" that clarifies the rhythmic clash between the ternary sesquialtera and the binary measure in other parts. Moreover, there would be no "inequality" if the sesquialtera were to turn binary according to Collins's theory.

    The same applies to a passage in Banchieri, who in 1609 also referred to the sesquialtera as a "proportion of inequality" when juxtaposed with binary measures in other voices, "because singing the parts unequally, one singer sings two notes, and the other three, under the same amount of time." Again, without the mention of any kind of rhythmic adjustment, the evenness of the three notes is understood, and with it, the resulting rhythmic clash. Earlier in the same passage Banchieri confirms this interpretation by referring both to the difficulties that singers experience in such cases for lack of practice, and to the reluctance of composers to be inconvenienced in public.[52] Neither lack of practice nor the ensuing "inconvenience" would be a factor in the case of rhythmic assimilation that would eliminate all difficulties of performance.

    Collins then quotes Picerli in the belief that the latter advocated with "crystalline clarity" the kind of rhythmic assimilation that changes triplets into binary figures. The text, however, does not justify this assumption. When, so Picerli writes in 1630, a sign signifying a ternary measure appears in some but not in all the parts, equal beat prevails ("demostrano solo la battuta uguale") placing two notes within the first half of the beat and the third one within the second part "without changing the beat from its natural and even character" ("dando similmente due note alla prima, & un' altr' alla seconda parte della battuta, senza mutarla dell'esser suo naturale, & uguale").[53] Now if one performs three even notes against two beats, the first two of the three notes do fall within the first beat and the third falls within the second beat, and that is exactly what Picerli wrote. His warning of not letting the execution interfere with the evenness of the beat makes sense only in the case of a rhythmic conflict: there is no way in which a binary resolution could deflect the equal binary beat from its "natural and even character." As a consequence, Collins's "resolutions" of Picerli's specimens of rhythmic conflict (given in his ex. 5, p. 15) are a misunderstanding.

Notes

1. This rhythmic combination occurs at the start of Schubert's Piano Trio in B♭ Major. In performance the strings, playing in unison, almost invariably square the triplet into an anapest; the common impulse to do so is reinforced by the thumping eighth notes of the piano.

2. I am grateful to Professor James Erb for this information.

3. For the theories of Michael Collins, see "The Performance of Sesquialtera and Hemiolia in the 16th Century," *Journal of the American Musicological Society* 17, no. 1 (Spring 1964): 4–28; and "The Performance of Triplets in the 17th and 18th Centuries," *Journal of the American Musicological Society* 19, no. 3 (Fall 1966): 281–328 (hereafter referred to as Collins I and Collins II, respectively). Bach's Prelude XIV is discussed in Collins II, pp. 311–13.

4. Arthur Mendel, "Some Ambiguities of the Mensural System," in *Studies in Music History: Essays for Oliver Strunk*, ed. Harold Powers (Princeton, 1968), pp. 137–60; see especially pp. 149–52.

5. Ibid., p. 152.

6. In speaking of Collins, Mendel asks probingly, "One wonders when he thinks 3-against-2 performance began." Ibid., p. 152, n. 20.

7. Collins I and Collins II, as listed in n. 3 above.

8. Collins I, p. 22.

9. Ibid., p. 7; see also p. 28.

10. Ibid., p. 28.

11. Ibid., p. 22.

12. Ibid., p. 21.

13. Collins actually applies this belief to triplets found in Bach's binary meters. He offers seven complicated rules, illustrated by thirty-four (!) equations to show how triplets, depending on their melodic shape, must sometimes be transformed into dactyls, sometimes into anapests, and sometimes could go either way. He believes that these rules "represent the common practice of the period." See Collins II, p. 315, n. 39, and the rules he lists on pp. 315–17.

14. Stefano Vanneo, *Recanetum de musica aurea* (Rome, 1533; reprinted in facsimile, Kassel, 1969), fol. 65^r, quoted in Collins I, p. 22, n. 30.

15. Collins I, p. 22. The inserted phrase in brackets is part of Collins's translation.

16. See the entry *quilibet* in Charlton T. Lewis and Charles Short, *A Latin Dictionary* (Oxford, 1879).

17. Gregorius Faber, *Musices practicae erotematum*, vol. 2 (Basel, 1553), p. 208 (my translation).

18. Martin Agricola, *Musica figuralis deudsch* (Wittenberg, 1532), chap. 12 (my translation and italics). This and several other treatises cited below are unpaginated.

19. It is important to note that in unequal beat the downbeat is twice as long as the upbeat (down for "1" and "2," up for "3").

20. Gioseffo Zarlino, *Le Istitutioni harmoniche* (Venice, 1562), part 3, chap. 48, p. 208, quoted in Collins I, pp. 9–10. The passage Collins quotes may also be found in the edition of 1558 (reprinted in facsimile, New York, 1965). Part 3 of the edition of 1558 has been translated by Guy Marco and Claude Palisca as *The Art of Counterpoint* (New Haven, 1968).

21. Lodovico Zacconi, *Prattica di musica*, vol. 1 (Venice, 1596), book 1, chap. 53, fol. 42^v, quoted in Collins I, p. 12. This and subsequent quotations from Zacconi may also be found in the edition of 1592 (reprinted in facsimile, Bologna, 1967).

22. Zacconi, book 3, chap. 36, fols. 153^r–153^v, quoted in Collins I, pp. 11–12.

23. Ibid., chap. 73, fol. 183^v (my translation).

24. Ibid., fols. 184^r ff.

25. Hermann Finck, *Practica musica* (Wittenberg, 1556), book 2. (In this and the succeeding quotations, the italics for the word "contra" are mine.)

26. Lucas Lossius, *Erotemata musicae practicae* (Nuremberg, 1563), book 2, chap. 12.

27. Michael Praetorius, *Syntagma musicum*, vol. 3 (Wolfenbüttel, 1619; reprinted in facsimile, Kassel, 1958), p. 29.

28. Adriano Banchieri, *Cartella musicale* (Venice, 1614), p. 31.

29. See Collins I, pp. 12–15; his footnotes document the treatises in detail.

30. Nicolaus Gengenbach, *Musica nova: Newe Singekunst* (Leipzig, 1626), pp. 64–65 (my translation).

31. Daniel Friderici, *Musica figuralis* (Rostock, 1619) (my translation). The succeeding example from Friderici's treatise is found verbatim in Daniel Hitzler's *Extract auss der Neuen Musica oder Singkunst* (Nuremberg, 1623), p. 52.

32. Johann Crüger, *Synopsis musica* (Berlin, 1630), chap. 4.

33. The treatise is preserved only in German translation; the passage referred to here is on p. 11 of the edition published in Augsburg in 1693.

34. Wolfgang Michael Mylius, *Rudimenta musices* (Muhlhausen, 1685).

35. Franz Xaver Anton Murschhauser, *Fundamentalische . . . Handleithung sowohl zur Figural als Choral Music* (Munich, 1707).

36. I give two representative patterns from Collins I, p. 23, ex. 11.

37. Girolamo Frescobaldi, *Il primo libro delle canzoni* . . . (Rome, 1628). For the text of Grassi's preface, see Gaetano Gaspari, *Catalogo della Biblioteca Musicale G. B. Martini di Bologna*, vol. 4: *Musica Strumentale* (Bologna, 1961), p. 45.

38. Frescobaldi, *Il secondo libro di toccate* . . . (Rome, 1637).

39. For an interesting specimen, see Johann Kaspar Kerll, *Ausgewählte Werke*, part 1, ed. Adolf Sandberger, in *Denkmäler der Tonkunst in Bayern*, series 2, vol. 2 (Leipzig, 1901), pp. 9–12 (Toccata No. 3). See also p. lxxiii (Revisionsbericht).

40. See the *Fitzwilliam Virginal Book*, ed. J. A. Fuller-Maitland and W. Barclay Squire (Leipzig, 1894–99; reprinted New York, 1963), vol. 1, p. 162, staves 2 and 3. (The manuscript of this collection, whose latest item—by Sweelinck—dates from 1612, was presumably completed in 1619.) In their notes to this passage (p. xxiv), the editors write that "the complicated cross-rhythms . . . are very carefully indicated in the MS where each triplet is preceded by '61' [6 = 1] or '32' [3 = 2], sometimes by both together, and each pair of even crotchets by the sign '**C**.'" Similar cross-rhythms may be found in Variation 15 of John Bull's *Ut, re, mi, fa, sol, la*; see vol. 1, pp. 186–87, and the facsimile page of manuscript reproduced as the frontispiece to the volume (see also p. xv).

41. See J. S. Bach, *Neue Ausgabe sämtlicher Werke*, Supplement: *Bach-Dokumente*, vol. 3, ed. Hans-Joachim Schulze (Kassel, 1972), p. 206, no. 757 (my italics).

42. In this particular case, Bach may have used this notation as a makeshift substitute for the $\frac{12}{8}$ meter signature, which he could not squeeze into the crowded score.

43. Berlin, Deutsche Staatsbibliothek, Mus.ms.Bach P 99.

44. Berlin, Deutsche Staatsbibliothek, Mus.ms.Bach P 283; for a facsimile see J. S. Bach, *Orgelbüchlein*, ed. Heinz-Harald Löhlein (Kassel, 1981).

45. Ibid.

46. Berlin, Deutsche Staatsbibliothek, Mus.ms.Bach St 130; for a facsimile see J. S. Bach, *Brandenburgisches Konzert Nr. 5 D-dur BWV 1005*, ed. Hans-Joachim Schulze (Leipzig, 1975). The figures shown in ex. 3.11 are written the same way in the autograph score (Berlin, Deutsche Staatsbibliothek, Am.B. 78); for a facsimile see J. S. Bach, *Brandenburgische Konzerte*, ed. Peter Wackernagel (Leipzig, 1950).

47. See n. 44 above.

48. Berlin, Deutsche Staatsbibliothek, Mus.ms.Bach P 153.

49. Berlin, Deutsche Staatsbibliothek, Mus.ms.Bach St 92.

50. The autograph of the *Clavierbüchlein* of 1725 for Anna Magdalena is held by the Stiftung Preussischer Kulturbesitz in Berlin (Mus.ms.Bach P 225). The original print of the six Partitas, *Clavir Ubung bestehend in Praeludien, Allemanden, Couranten, Sarabanden, Giguen, Menuetten, und andern Galanterien . . . Opus 1*, appeared in 1731. (The Partitas were published individually before that date, but no copy of Partita No. 6 has survived.)

51. Collins I, p. 8; his translation of Orazio Tigrini, *Il compendio della musica* (Venice, 1588), pp. 129ff.

52. Ibid., pp. 8–9, quoting Adriano Banchieri, *Conclusioni del suono dell'organo* (Bologna, 1609), pp. 36–37. The "inconvenience" is clearly the embarrassment of poor execution.

53. Ibid., pp. 14–15, quoting Silvero Picerli, *Specchio primo di musica* (Naples, 1630), p. 26. In Collins's translation the word "disparate" should be replaced by "an odd number."

4

The *Notes Inégales* Revisited

Nearly a quarter century ago I published a lengthy essay on the *notes inégales* with the express purpose of protecting Bach from misguided attempts to subject his music to the principles of the French convention.[1] The article elicited a lively response from several scholars. I answered the first of the critics, Robert Donington, in a later issue of the aforementioned journal.[2] Then three more colleagues joined the polemic: Sol Babitz, John Byrt, and Michael Collins, who responded in the next volume of that publication.[3] Finding their arguments wanting I was eager to set forth my differences, but the then editor called a halt, preferring to end the exchange with what he called (with reference to the *Rosenkavalier*) the "Schlussterzett." Now, rereading the "Schlussterzett" after these many years I find that I have lost, not the ability to answer, but the sense of need.

What prompts me today to return to the topic are different reasons. One is that, on reconsidering the convention after a long interval, I have gained a new insight into its nature that reveals its complex structure as a unified, fully integrated, organic unit. Seeing the convention in this new light I now realize why it has no counterpart in any other country and stands distinctly apart from any other kinds of inequality that abound in the music of all nations (including France). This perception had, at least in part, escaped me before, as it seems to have escaped others.

The second reason is the recent publication of an important essay on the subject by David Fuller, first appearing in *The New Grove Dictionary* (s.v. *Notes inégales*), later, with negligible changes, in *The New Grove Dictionary of Instruments* and then in a condensed version in *The New Harvard Dictionary*. The valuable study, written with well-tempered objectivity, clarifies many important aspects of the subject. But it has some flaws. One of these could encourage those who believe in the international currency of the convention in having found an important champion of their cause. Though Fuller hedges a bit on this

---

This article originally appeared in *The Journal of Musicology* 6 (1988): 137–49. Reprinted by permission of the publisher.

issue, his implication is nevertheless that of a much wider geographic distribution than I believe to be justified. I had hoped to have laid this idea to rest, but now that it has surfaced again in publications by an important scholar, it is necessary to address this particular issue once more. Furthermore, there is another important point touching on the actual performance of *notes inégales* on which I believe Fuller to be mistaken.

I still stand by every word of my original article and of others in which I dealt with the subject.[4] Here I am adding, not retracting. Above all I emphatically reaffirm that, semantically and logically, the concept of *notes inégales* makes sense only in reference to notes that are written equal but rendered unequal, and more specifically to such notes that are subject to long-short rendition by the principles of the French convention. To include, as Fuller did, the written dotted note under the label of *notes inégales* is a dangerous assumption that opens the door to terminological and, with it, to conceptual confusion. It was this inclusion of the dotted note that led Fuller to infer the use of *inégalité* by non-French masters. "To insist," Fuller writes, "that *notes inégales* are, by definition, always written equal is to mask a great deal of evidence that can help in mapping the geographical extent of the convention, and in deciding whether or not it affected only music in French style." The evidence that is being "masked" is deceptive as we shall presently see. However, before I can elaborate on this matter I must put the nature of the convention into proper focus.

The *notes inégales* are a special case of rhythmic alteration that is related to agogic accents and to rubato. Across the borderline of rhythmic alteration, they bear a resemblance to the dotted notes with which they must not be confused. It is advisable to limit the term of *notes inégales* to a specific French convention that, growing from only dimly perceived origins, emerged clearly structured by the mid-seventeenth century and remained so until about the end of the eighteenth. Characteristic of the convention is that only specific, evenly written note values in specific meters were subject to being rendered unequal, such as sixteenth notes (but not eighth notes) in C meter, or eighth notes (but not quarter notes) in such meters as 2 or 3, quarter notes (but not half notes) in meters such as $\frac{3}{2}$. Inequality was long-short in a ratio that for all practical purposes ranged from a barely perceptible 7:5 to about 2:1, rarely going beyond this limit. The notes involved had to be binary, never ternary, had to be subdivisions of the beat, never the beat itself, and had to move basically in stepwise motion. Whenever the conditions were right, *inégalité* was mandatory unless the composer canceled it either by placing dots or dashes above the notes or by such words as "marqué," "détaché," or "notes" or "croches égales."

On first sight, these principles seem to be an arbitrary assembly of rules. Yet there is method in them and once we discern it, the system makes perfect sense with all the details falling readily into place. The purpose of the convention was ornamental. The rhythmic lilt was to add grace and elegance to a musical line without impairing its structural guideposts. It was, as it were, a further embellishment of ornamental notes. The limitation to subdivisions of the beat assures that the notes that do fall on the beat and are most likely to be structural may be lengthened, which adds emphasis, but cannot be shortened, which would endanger their proper rhythmic weight. The rule about the meter-note relationship insures that only those notes that are likely to be the fastest in the piece, and therefore also likely to be ornamental in character, will be subject to rhythmic modulation. Thus we can understand that in meters that were beaten fast or fairly fast, such as, for instance, 2, 3, $\frac{3}{8}$, $\frac{6}{8}$, the first subdivisions were subject to *inégalité,* because they could be and often were the fastest notes in the piece; whereas in a slow meter such as C or $\frac{2}{4}$, the eighth notes as first subdivisions of the beat were leisurely enough to have structural meaning, so that the ornamental function devolved on the second subdivision, the sixteenth notes, which generally abound in this meter. (Henceforth I shall use the term *inégalité* solely with reference to French *notes inégales.*) The principle of the predominantly stepwise progression that favors, versus angular lines that disfavor *inégalité* completes the picture: ornamental figurations tend to move by steps, whereas in an angular line the individual notes will tend to assume melodic-structural importance. Seen from this vantage point we can make a reasonable judgment when a line is and when it is not hospitable to *inégalité:* it need not proceed solely by steps; it can circumscribe a chord and can still be perceived as ornamental, if such progressions have the character of an arpeggio. When, however, the single notes assume melodic substance then *inégalité* will be improper.

We see that the French convention was a unified system whose parts fitted together into an organic, logical whole. Logical, because in terms of its function it all makes perfect sense and the individual principles complement each other. And this inner logic was the cement that held this complex, sophisticated system together over a period of a century and a half, during which all the many writers of manuals—according to David Fuller no fewer than eighty—agreed and kept agreeing on all important points.

A striking document from the mid-sixteenth century sheds some light on the otherwise obscure early stages of this evolution. Loys Bourgeois in 1550 explains how to sing with good taste ("la manière de bien chanter") a series of semiminims (quarter notes) in these signs: $\Phi \quad \textcent \quad O_1^2 \quad C_1^2 O_2 C_2$ by grouping them in twos and somewhat lengthening the first and shortening the second of each pair ("de deux en deux, demourant quelque peu de temps dauantage sur la première, que sur la seconde"). Analogous treatment is to be given a sequence of *fusae* when they occur under these signs: $O \quad C \quad O_2 \quad C_2$.[5]

What is fascinating about this document is that it already contains four important ingredients of *inégalité:* the long-short sequence, the dependence of inequality on note-value and meter relationship; the mildness of the inequality; and the reference to its ornamental function in that Bourgeois justifies the procedure by pointing to the first note as normally being a consonance, the second as usually being a dissonance ("un discord, ou [comme on dit] un faux accord"). What he implies is that the second note is a passing note, hence ornamental in function. This is confirmed by his examples, which show for both denominations a stepwise sequence both rising and falling. There is little doubt that we see here already the main features of *inégalité*, perhaps at or near its fountainhead.[6]

All these features set Bourgeois's principles clearly apart from Italian or Spanish references to inequality, just as the fully developed system is clearly set apart from deceptively look-alike unequal treatment of equal notes to be found in the music of all times and all nations.

This fully developed and integrated French system could work only in France, where every musician, from his childhood training on, began absorbing the principles of the convention until they became so much part of his musical consciousness that he had them as it were in his blood and bones; where it could work in an orchestra with the conductor or concertmaster indicating the ratio of *inégalité* wherever applicable. Of course when Frenchmen traveled or worked abroad they carried this legacy with them. And where such French musicians taught students abroad they imparted the knowledge of *inégalité* to chosen individuals.

Yet apart from a few such individuals the convention was unknown to the rank and file of musicians outside of France. And it is this rank and file, not one or the other field marshal, that mattered for the question whether *inégalité* was, or indeed could have been, not just a French but an international convention. The common musician outside of France could not have been acquainted with it. Its very complexity and its inner unity required a thorough grounding in its principles. Whereas all French texts without exception, especially those addressed to children, explained the system, there is no counterpart to such thorough conditioning anywhere abroad. In fact, with the exception of Quantz and Georg Muffat, who liked the French convention and tried—unsuccessfully—to introduce it to their German readers, there is no mention of a comparable system anywhere outside of France.

Yet, ever since Dolmetsch in 1915 demonstrated how to apply *inégalité* to certain Bach and Handel works, the issue was up for debate. Robert Donington followed Dolmetsch's lead and so did, with great fervor, Sol Babitz and Michael Collins. The stakes are high and comprise the question of whether *inégalité* can or indeed must be applied to Bach, Handel, Vivaldi, and their contemporaries; to the sons of Bach, and perhaps to Haydn and Mozart. A closer look at the controversy reveals that either faulty reasoning or mistaken identities were at the root of the internationalist creed.

The faulty reasoning had to do with: 1) the misinterpretation of the fact that two German masters, Georg Muffat in 1698 and Quantz in 1752 recommended the French convention to their German readers; 2) the belief that the metrical alternation of strong and weak beats was identical with the long-short alternation of the *notes inégales*—a belief fostered by old German theorists who misleadingly referred to the metrical strong-weak pattern as "long" and "short," albeit invariably qualified by adverbial expressions such as *quantitate intrinseca* or *virtualiter* or *innerlich*; 3) references to agogic accents for the first note under a slur; and 4) old keyboard fingerings that were believed to be designed to produce unevenness of performance. I have dealt with all these points at length in my article in 1965, and since David Fuller seems to agree, or at least not to disagree with me on these matters, I see no need to recapitulate here my arguments. I simply refer the interested reader to this earlier study.

Things are different with regard to the "mistaken identities." I shall have to deal with them here in some detail, because Fuller did not escape their pitfalls. *Mistaken identities* are mainly of two kinds: 1) various cases of evenly written notes that are rendered unevenly for reasons other than *inégalité,* and 2) written-out dotted notes misinterpreted as *notes inégales*.

1) Inequality other than *notes inégales*. There are many cases in the music of all times and all nations where a soloist has rendered equally written notes unequally, mostly long-short, occasionally short-long. There are "agogic accents" for the sake of expression or emphasis: a singer or a violinist following his artistic instinct in modulating the rhythm according to the strivings, the stresses and releases of melody or harmony; an organist or harpsichordist, incapable of accentuation, lengthening a note that called for emphasis, be it metrical or otherwise. There is furthermore rubato playing or singing where usually more than two notes are involved in often irregular patterns of rhythmic manipulation, but where occasionally modulations resembling the *inégalité* pattern will occur.

Considering that the more we go back in time, notation becomes less and less precise, while the solo performer was more and more at liberty to deviate from the letter of the score, it is certain that rhythmic modulations were a commonplace occurrence without any connection with, or inspiration from, the *notes inégales*.

The Spaniard Tomás de Santa Maria, who is often quoted in this connection, gives in his remarkable treatise on the clavichord of 1565 three rubato patterns for the graceful playing of *fusae* (eighth notes) and one for semiminims (quarter notes) that in its alternation of long and short notes resembles the *inégalité* pattern, as does one of the three rubato designs for the *fusae*.[7] The pattern for the semiminims comes closest to *inégalité*, though the important meter—note-value relationship, already present in Bourgeois, is missing; and for the *fusae* alone, the choice of three manners shows a difference in kind.

The same is true of the directive by Frescobaldi in his famous preface to the Toccatas of 1614 that sixteenth notes in one hand set against eighth notes in the other hand, should be played with mild short-long unevenness ("alquanto puntato"). This special case hinging on two different, simultaneous rhythms is totally foreign to the French convention, not to speak of its short-long inequality.

Giulio Caccini has been referred to by several scholars as directing rhythmic alteration allegedly related to *inégalité*. Yet in Caccini's examples the equally written notes are manipulated in various manners, arbitrarily chosen by artistic judgment. No regularity, no principle, no convention is involved.[8]

The resemblance of all these species of inequality to the French convention is only superficial, since none of them is part of a closed, integrated system. Their common denominator is simply a less literal attitude in the interpretation of the score than we are trained to apply today, and of course the greater freedom given the soloist who alone is involved in all these non-French examples. We must beware not to see in them a proof for either the spread of the French convention beyond its borders or of a spontaneous germination of the same ideas in various nations.

2) Dotted notes mistaken for *notes inégales*. The idea of several scholars to include written-out dotted notes under the *notes inégales* label is not a happy one, because it gives a distorted picture of the currency of *inégalité* in and outside of France.

Of course, a dotted note and its companion with their 3:1 ratio are uneven quantities, but so are all notes of different denominations. To call them uneven notes or, in French, *notes inégales,* is a tautology, and as with every tautology it is true but pointless. Since practically all music contains notes of different lengths are we to say that all music consists of *notes inégales?* That clearly makes no sense.

Certainly dotted notes bear a resemblance to *notes inégales,* and the idea of their actual identity was encouraged by the way some theorists and authors of manuals explained *notes inégales* with dotted note illustrations. There was

at the time— $\quad \downarrow \; ^3 \; \downarrow$ being unknown—no other graphic device available to suggest *any* kind of long-short unevenness. To do so was a reasonable, if exaggerated approximation. Already Bourgeois, and as we have seen, Santa Maria and Frescobaldi used the dotted illustration for what they verbally described as mild unevenness. And later theorists, among them Georg Muffat, Hotteterre, Montéclair, and La Chapelle, who used the same pedagogical device, misled some modern scholars into taking this makeshift device on its 3:1 face value, giving both a misleading idea about the sharpness of *inégalité* and about the identity, or at least the overlapping, of dotted notes and *notes inégales.*[9]

Another source for the mistaken identity is the, at the time, common use of the term *pointer* for lengthening a note, indicating an increment of indeterminate and sometimes minuscule size. Bénigne de Bacilly, author of a famous vocal treatise of 1668, in recommending *notes inégales* for improvised diminutions, speaks of *points alternatifs* but cautions that they be applied with such subtlety that the "dotting" is hardly noticeable ("notes pointées si finement que cela ne paroisse pas").[10] Hotteterre defines *pointer* as the making (in **C** meter) of two sixteenth notes one long and one short ("une longue et une brève"), which certainly falls short of suggesting a 3:1 ratio. Duval, concerned about the misleading use of the word *pointer,* says; "'dotting' is an improper term for *inégalité.*"[11] Couperin directs in one of his pieces (the allemande *La Laborieuse*): "the sixteenth notes ever so slightly dotted" ("Les double croches un tant soit peu pointées") and half a century earlier Nivers in his *Livre d'orgue* of 1665 speaks of "half-dotting" ("faire comme des demipoints") the first, third, fifth, and seventh of eight eighth notes in a measure by lengthening them "a little bit" ("augmenter tant soit peu") and by proportionally shortening the companion notes. In other words, the term *pointer* can mean standard dotting, but can also mean an indeterminate lengthening, and where it means the latter, it might be best to translate it as "extending" or "lengthening" rather than "dotting" because in English the term "dotting" evokes the standard 3:1 ratio.

The deceptiveness of the dotted illustrations and of the term *pointer* is confirmed by other important theorists who specify the mildness of the *notes inégales* thereby setting them clearly apart from regular dotted notes. Loulié makes this difference very clear when he distinguishes two types of unevenness. The first, contingent on stepwise motion—the proper climate for *inégalité*—he calls *lourer,* where the first of an equal pair of notes is held "a little longer"; the second type in which the first note is "much longer than the second," he calls *pointer* or *piquer* but here the note has to have a dot ("doit avoir un point"). The implication is clear: under the principles of *inégalité* the lengthening is only mild; any strong lengthening crosses over into the realm of standard dotted notes and is marked accordingly. To avoid the danger of exaggerating the ratio of *inégalité,* Loulié, in manuscript supplements to his treatise, indicates the mildness of this ratio by the ingenious design ♪. ♪♪ ♪ .[12]

Montéclair in 1709 illustrates *inégalité* with dotted notes: **2** ♪♪♪ like ♪. ♪♪ ♪ while explaining that the first note should be held "a little longer" ("un peu plus longue") than the second one, clearly belying the literal meaning of the dots.[13]

Other eminent theorists concurred in the mildness of *inégalité.* To list just a few among many, Villeneuve says: "one renders the second eighth note a little faster" ("un peu plus vite"); Choquel: "the first of two even notes that form a beat must be held a little longer than the second" ("la première des deux qui forment un temps doit estre tenue un peu plus longtemps que la seconde"); Mercadier de Belesta: "the first a little longer than the second" ("la première un peu plus longue que la seconde"); Jean-Jacques Rousseau: "In French music . . . the eighth notes are equal only in C meter; in all others one lengthens (literally: dots) them always a little" ("on les pointe toujours un peu").[14]

The mildness of *inégalité* is further confirmed by Père Engramelle in both his *Tonotechnie* and his essay for Bedos de Celle's book on organ building.[15] Though in theory he stakes out a range for *inégalité* from a barely noticeable 7:5 to 3:1 ratio, the latter being reserved for marches and their like, in practice, in the given examples, even in the *Marches du roy,* Nos. 1 and 2 from the *Tonotechnie* and in the cylinder notations in *L'Art du facteur d'orgue,* the sharpest ratio to be found is 2:1. We find the latter in the marches and in assimilation to triplets, whereas elsewhere the ratio throughout is milder.

We can gather from this evidence derived from eminent authorities that the modern idea of vigorous *inégalité* equivalent to and exceeding a dotted note is a misunderstanding. David Fuller, who earlier had himself pointed to the basic mildness of *inégalité,* reversed himself in the *Grove* articles by writing that, "contrary to what is now often said, French inequality ran the gamut from barely perceptible to extremely dotted." He let himself be swayed by a sentence in an anonymous seventeenth-century manuscript treatise referring to one specific piece that is to be extremely dotted. The treatise, reproduced by W. Pruitt in *L'Orgue* (112 [1974]:107) is written in primitive prose with a spelling that even in a time of orthographic latitude seems near-illiterate. To base a new thesis on the nature of *inégalité,* one that is at odds with the statements of a large array of prominent artists and theorists, one, moreover, deriving from an individual of unknown competence, whose style does not speak well for his education, is dangerous to the point of unreasonableness. It is the kind of anonymous testimony that would be thrown out of court in any civilized society. Certainly there always have been and always will be performers who tend to eccentricity, and given the unlimited freedom with which keyboard players, as opposed to members of an ensemble, can manipulate the musical materials, worse things must have been perpetrated than the extreme dotting of evenly written notes. But extremes and eccentricities should not influence our notions of what was intended by the important masters at a given time and place, of what was at the center, not the periphery, of a musical scene. It may have been the unjustified trust that Fuller placed in this single sentence that misled him to include dotted notes within the concept of *inégalité:* if the latter ranges from barely noticeable to extreme dotting, then, of course, the plain dotted note finds itself comfortably ensconced in the middle of this range, whereas in fact, it was near to, but outside the realm of *inégalité* as understood by the consensus of many voices of commanding authority.

Also, the dotted note was of an entirely different kind, a different species altogether. It occurred in the music of all times, of all Western nations, for any kind of note values, from breves and whole notes, to the shortest values, in all melodic contexts with no immanent organic connection to ornamental functions. To include the dotted note within *inégalité* is a major methodological error, because it leads to mistaken inferences about the validity of the *inégalité* convention far beyond its true realm.

We find this kind of reasoning in Donington, who prints the starting measure of Handel's Sonata, op. 1, no. 1 "first in mainly equal notation, later in unequal notation" (see ex. 4.1a).[16] "There can be," he continues, "no reason other than inadvertence." He sees in this discrepancy a proof that Handel practiced *inégalité* and that the first measure should be played like the twelfth. I submit that a more plausible reason for the discrepancy was a wish to vary the theme on its repeat. When Beethoven writes in the Finale of the Spring Sonata the rhythmic configuration shown in example 4.1b, then, later in the movement the one shown in example 4.1c, the discrepancy is neither proof that he too practiced *inégalité,* nor that the equal notation of the first measure was due to inadvertence or laziness, and that the theme should throughout be played in the dotted style. The example might seem extreme, but it does point up the danger of finding evidence in the notation of parallel spots; the same applies to simultaneous discrepancies of voices and instruments, another of Donington's arguments. The latter discrepancies (between rounder vocal and sharper instrumental rhythms) are frequent because composers who knew how to write for the voice often adjusted the rhythms to the demands of the vocal idiom for less angularity. The resulting clashes may look surprising on paper, but in performance they are totally innocuous.

Example 4.1a.   G. F. Handel, Sonata, op. 1, no. 1, first movement

Example 4.1b.   L. van Beethoven, Spring Sonata, Finale

Example 4.1c.   L. van Beethoven, Spring Sonata, Finale

In a similar vein Fuller comments on the question of whether Bach and other non-French composers used *notes inégales* and affirms that *"countless scores show that they did"* [italics mine].[17] There are, I believe, only two ways in which those countless scores could, in Fuller's eyes, prove that their authors used the *notes inégales:* one would be the occasional use of the directive *"notes égales"* or its equivalent, which, by canceling *inégalité* for a specific piece implicitly proves its presence; the other would be the writing of dotted notes, and that is what Fuller must have had in mind. The directive *"notes égales"* is nowhere to be found in Bach, nor, to my knowledge in the scores of any other non-French composer. Dotted notes are of course as I have mentioned earlier, found everywhere with everyone from the Middle Ages to the present, which therefore proves nothing.

The French in particular were notoriously fond of the dotted pattern, which prompted Mattheson to say that a Frenchman without a dot is like a cock without a comb. They used the pattern ubiquitously, as did composers of other nations, only more so. Its typical appearance in overtures and *entrées* was one of many signs of this predilection. This rhythmic genre neither proved that *inégalité* existed (which of course it did) nor had anything to do with it: it occurred on all rhythmic levels, as said before; it was independent of meter–note-value relationships, it was structural, not ornamental, not limited to subdivisions of the beat, and occurred in ternary as well as binary figures (such as the typical French

gigue pattern: ♪♫ ♪♫). Moreover, dotted notes, by their innate rhythmic angularity, favor melodic angularity as well, often evident in large leaps,[18] just as the rhythmic gentleness of the *notes inégales* favored, and was congenial to, melodic smoothness, the often-listed "stepwise progressions"; the sharp edges of the dotted notes moreover readily admit sharp staccato articulation, as the soft lines of the *notes inégales* thrive in legato environment. All of which reaffirms a difference in kind, not just in degree, between dotted notes and *inégalité*.

The way some scholars mixed all kinds of unequal notes, be they written even or uneven, as if they were members of one big family, was the unavoidable upshot of the logical fallacy of equivocation. Rubato, agogic accents, and the uneven rendition of evenly written notes mentioned in Spanish and Italian sources involved inequality of course, and so did the 3:1 ratio of the dotted note, or any other ratio between notes of different denominations. There was inequality and since inequality translates into *inégalité* we are ready for a smooth and treacherous glide into the logical trap of inferring from linguistic double meaning and acoustic resemblance an identity of substance. Among the massive fallout from such a logical aberration is the belief that a dotted notation by a master proves that he practiced *inégalité*.

It is regrettable that Fuller, by joining Donington in falling victim to this snare, flawed his presentation and gave support to what he called the "leftist" (would-be progressive) scholars who had proclaimed the international validity of the French convention.

On the other hand, we should be grateful that Fuller parts company with the "leftist" innovators when they see in the "good" and "bad" notes as well as in the agogic accents for first notes under a slur a manifestation of *inégalité*. Thus in important matters Fuller has clarified the issues. If only he would rethink his insistence on including in the principle of *inégalité* dotted notes and other inequalities that are alien to the integrated French system, his contribution would be enhanced.

This is not a hairsplitting discussion of semantic subtleties. It all boils down to the intensely topical issue of how these matters affect the proper performance of Bach, Handel and other non-French masters of the time. As to rhythmic alterations, say, with Bach, there certainly were, in soloistic performance, agogic accents, and there were, in appropriate contexts, rubato freedoms. By contrast, a transplant of the complex, well-integrated French convention to his music is improbable to such a degree that we can dismiss it as a historically unacceptable choice.

The same is true of Purcell, of Handel, of Vivaldi and other non-French masters other than those who like Quantz, Reicha, and perhaps Franz Benda, moved within the orbit of the French performance style. (The fact that a composer wrote French overtures, or French-derived dances—and most of them did—does not allow the inference that they also adopted French performance manners and mannerisms.) Other than for such exclusively French-oriented masters who happen to occupy a negligible space in today's living repertory, it would be advisable to limit the use of *inégalité* to French composers prior to the Revolution. For them *inégalité* should be used for both solo and ensemble music, including opera and ballet, whenever the circumstances are right, such as proper meter—note-value relationships and basically stepwise motion. It would be further advisable to be discreet, and to stay well within the limit of a 2:1 ratio, never exceeding the latter.

Addendum

David Fuller published an answer to the above essay under the title "Notes and *Inégales* Unjoined: Defending a Definition" (*Journal of Musicology* 7, no. 1 [Winter 1989]: 21–28). In it he tries to defend, with more wit than persuasiveness, his idea of the overlap of dotted notes and *notes inégales*, while failing altogether to address the *central* issue of my thesis: that the principles of the French convention do not apply to the music of J. S. Bach.

Notes

1. "The French *Inégales*, Quantz, and Bach," *Journal of the American Musicological Society* 18 (1965): 313–58. Reprinted in *Essays in Performance Practice* (Ann Arbor, 1982), chap. 3.

2. Donington's "Communication to the Editor" appeared in *Journal of the American Musicological Society* 19 (1966): 112–14; my answer in *Journal of the American Musicological Society* 19 (1966): 435–37; reprinted in *Essays*, chap. 4.

3. *Journal of the American Musicological Society* 20 (1967): 473–85.

4. Among others: "External Evidence and Uneven Notes" and "Facts and Fiction about Overdotting," both reprinted in *Essays*, chaps. 5 and 8, respectively.

5. *Le droict chemin de musique* (Paris, 1550), chap. 10.

6. Significant too is that the illustration of these long-short sequences as a series of dotted notes is revealed as a substitute for an only mild inequality ("quelque peu de temps dauantage"). Owing to the lack of a more appropriate graphic device, the same dualism of dotted illustration and verbal qualification runs like a red thread through the whole history of the convention.

7. *Libro llamado Arte de tañer fantasia* (Valladolid, 1565), chap. 19.

8. *Le nuove musiche* (Florence, 1602) (the year 1601 on the print refers to the Florentine calendar and corresponded to 1602), preface.

9. It is an age-old pedagogical device to explain something unknown with the help of something known. In an Italian elementary introduction to English the pronunciation of "father" and "daughter" is explained as "fadza" and "dota." As a reasonable approximation this is a counterpart to the dotted illustration of the *notes inégales*.

10. *Remarques curieuses sur l'art de bien chanter . . .* (Paris, 1668), p. 232.

11. Jacques Hotteterre, *L'Art de préluder sur la flûte traversière* (Paris, 1718), p. 57. Duval, *Méthode agréable et utile pour apprendre facilement à chanter . . .* (Paris, 1775), p. 15.

12. These fragmentary supplements were first published as inserts in the English translation and edition by Albert Cohen, *Elements or Principles of Music* (Brooklyn, N.Y., 1965). The design for the *lourer* is on p. 67.

13. Michel Pignolet de Montéclair, *Nouvelle méthode pour apprendre la musique* (Paris, 1709), p. 15.

14. Alexandre de Villeneuve, *Nouvelle méthode . . . pour apprendre la musique . . .* (Paris, 1733), p. 4. Henri-Louis Choquel, *La Musique rendue sensible par la méchanique . . .* (Paris, 1762), p. 106. Jean-Baptiste Mercadier de Belesta, *Nouveau système de musique . . .* (Paris, 1776), p. 67. Jean-Jacques Rousseau, *Dictionnaire de musique* (Paris, 1768), s.v. *pointer*.

15. *La tonotechnie ou l'art de noter les cylindres . . .* (Paris, 1776); Bédos de Celles, *L'Art du facteur d'orgues* (Paris, 1778), vol. 4. The section on the mechanical organ is written by Engramelle.

16. *The Interpretation of Early Music*, new edition (London, 1974), p. 461.

17. *New Grove Dictionary of Instruments*, s.v. *notes inégales*, p. 779.

18. See for instance Couperin, XIIIe Ordre, *Les folies françoises*, 3e couplet; or XIe, *Les fastes*, act 4; or for that matter, Beethoven's Grosse Fuge, or the consistently double-dotted Qui tollis of Mozart's C-Minor Mass, with its rugged leaps.

5

Graham Pont's "Paradigm of Inconsistency" and the Interpretation of Handel's Overtures

The following essay deals with an attempt by Graham Pont to rescue a fraction of the French overture style from the consequences of my criticism (see my Essays *of 1982, chapters 5–9). Pont agrees with me that the belief of what he calls the "traditionalists" in the French overture style is mistaken, but he sees a compromise, a "third alternative," derived from his own doctrine, the "Paradigm of Inconsistency." He argues that overdotting, one of the three aspects of the overture style (the other two being upbeat contractions and synchronizations) should be used here and there,* inconsistently, *while elsewhere literalness prevails. Perfectly feasible for a keyboard soloist who can improvise at will, the idea is unrealistic for an orchestra.*

Graham Pont's article, "Handel and Regularization: A Third Alternative" (*Early Music* [November 1985]: 500) is the latest skirmish in his campaign aimed at leading to victory a "Revolution in the Science and Practice of Music." His battle cry is the "paradigm of inconsistency" that, he predicts, will supplant the pre-revolutionary "paradigm of consistency."[1] I shall attempt here, in the limited space available, to take a look at Pont's doctrine and at his "third alternative."

Two issues are involved here. One is the "paradigm" proper; the other is its role in Pont's proposed synthesis between the "traditionalists" who practice sharp rhythmic contractions in French overtures, dances, and other music vulnerable to such treatment, and, at the other pole, my contention that these practices are historically false and that the rhythms were intended to be rendered as written.

First, what is the paradigm of inconsistency? Pont and his collaborator Dene Barnett have noted that many composers—Bach, Handel, Haydn, and

This article originally appeared in *Early Music* (August 1986): 403–6. Reprinted by permission of the publisher.

Mozart among them—were inconsistent in the sense that the same musical figure on its repeat or in simultaneity in another voice often showed divergencies in notation. Pont concluded that such inconsistencies, which he assumed to be always deliberate, are of the musical essence. He castigates those editors who find some of these inconsistencies untidy and remove them by analogy. Pont forcefully objects to what he calls regularization and insists on preserving the integrity of any such discrepancies. In other words, he demands absolute literalness whenever inconsistency is spelled out, and herein he finds the focus of his "revolution."

So far the doctrine is relatively harmless: literalness is the safest first approach to interpreting a score since it is much more probable that a composer meant what he wrote than that he did not. But several dangers lurk for Pont's paradigm. First, the composer, human after all, may make mistakes, and create an inconsistency by forgetting a slur, an accidental, a dynamic marking, an ornament, by writing a wrong note, and so on. To take him on his word on such occasions where he obviously did not mean what he wrote, results at best in pedantry, at worst in silliness and absurdity. This would produce a "paradigm of human frailty."

Second, there is a hierarchy among the musical elements that ranges from the vital to the negligible, as from heart or brain to the earlobes or the mustache. When a composer wishes to repeat a phrase he will be consistent about the essentials, notably the pitches and the rhythm, but may be careless about the things that matter little. Creative artists in all fields vary a great deal in the degree of care they bestow on minor matters. The masters of the Baroque had generally an easygoing attitude towards notation: Bach's keyboard works have only very sporadic articulation marks.

There is also a range from important to unimportant within each musical element, as in articulation, ornamentation, dynamics etc. Thus it matters whether a phrase is all staccato or all legato, but within a general legato context the exact disposition of the slurs may be immaterial. The Allegro theme from Mozart's great E♭ Symphony has such a basic legato articulation, yet the disposition of its slurs differs in the first statement in measures 26ff. from the melodically identical recapitulation in measures 184ff., as shown in example 5.1 (above and below the notes respectively). Musically the discrepancy is not noticeable enough to be seen as an intentional variant and unquestionably was due either to oversight or to indifference. The paradigm involved here is not one of inconsistency but of indifference.

Example 5.1.　W. A. Mozart, Symphony No. 39 in E♭, K. 543, first
　　　　　　　 movement

Furthermore, even some pitches and some rhythms are clearly more important than others. Some ornamental pitches that fall off the beat can be left out
without being missed. The rhythm of some ornaments can be modified without
harming the musical substance. The rhythm of an upbeat can be slightly varied
and make little difference.

We find convincing evidence for the unintentional nature of some inconsistencies when we compare the incipits of Mozart's autograph Index of his works[2]
with the respective measures of the autograph scores. In view of the Index's
purpose the many discrepancies are obviously due to carelessness.[3]

Pont and Barnett place much emphasis on inconsistencies in Bach's articulation, yet many of these are of little or no moment. In one of his most calligra-
phically outstanding manuscripts, Bach articulates a pervasive theme in the
second movement of the Fifth Brandenburg Concerto on each of its many
appearances, haphazardly either by twos or by fours. Example 5.2 shows the
motive in both sequence and simultaneity (with a case of forgotten slurs in the
violin part added for good measure). There is no conceivable musical reason for
the difference, which was clearly a matter of unimportance (a "paradigm of
insignificance").[4]

Example 5.2.　J. S. Bach, Brandenburg Concerto No. 5, second
　　　　　　　 movement

Idiomatic considerations may be involved in cases where Bach articulates differently for voice and for melody instruments, and where the differentiation is consistent, hence clearly deliberate. When Bach slurs dotted notes, he does so for strings or winds always on the downbeat and mostly by twos. We find this pattern in the first movement of Cantata No. 84, *Ich bin vergnügt,* whereas he articulates the voice on the upbeat (see ex. 5.3).

Example 5.3.   J. S. Bach, Cantata No. 84, *Ich bin vernügt*, first
            movement

In many other cases, where the articulation of the voice, as determined by diction, differs from that of unison melody instruments, the reason may be idiom, may be indifference, may be the wish for a better blend, or other musical effect. In all these cases we do well not to regularize but to follow the letter of the score, since here, too, the discrepancies may have been deliberate.

Next we have to ask the question: where does inconsistency end and thematic elaboration or variation start? Both repetition and elaboration are fundamental principles of musical structure. When a composer manipulates the thematic material by spinning it out, by adding ornamental figurations, by fragmenting or polyphonically elaborating, we are not seeing inconsistency but variation. The concept of inconsistency might conceivably be stretched to comprise, at its outer limits, Bach's discrepant articulation of voices and unison instruments, but it ends when the deviation is noticeable enough to be perceived as thematic variant. A change of rhythm, such as the shift from single-dotted to double-dotted notes or vice versa, that alters the physiognomy of a theme or the character of a passage, provides so striking a contrast that it cannot by any stretch of semantic imagination be called an inconsistency.

Thus we see that the legitimate scope of inconsistency is very small to begin with. If we consider that within this scope a great, perhaps the greatest, number of discrepancies is not deliberate but due to negligence or indifference, what remains can only range from marginal to negligible. By enormously exaggerating with his paradigm the role of inconsistency, Pont has made a mountain out of a molehill. The molehill is real, but hardly the stuff of which revolutions are made.

As to Pont's application of his paradigm to Handel's overtures, I am glad that he agrees with me about the mischievous nature of the rhythmic-contraction-cum-synchronization performance ritual that, ordained by the synoptic gospels of Dolmetsch, Dart and Donington, keeps being reverently celebrated by all the faithful. They sincerely believe they unveil an old masterwork in its pristine shape, when in fact they distort it into a caricature.[5] Pont justly castigates these faithful by asking: "How long will the traditionalists persist in treating Handel as if he did not know how to write his own music—or as if he employed a completely irrational system of notation?" (p. 503). A very good question indeed: it clearly implies that Handel, who knew how to write single-dotted and double-dotted rhythms, upbeat figures of eighth notes, sixteenth notes, or thirty-second notes, meant what he wrote and expected his notation to be respected.

I seem to have found an ally. But, in a surprising about-face, Pont turns to castigating me for respecting Handel's notation, when he took the traditionalists to task for failing to do so. To explain this contradiction we have to realize that Pont has become captive of his own doctrine of inconsistency and needed to show that Handel adheres to the paradigm. Where Handel's rhythms contain milder and sharper designs in a mix that could conceivably be associated with inconsistency, his notation is certified as being rational and must be taken literally. But when Handel forgets to honor the paradigm by using consistently the same rhythm, say, a dotted note, his notation becomes irrational: he could not have meant what he wrote; it is up to us to achieve the needed inconsistency by inserting here and there some double dots. To justify such intervention Pont invokes "*some kind* [my italics] of conventional rhythmic alteration" (p. 502) and claims "considerable evidence" for such action. The alterations he refers to are apparently rhythmic contractions and *notes inégales*. But what is his evidence?

At the *Messiah* Symposium in Ann Arbor, Michigan (December 1980), Pont presented as such evidence a tape of an overture played on the harpsichord with a mixture of sharp and mild rhythms that apparently were not specified in the original score. What did it prove? No more than that a keyboard player can manipulate musical material in any manner he wishes. He can transform an overture into a waltz, march, jazz or rock-and-roll or what have you. Compared with such transformations, the mere change of a few rhythms is child's play. Two hundred fifty years ago, Mattheson, in discussing rhythms derived from poetic meters, illustrated how one can change a chorale melody into any kind of a dance: a gavotte, sarabande, polonaise, minuet, etc. and vice versa, how to change a dance into a chorale melody.[6] He did not suggest that this is how a chorale, or how a dance is to rendered.

Given the unlimited freedom of a soloist or arranger to add, detract, or paraphrase, we are not entitled to assume that keyboard versions of Handel overtures, dances, and so on, which deviate from the original, reveal the composer's true intentions. Least of all when the arrangements originated 75 years or more after the works were composed. Such is the case with Pont's crown witness. He is somebody who Pont hopes—but is not sure—is Jonathan Battishill, a minor composer of sacred music. In a Wright edition of ca. 1785 of Handel overtures transcribed for the clavier, this scribe entered, perhaps in the 1790s, some variants, involving mostly rhythmic sharpenings. He did so erratically, hence, to Pont's joy, inconsistently. In some overtures he entered no changes, in some only very few, in some a goodly number. Of the last category Pont has offered illustrations in a previous article.[7]

Pont sees in these irregular, desultory rhythmic alterations a perfect manifestation of his paradigm and finds in them the chief evidence for his mysterious "kind of conventional rhythmic alteration." Now these entries can tell us something about the scribe's skill, taste, and idiosyncrasies—a matter of supreme unimportance—but as evidence for Handel's intentions they have no value; the less so since their style is in sharp contrast to Handel's own keyboard transcriptions and to those of his contemporaries. Handel's own versions (presumably done for the use of royal students) are simple and straightforward, show occasional ornamental additions, as well as small idiomatic adjustments, but no rhythmic sharpenings of any consequence; on the contrary, Pont himself points to *Riccardo I* where Handel altered a series of thirty-second note upbeat figures by softening them to sixteenth notes[8] and doing so consistently (probably to make them easier to play). Besides I have offered samples of such transcriptions of Handel overtures, one from his copyist and amanuensis, J. C. Smith, from ca. 1720, others from an important manuscript collection dating from ca. 1729. In all of these, calligraphic vertical alignment as well as horizontal spacing leave no doubt about the consistently literal meaning of Handel's rhythmic notation.[9]

Furthermore, Pont's "third alternative" of inconsistent alterations, no problem for the keyboard, is utterly impossible for orchestra or chorus. The question of when to be literal, and when not, and if the latter, how to change the rhythms is unanswerable by the members of an orchestra or chorus. Imagine the director instructing his musicians: "Play some rhythms as they are written, play some others twice or three times as sharp; take your choice but don't be consistent." Such a scenario is of course absurd. Small wonder that when I asked Pont in Ann Arbor how exactly the *Messiah* overture is to be played according to his paradigm he did not answer.

In formulating his "third alternative" Pont forgot, I believe, first to consider its feasibility outside the keyboard; second, to see the contradiction between his criticism of the traditionalists for not acknowledging the rationality of Handel's notation, and his own assumption of Handel's irrationality. A notation is certainly irrational when, according to the "third alternative," passages that mean what they say arbitrarily alternate with others that disguise their meaning and have to be transformed in performance without the benefit of any clear guidance as to how this should be done. Pont ought to readdress to himself his above-quoted rhetorical question to the traditionalists!

The contradictions show how gratuitous is Pont's charge of a "fatal weakness" in my reasoning (p. 502) when I "tacitly assumed" that a composer who knew how to notate a double-dotted ratio would want a single dot to be taken literally. This is indeed my argument, and I repeat that the presumption for a text is that it means what it says. It is for those who deny that the text should be taken literally to prove their case.[10] Yet such proof is impossible for Pont's "third alternative" since orchestrally or chorally it is unperformable—unless the parts are rewritten. But the need to rewrite the parts condemns the theory. Not only is it unhistorical: parts were always copied mechanically from the score without being recomposed; rewriting also belies the existence of Pont's "some kind of convention," which is revealed as unable to stand on its own feet.

Notes

1. For a detailed exposition of Pont's "paradigm" see G. Pont, "A Revolution in the Science and Practice of Music," *Musicology* 5 (1979): 1–66.

2. *Verzeichnüss aller meiner Werke vom Monath Febrario 1784 bis Monath . . .* [Nov. 1791] (autograph at the British Library; facs. eds. Vienna, 1938; New York, 1956).

3. The discrepancies are fascinating because they often offer revealing clues to performance. Among such clues are differences in tempo indications: the Allegro of the F-Major Piano Concerto, K. 459, becomes Allegro vivace; the Allegro of the C-Major Concerto, K. 467, becomes Allegro maestoso, which reveals that it is mostly played too fast; the Presto of the *Figaro* overture (in ¢ meter) becomes Allegro vivace, which reveals that it is *always* played too fast; the Andante of the overture to *Così fan tutte* becomes Andante maestoso; the apparently sudden forte in the second measure of the F-Major String Quartet, K. 590, turns to sforzando and its original ¢ signature is changed to ¢, which shows that Mozart may often have felt a ¢ Allegro in twos rather than fours. The slur of the first two measures of the C-Minor Piano Concerto is missing; so are the slurs at the start of the D-Major String Quintet; the eighth-note graces in "Das Veilchen" are written as sixteenth notes; conversely the sixteenth-note graces in the D-Major String Quartet, K. 575 are written as eighth notes, etc.
    A major discrepancy is at the start of the overture to *Don Giovanni* where, in measures 2 and 4, the basses keep reverberating ominously after the rest of the orchestra, whereas in the Index the basses are synchronized. Mozart must have momentarily forgotten his stroke of genius in a "paradigm of memory failure."

4. When he articulates in Cantata 107/6 the melodically unison flutes and violins differently, it was, as so often with Bach, a matter of choosing the idiomatically ideal bowing pattern ("paradigm of idiom"). This, incidentally, like the sample from the Brandenburg Concerto, proves that those are wrong who believe that two-by-two slurring has to result always in accentuation of the first and shortening of the second note. Applied to cases like those mentioned, such a principle would make no sense.

5. See on this matter five articles of mine, reprinted in *Essays in Performance Practice* (Ann Arbor, 1982), as chaps. 6–10. As to chap. 9, an answer to David Fuller, the reprint contains a number of important passages that had been omitted for lack of space in its original appearance in *Early Music* 7 (January 1979): 39–45.

6. *Der vollkommene Capellmeister* (Hamburg, 1739; facs. ed. Kassel, 1954), pp. 161–64.

7. G. Pont, "Handel's Overtures for Harpsichord and Organ," *Early Music* 11 (July 1983): 309–22, exx. 5c and 6b.

8. Ibid., p. 317 and ex. 7a.

9. For the Smith MS (New York Public Library, Drexel 5856) see my *Essays*, p. 166; for the other contemporary MS (British Library, RM.18.c.1.), ibid., pp. 140–41, first published in *Early Music* 7 (January 1979): 43.

10. I am of course aware that there occur discrepancies based on genuine, undisputable conventions (such as the composer's wish for impromptu addition of ornaments) not on conventions made up *ad hoc* to support a theory.

6

The Rhythm in
"Behold the Lamb of God"

The following essay was presented at the Messiah *Symposium of December 1980 in Ann Arbor, Michigan. There Graham Pont expounded his "Paradigm of Inconsistency" and its application to Handel's overtures—the subject of the preceding essay.*

In Handel's music we face certain problems of rhythm, but they are neither as numerous nor as complex as some modern interpreters believe them to be. Thus, in the chorus "Behold the Lamb of God" from *Messiah,* we meet problems of tempo, articulation, ornamentation, dynamics, phrasing, balance—but not of rhythm. The piece, I believe, should be rendered as written.[1] Yet some editors suggest, and some conductors introduce, various rhythmic alterations. Foremost among their reasons for so doing is their belief in what is commonly called the French overture style with its multiple ramifications of overdotting, other forms of rhythmic contractions, and synchronizations. In a series of five articles I hope to have succeeded in showing that the French overture style is a fiction created by improper research procedures and that the alleged evidence is spurious.[2]

Among the rhythmic changes that I found applied to our piece in recordings, live performances, or editions are: (1) overdotting; (2) contraction of all eighth-note upbeats into sixteenth notes; (3) dotting of plain eighth-note patterns to synchronize them with simultaneous dotted ones; (4) dotting of *all* plain eighth notes including those not resulting in a clash with another part; (5) for measures 19, 20, 24, and 25, the change of the bass rhythm as shown in example 6.1, adjusting its pattern to that of the alto part. I shall address these changes now in the order listed.

This article originally appeared in *American Choral Review* 28 (October 1986): 18–22. Reprinted by permission of the publisher.

Example 6.1.   G. F. Handel, *Messiah*, "Behold the Lamb of God,"
                mm. 19–20

Original form   Watkins Shaw edition

that ta - keth a - way   the   sin.   a - way ___ the

(1) For my contention that overdotting is not justified, I have to refer the reader to the mentioned articles.

(2) In connection with the shortening of upbeats, interpreters may conceivably be guided by the similar pattern ♪ ♫♫ which often *was* an imprecise notation for ♪ ♫♫♫ . The only theoretical confirmation that I am aware of comes from the famous essay of Johann Joachim Quantz where this manner is limited to dotted *sixteenth* notes that *follow* a rest on a heavy beat without any mention of either dotted *eighth* notes or upbeats that *precede* heavy beats.[3] In instrumental music the actual use of Quantz's pattern is confirmed by evidence, such as the duet in Bach's Cantata No. 91, where in an early version an ever-recurring string passage is written ♪ ♫♫ throughout, and in the final version ♪ ♫♫♫ throughout.[4] It is likely that Handel had the same adjustment in mind for the violin passages in the chorus "Surely, surely."

We can find an explanation for such imprecise notation in the fact that eighteenth-century orchestra players yielded more readily to spontaneous tendencies of doing what comes naturally than do the intensely trained players in today's virtuoso orchestras.[5] This is the reason why composers could use the more convenient, imprecise notation with a reasonable prospect of achieving the desired result.

On the other hand, in a slow tempo and with dotted eighth notes rather than sixteenths, the tendency to assimilate disappears. Also, there are many passages written by composers of the time where in the pattern ♪ ♫♫ the integrity of the first eighth note is clearly of thematic-rhythmic essence.[6] This is true for instruments and, to a higher degree, for voices whose idiomatic impulse favors a longer over a shorter upbeat, especially when a leap and change of register is involved, as is the case in our piece.

There is, moreover, the matter of diction. Handel considered the *be-* in "behold" a long syllable, as shown in measure 5 where he articulates the alto part

rather than

and in measure 11 where the syllable is placed in the tenor as a quarter note:

Apart from these two cases, the word occurs in seventeen further cases, and in all of these the *be-* is set as an eighth note, never as a sixteenth.

Another argument for the upbeat contraction is an assumed need for synchronization, e.g., at the end of measure 1, in the middle and at the end of measure 2, and many times thereafter. True, there *are* contexts where rhythmic clashes make little musical sense, notably when two voices are closely tied to one another in either unison or strict parallel progression. In keyboard pieces the composer could count on the understanding of the single player involved to recognize the need for matching voices. For orchestra or chorus such expectations were harder to fulfill. Sometimes the desirable adjustment may have been made, more often probably not, the result remaining within the era's tolerance level for ensemble precision.

The situation changes when we move from parallel voices to a genuinely polyphonic setting. Here, a forcible unification of discrepant rhythms is undesirable because it obscures and impairs the independence of parts and, in fact, the polyphonic essence. Genuine polyphony implies independent melody *and* independent rhythm. By rendering the upbeats in our pieces in their notated value, the imitative entrances emerge with true polyphonic plasticity that is lost in rhythmic assimilation.

I owe a further argument to Alfred Mann who pointed out to me that upbeat contraction corrupts the part writing in a few spots. For instance, at the end of measure 2 the viola part enters its upbeat logically on a consonance. By rhythmic contraction, the counterpoint turns faulty, as consonance changes to dissonance (see ex. 6.2); a stylistically impeccable clash of rhythm would be replaced by a contrapuntally illegitimate and stylistically incongruous clash of sound.

An analogous situation occurs in measure 5 with the upbeat in the alto and in measure 7 with the upbeat in the soprano part.

Example 6.2.   G. F. Handel, *Messiah*, "Behold the Lamb of God," mm. 2–3

(3) Synchronizing rhythmic disparities in mid-phrase (see ex. 6.3) entails similar liabilities. In both cases we would lose the charm of rhythmic diversity. In measure 6, moreover, the dotting of the tenor part would again adulterate the part writing and produce an unpleasantly sharp harmonic clash. In turn, requisite integrity of the second eighth note in the tenor confirms the eighth-note value of the upbeat in the bass.

Example 6.3.   G. F. Handel, *Messiah*, "Behold the Lamb of God," mm. 6, 7, 9

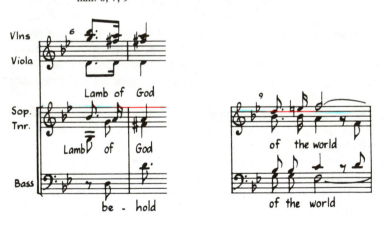

(4) More serious—because of stronger impact on the music—is the category of horizontal assimilation: the dotting of plain eight notes even if they occur simultaneously in all voices. Since for various reason the practice of *notes inégales* cannot be a factor here,[7] the only reason for such manipulation would seem to be the conviction that rhythmic variety in any form is illicit and has to

be purged. Such a proposition implies that once a composer starts a movement or section with a certain rhythmic pattern, he becomes its captive and is compelled to persevere with it to the end. A rule to that effect would flout every principle of aestheticism by denying the composer his freedom of thought and his right to diversity.

(5) An extreme case of rhythmic synchronizing was shown above in example 6.1. Here the wonderful bass line of measure 19 (repeated three times), whose syncopation should seem to be immune to manipulation, has been transformed in Watkins Shaw's edition into an un-Handelian, indeed, un-eighteenth-century, jazzy rhythmic design. Its contrived complexity alone leads the whole principle of obligatory rhythmic assimilation *ad absurdum*.

The effort to enforce homogeneity of rhythm is particularly illogical in this piece in view of the prevailing variety of its thematic and textural design. The descending theme of the beginning and end is contrasted by an ascending theme in measures 13–14, and, slightly modified, in measures 18–25 against a pedal note in the soprano. The prevailing polyphonic texture yields to homophonic texture briefly in the cadence of measure 15, and then more decisively in the last three-and-one-half measures of the choral score. It is no coincidence that in these very measures all the eighth notes shed their dots with magnificent effect. It is their very evenness that, in a purely chordal setting, lends a feeling of broadening to the cadence in measure 15, and conveys a sense of sovereign tranquillity to the final measures.

In this wonderful chorus the variety of dotted and even rhythms, of parallel rhythmic motion and clash, adds a dimension of depth to the musical fabric that is superbly integrated with theme, texture, form, and words. Forcible rhythmic assimilation wipes out this added dimension and severely diminishes the communicative power of the work.

Notes

1. A probable, very minor exception occurs in measure 27 where, at the final cadence of the chorus, the first violins, doubling the sopranos, sound the last note, g'—but before the voices. Whether or not the players made the logical adjustment apparently mattered little at the time. Today it will be advisable to change the eighth note to a sixteenth.

2. The five articles are reprinted in my *Essays in Performance Practice* (Ann Arbor, 1982), chaps. 6–10.

3. Johann Joachim Quantz, *Versuch einer Anweisung die Flöte traversière zu spielen* (Berlin, 1752), chap. 17, ii, 16. English ed. by Edward Reilly (New York, 1975).

4. Both versions are given in the *Neue Bach Ausgabe* I/2, pp. 164–69 and 157–62, respectively. See also *Kritischer Bericht* I/38, p. 130; cantatas 19/1 and 198/1 (*Trauerode*).

5. Even today's finest virtuoso orchestras occasionally yield to the instinct of doing what comes naturally in deviating from the prescribed rhythm. I have yet to hear in Beethoven's Seventh Symphony the pervasive rhythm of the first movement in its proper note values. It is invariably

changed, for the simple reason that the written rhythm is extremely difficult in the prescribed lively tempo.

6. A striking illustration appears in the third movement of Bach's Cantata No. 119 where (as shown at the place marked by an asterisk) Bach had at first written a dotted pattern, then corrected it to even notes; the same correction appears at the parallel passage in measure 30:

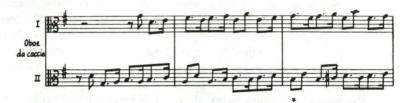

7. Some of the reasons: (1) the *notes inégales* represent a French convention, and no evidence permits us to assume that they were widely known and applied by English musicians; (2) under the rules of the convention, eighth notes were strictly equal in $\frac{4}{4}$ meter; (3) the *notes inégales* cannot be counted upon to result in a 3:1 ratio: their inequality varied and was generally much milder; (4) if the eighth notes had become dotted through *inégalité*, the original dotted notes would have had to be double-dotted, which is not only antivocal but contradicts the gentle affection of the piece.

Part Three

Problems of Ornamentation

7

Remarks on Haydn's Ornaments

The following essay was a paper presented in German at the International Joseph Haydn Congress in Vienna in 1982 and published within the Proceedings of the Congress by the Henle Verlag in 1986. It is presented here in English translation, preceded by my contribution to the discussion in form of a brief answer to László Somfai's paper "How to Read and Understand Haydn's Notation in Its Chronologically Changing Concepts." In this paper Professor Somfai had reaffirmed his belief in the orthodox precepts for Haydn's ornamentation that, with the exception of the turn for which the symbol is written after the note, all other ornaments have to fall on the beat, and all trills have to start with the accented upper note.

"The focus of my differences with my colleague Somfai resides in the question of rhythmic disposition. He insists for Haydn on the orthodox principle of the downbeat start for every ornament and of the trill's start with the auxiliary. This principle has its main origin in a number of ornament tables that scholars have taken too literally. In so doing they committed the logical sin of confusing the abstract with the concrete. A theoretical model is a pure abstraction, totally detached from any actual musical situation. It is, as it were, the Platonic idea of an ornament that assumes innumerable differing shapes in practice. These varied shapes grow out of a specific musical situation to which they ought to adapt spontaneously, guided by instinct, taste, and intelligence. If instead one concretizes this abstraction unyieldingly and literally, one compounds the logical sin with an aesthetic one: by the unmerciful repetition of a mechanically regulated ornament, one stiffens and hardens the musical fabric instead of loosening and lightening it; one annoys with immutable predictability, bores with literal repetitions, while forgetting that one of the principal functions of ornament is variety, the unexpected turn with a breath of fresh air. Ornaments

---

The text of this chapter is a translation of a paper that originally was published in the *Proceedings* of the Joseph Haydn Congress of 1982 (Munich: Henle, 1986). Reprinted here by permission of the publisher.

are children and grandchildren of improvisation and must never deny this origin. That is true for J. S. Bach, for Mozart, and certainly also for Haydn."

After the publication of my book on the ornamentation of J. S. Bach (Princeton, 1978) I started writing a study on the ornamentation of Mozart (Princeton, 1986). In the course of its preparation I have also collected some autograph material on Haydn that I trust will provide sufficient substance for this small paper. Within the narrow time frame of twenty minutes allowed I shall limit myself to two points: first, a critical look at the widely-held idea that all of Haydn's ornaments have to fall on the beat, and second, a contribution to the question of the so-called "Haydn ornament."

The Downbeat Rule

Recently I realized again the importance of the first point when an eminent Haydn scholar, László Somfai, took the downbeat rule for Haydn's ornaments as a matter of course and subjected to its jurisdiction even phrases like those shown in examples 7.1a and 7.1b. In example 7.1a from the String Quartet, op. 77, no. 1 (Hob. III:81) the *Vorschläge* preceding dotted eighth notes in a brilliant march rhythm are placed on the beat and in example 7.1b from the sister Quartet, op. 77, no. 2 (Hob. III:82) the turn, both in its notation as three little notes, and in that of the synonymous symbol, is given the same treatment. To see this happen has saddened but not surprised me: I am aware how many scholars share the belief in the uncompromising downbeat rule and how many historically oriented performers follow its principle. A much-quoted remark of Haydn's in praise of C. P. E. Bach, the leading prophet of the downbeat dogma, was widely interpreted as an endorsement of *all* of the older master's doctrines.

Example 7.1a.   String Quartet, op. 77, no 1. (Hob. III:81),
first movement

Example 7.1b.   String Quartet, op. 77, no. 2 (Hob. III:82),
third movement

Of course, many ornaments are intended to be rendered on the beat, especially those that have either the function of enriching the harmony or conveying a nuance of warmth, tenderness, or similar emotion. But ornaments have many facets and one rigid rule cannot do justice to all of them. There are types of ornaments whose function is to add luster and emphasis to the principal note. Others again serve the purpose of smoothing the transition between principal notes, filling the space between notes more engagingly and gracefully, or performing similar functions. In these and related cases the ornament can fulfill its function only if placed unaccented and unobtrusively in the time between the beats. If one makes the effort to render such ornaments on the beat, one frequently turns the musical priorities upside down: one elevates what is accessory to what is essential and vice versa; one alters the physiognomy of the melody, blurs the contour of the musical structure, and disfigures rhythmic designs. Let us reserve such treatment of ornaments for C. P. E. Bach and his followers who apparently wished to abide by such an artificial rule, but let us protect Haydn and Mozart from the consequences of a law whose unbending rigidity runs counter to the very spirit of ornamentation.

The rule of playing *all* ornaments on the beat is unnatural, as can be gathered alone from the vocal portamento, perhaps the oldest and most frequent of all ornaments. This spontaneous manifestation of the vocal impulse in connecting distant pitches, is invariably done *before* the beat. It so happens that several instrumental ornaments are direct descendants of the vocal portamento. The short *Vorschlag* (especially the upward-leaping one), the slide, and the arpeggio are basically stylized forms of the vocal portamento and as such carry the genetic trait of anticipating the beat. For a characteristic illustration, example 7.2a from the String Quartet, op. 64, no. 2 (Hob. III:69) shows leaping *Vorschläge*, where the wish for an audible portamento is indicated by the original fingerings. Example 7.2b consists of three separate instances taken from the Symphony No. 101.

Example 7.2a.   String Quartet, op. 64, no. 2 (Hob. III:69),
                 third movement

Example 7.2b.   Symphony No. 101 (Hob. I:95),
                 second movement

The next excerpt, example 7.3a from the Symphony No. 95, shows slides whose undeniable connective function suggests anticipation. In example 7.3b from the Symphony No. 103 the need for anticipation is doubly underscored: first by the *sforzando* sign that Haydn had clearly placed under the principal note and second, by the ugly parallel unisons with the second violins that would result from downbeat execution of the slide. Similar objectionable parallels in example 7.3c from the Symphony No. 99 can only be avoided by anticipation of the slide.

Example 7.3a. Symphony No. 95 (Hob.I:95),
                second movement

Example 7.3b. Symphony No. 103 (Hob. I:103),
                third movement

Example 7.3c. Symphony No. 99 (Hob. I:99),
                second movement

For the third kind of portamento descendants, the arpeggio, we can see in example 7.4 how a downbeat with an accent on the lowest note would subvert the musical priorities inasmuch as the melody leaps from E upward to C and not downward a ninth to the D that is only a harmonic filler—not to speak of the *sforzando* sign that Haydn, here too, had set unequivocally under the principal note.

Example 7.4.   Symphony No. 104 (Hob. I:104),
                     second movement

Whoever believes that anticipation of little notes is forbidden as a matter of principle should study example 7.5, from *L'Anima del Filosofo,* where Haydn in short succession writes an anacrusis in the same motive first with a small, the second time with a regular note. This example alone should suffice to break for Haydn the spell of the downbeat fixation.

Example 7.5.   *L'Anima del Filosofo,* Overture

The Haydn Ornament

My second important point concerns the so-called Haydn ornament: this term must have several meanings since a solution that fits one situation is obviously wrong for another one and vice versa. The ambiguity of this ornament has caused discomfort to scholars because it does not accommodate the modern striving for greatest textual fidelity. Here we forget too easily that very few ornamental symbols are free from any ambiguity and neither can nor ought to be resolved in mathematical terms.

Regarding the Haydn ornament, Georg Feder writes that it normally means

♫ but, depending on circumstances, it can also mean ♪ , hence assuming either the form of a turn *before* the note, or that of a mordent. Yet even if we allow these two melodic designs the widest rhythmic and dynamic leeway they still do not exhaust the potential of this ornament, and in the following I shall pass in review the varied alternatives for its interpretation.

In the case of the turn, the Haydn ornament can be synonymous with the meaning of ∾ both when written on top of the note or after the note. Such identity becomes clear when Haydn casually and unconcernedly interchanges the two symbols for the very same motive when the intention of a variant is highly improbable. For a turn *after* the note we see such interchange in examples 7.6a from the *Missa brevis* in B♭ and in 7.6b from the Piano Sonata in A Major (Hob. XVI:26). Example 7.6c, from the Cello Concerto in D Major (Hob.

VIIb:2), shows the Haydn ornament in the unmistakable meaning of a turn *after* the note whose connective function and interbeat rendition is unquestionable.

Example 7.6a. *Missa brevis* in B♭ (Hob. XXII:7),
              Benedictus

Example 7.6b. Piano Sonata in A Major (Hob. XVI:26),
               first movement

Example 7.6c. Cello Concerto in D Major (Hob. VIIb:2),
               first movement

For a turn symbol written *above* the note, the synonymity of the two symbol types is apparent in example 7.7a, from the Variations in F Minor (Hob. XVII:6), known as *Un piccolo divertimento*.

Example 7.7a. F-Minor Variations (*Un piccolo divertimento*)
               (Hob. XVII:6)

These cases allow a wide range of interpretive options, as I tried to show in example 7.7b without exhausting all possibilities. The numbers 1) and 2) show the textbook solutions with the start of the upper note on the beat. Number 3) shows anticipation; number 4), the start with the main note in the sense of C. P. E. Bach's "geschnellter Doppelschlag."

Example 7.7b.   Possible Interpretations of 7.7a

Not all of these alternatives are always available, and sometimes anticipation is the only indicated solution. The latter is, for instance, unmistakable in
example 7.8, from the Symphony No. 90, where the turn is at first written with
three little notes (a). Then in (b), (c), and (f) the slur to the preceding note
establishes their *Nachschlag* character and with it their placement before the
beat. The same rhythmic disposition is unquestionable when the motive recurs,
as shown in examples (a), (d), (e), and (g), and, most importantly for us, in (h)
where the turn is written with the Haydn ornament.

Example 7.8.   Symphony No. 90 (Hob. I:90),
                first movement

What we have here is not an isolated case, and it is most probable that in
many, if not in most, other occurrences in Haydn's work, the three little notes
that form a turn should be understood in the sense of Tartini's and Leopold
Mozart's anticipated "mordente" (for us a misleading term for a prebeat turn).
It is in this sense that such rendition, in example 7.9 from the String Quartet,
op. 71, no. 3 (Hob. III:71), a is to be given in analogy to the parallel spot of b,
where it is written with the clearly synonymous Haydn ornament.

Example 7.9.   String Quartet, op. 71, no. 3 (Hob. III:71),
                        second movement

The same applies to countless other instances where musical reasons suggest or demand anticipation. Two such typical specimens are given in example 7.10a, from the Symphony No. 102, and 7.10b from the String Quartet, op. 77, no. 1, where the strong downbeat accents of the dance need to fall on the principal note. When so rendered, the turn adds luster to this note; when done accented on the beat it effectively blurs, indeed distorts, the melodic outline.

Example 7.10a.   Symphony No. 102 (Hob. I:102),
                        third movement

Example 7.10b.   String Quartet, op. 77, no. 1 (Hob. III:81),
                        third movement

By contrast, we often encounter cases that favor or demand the standard textbook solution of the turn starting with the auxiliary on the beat. Two such specimens are shown in examples 7.11a and b, the first from the Variations in F Minor, *Un piccolo divertimento;* the second, from the Cello Concerto in D Major (in this second example interpretation as a trill—rather than as a turn—is a possibility).

Example 7.11a.   F-Minor Variations (*Un piccolo divertimento*)
                        (Hob. XVII:6)

Example 7.11b.   Cello Concerto in D Major (Hob. VIIb:2),
first movement

Mordent meaning for the symbol occurs but is relatively rare and seems to be limited to the clavier. For a characteristic case see example 7.12, from the Piano Sonata in B Minor (Hob. XVI:32), with the mordents first indicated with—rhythmically ambiguous—little notes, and then replaced by the Haydn ornament. (The source is not an autograph; Haydn quite certainly wrote the little notes with three, not two beams.)

Example 7.12.   Piano Sonata in B Minor (Hob. XVI:32),
first movement

Very often the symbol has trill meaning, and this intention is often graphically clear when for the very same motive Haydn—unthinkingly, so it seems—interchanges the trill symbol with the Haydn ornament. We see such a case in example 7.13, from the Trumpet Concerto (Hob. VIIe:1), where we find the Haydn ornament in the first measure, the trill symbol in the third and fifth measures, and an unmarked but understood continuation of the trill in the seventh measure.

Example 7.13.   Trumpet Concerto (Hob. VIIe:1)

No less convincing is the graphic evidence of example 7.14, from the String Quartet, op. 17, no. 1 (Hob. III:25), where the trill signs in the first measure are replaced in the second by the Haydn ornament. Most likely these short trills start for motivic reasons with the main note and end for idiomatic and technical reasons without a suffix.

Example 7.14.   String Quartet, op. 17, no. 1 (Hob. III:25),
                first movement

For musical reasons the Haydn ornament will have trill meaning when, as in example 7.15a, from the Symphony No. 45 ("Farewell"), it follows a stepwise descending long appoggiatura. Such meaning is fully clarified in example 7.15b, from the String Quartet, op. 17, no. 2 (Hob. III:26), where the identical phrase has first the trill symbol and then the Haydn ornament.

Example 7.15a.   Symphony No. 45 ("Farewell") (Hob. I:45),
                 first movement

Example 7.15b.   String Quartet, op. 17, no. 2 (Hob. III:26),
                 third movement

The same will most likely be true when the ornament is slurred to a note placed one step higher on the strong beat, even if the latter is not a dissonant appoggiatura, as is the case in examples 7.16a, from the String Quartet, op. 20, no. 4 (Hob. III:34), or 7.16b, from the Symphony No. 50 in C Major.

Example 7.16a.   String Quartet, op. 20, no. 4 (Hob. III:34),
                 first movement

Example 7.16b.   Symphony No. 50 (Hob. I:50),
first movement

Trill intention can also be assumed when the time is too short to accommodate a turn, and when a mordent does not fit, as shown in example 7.17, from the Cello Concerto in D Major. Here a *Schneller* (a brief, one-repercussion main-note trill, sometimes referred to as "inverted mordent") offers the most logical solution.

Example 7.17.   Cello Concerto in D Major (Hob. VIIb:2),
first movement

In a spot like the one shown in example 7.18, from the String Quartet, op. 71, no. 1 (Hob. III:69) mordents fit musically well, but for two reasons are unlikely: the mordent symbol is foreign to strings, and the first two would-be mordents would have been expected to carry accidentals. Main-note trills seem to be the best solution here.

Example 7.18.   String Quartet, op. 71, no. 1 (Hob. III:69),
first movement

The variety of forms encompassed by the Haydn ornament, and the frequent uncertainty of its meaning, have far-reaching implications for the whole of Haydn's as well as other masters' ornamentation. It proves for instance that the *exact* melodic-rhythmic-dynamic design of this ornament (and in analogy of many other ornaments as well) was far less important to the masters than we usually assume to be the case. What often mattered to Haydn was to grace a note at a given place with a suitable ornament. Often only a clearly defined form was intended at a given spot, but not infrequently there will be one or more other options in which cases it will often not greatly matter which of the designs is being used. The freedom of such choice is only a pale reflection of the Baroque and Rococo manner of embroidering the composer's text freely with improvised ornamental figurations—a manner still widely practiced in Haydn's time by Italian and Italian-oriented performers.

From the large canvas of free improvised ornamentation and from the small one of the many-sided Haydn ornament, we can learn that the modern attempts to mathematically define an ornament's authenticity are misguided, inasmuch as the ornaments of Haydn, Mozart, and other great masters occupy in their dynamic-rhythmic-melodic dimensions a far wider range than today's scholars are willing to concede to them. It is possible that C. P. E. Bach and his circle, perhaps influenced by the Prussian *genius loci,* tried to militarize the ornaments and make them respond according to the book in drill-order fashion; but I am inclined to believe that in this field Philipp Emanuel did not, as the German saying goes, "eat as hot as he had cooked." For Haydn's music we certainly must replace mathematics and rigid rules with imagination, flexibility, taste, and musical intelligence. That is perhaps the most important lesson to be learned from the many-faceted nature of the Haydn ornament.

8

More on Haydn's Ornaments
and the Evidence of Musical Clocks

The preceding essay, presented as a congress paper, was by that very fact limited in length and scope. These limitations hit hardest in the first part of that paper, the one dealing with the question of the downbeat rule for Haydn's ornaments. Here I shall offer additional material on that controversial issue as well as on the evidence of musical clocks, which is significant because of the close connection of the clock maker to Haydn himself. The evidence is of particular interest with regard to the trill, besides shedding light on the mordent and the turn.

The Anticipated *Vorschlag*

The way in which Haydn writes a dynamic mark, such as *f,* *sf,* or *fz* often clarifies the placement and with it, the nature of an ornament. If he places the *sforzando* sign clearly and unequivocally below the principal note, as shown in example 8.1a, from the String Quartet, op. 64, no. 2, he strongly suggests that the accent, and therewith the beat, falls on this principal note and that the *Vorschlag* is to be rendered lightly and quickly before the beat. Had he wished an accented start on the *Vorschlag,* as shown in example 8.1b, he would have had to write it thus if he did not want the violinist to interpret the graphic design at face value. Here, as well as in many similar spots, anticipation of the *Vorschlag* is further supported by the articulation dashes that call for a brisk staccato. With the downbeat rendition of example 8.1b no effective staccato is feasible.

    The need for clear staccato articulation will similarly call for anticipation of the *Vorschläge* in example 8.1c, from the Finale of the String Quartet, op. 64, no. 4, as will the series of *fz* marks in example 8.1d, from the first movement of the Symphony No. 103 ("Drum Roll").

Music examples in this chapter have been cited from the *Joseph Haydn Werke* (Munich: Henle, 1958–) by permission of the publisher.

Example 8.1a.   String Quartet, op. 64, no. 2 (Hob. III:66),
                 third movement

Example 8.1b.

Example 8.1c.   String Quartet, op. 64, no. 4 (Hob. III:68),
                 fourth movement

Example 8.1d.   Symphony No. 103 (Hob. I:103),
                 first movement, mm. 66–68

In example 8.2, from the String Quartet, op. 74, no. 1, harmonic reasons call for the anticipation of the little note that precedes the trill. The tied-over C of the second violin is a suspension that resolves in mid-measure to the trilled half-note B. The first violin's dissonant D has to enter decisively on the beat to clarify the nature of the suspension and with it of the harmonic progression. For this purpose the *Vorschlag* on C has to be anticipated; if played on the beat, it would blur the harmony.

Example 8.2.   String Quartet, op. 74, no. 1 (Hob. III:72),
                first movement, mm. 16–18

The Arpeggio

The arpeggio being an ornament, many scholars and some performers who follow the orthodox line will subject it, along with the other ornaments, to the downbeat rule. This despite the fact that in the vast majority of cases, where the arpeggio precedes and leads to the melody note, such rendition is illogical and unmusical; it is perhaps the most striking of the cases mentioned in the preceding essay in which an onbeat rendition turns the musical priorities upside down: the melody, the master, has a claim to melodic and rhythmic integrity; the arpeggio, the helper, serves only as a foil that adds grace and highlights the melody note, but can do so only by remaining in the dynamic and rhythmic shade, which means anticipation.

Haydn often spells out the anticipated arpeggio in regular notes, which shows that he did not find this design objectionable. Three of such cases from the slow movement of the Piano Sonata in E♭ are given in example 8.3a and another written-out anticipated arpeggio extending over two octaves, from the Sonata in F, is given in example 8.3b. In the first movement of the E♭ Sonata we find the interesting graphic design of example 8.3c, where of three arpeggios over the ascending B♭ major triad the first, starting the measure, is written in little notes; the second and third show anticipation in regular notes. That the first has to be equally anticipated is a matter of elementary musical logic. The identical design recurs in measure 66.

Example 8.3d shows a similar series of arpeggios ascending along the same chord—here a dominant seventh—all written in little, unmetrical notes, whose anticipation is urged by the staccato marks over the principal notes that confer accents on them along with sharpness of articulation. Clearly the melody that needs to come out is F–B–D–F, and not G–D–F–B!

A different kind of proof for anticipation of an arpeggio, and simultaneously also of a *Vorschlag,* is offered in example 8.3e, from the slow movement of the String Quartet, op. 71, no. 1 (Hob. III:69), where all four strings play the same dotted siciliano rhythm preceded in the first violin by a three-note, in the cello a two-note arpeggio, and in the second violin and viola by simple *Vorschläge*. The principal (dotted) note has a *sforzando* marked in all strings. Clearly, these first accented notes have to enter simultaneously and can do so only if the preceding ornaments of one, two, and three notes are anticipated. Needless to say, the accentuation itself, again clearly marked under the principal notes, concurs in this requirement.

In the Minuet of the Quartet, op. 74, no. 1, the first violin plays as shown in example 8.3f. Surely the notes to be emphasized and given a metrical accent are E–F–G and not G–G–G. There are innumerable similar cases.

Example 8.3a.   Piano Sonata in E♭ Major (Hob. XVI:38),
                second movement

Example 8.3b.   Piano Sonata in F Major (Hob. XVI:29),
                first movement. m. 15

Example 8.3c.   Piano Sonata in E♭ Major (Hob. XVI:38),
                first movement, m. 19

Example 8.3d.   Piano Trio (Hob. XV:27),
                first movement, m. 3

Example 8.3e. String Quartet, op. 71, no. 1 (Hob. III:69),
second movement, mm. 41–42

Example 8.3f. String Quartet, op. 74, no. 1 (Hob: III:72),
third movement

The Turn and an Issue of Phrasing

In the preceding chapter I discussed Haydn's turn and offered at least one instance (see ex. 7.8) that provides incontrovertible evidence about the anticipation of a turn written by three little notes, as well as the analogous anticipation of a turn written with the Haydn ornament on top of the note.

Haydn often wrote the three little notes in the rhythmic design shown in example 8.4a, where they are followed by a dotted note on the same pitch as that of the preceding regular note, where it could be synonymous with the usual turn symbol ∞ placed *after* a double-dotted note (see ex. 8.4b). I said "could be" because Haydn's notation is more precise whereas the symbol would allow for a wider range of rhythmic disposition: it could for instance cause the turn to be rendered at the very end of the value of the double-dotted note. This may be the reason why Haydn resorted to the more cumbersome notation with the three little notes. Occasionally on-beat rendition will be a reasonable option, but very often, indeed mostly, whenever there was time enough, they were meant to be rendered *before* the following regular note. Apart from its graphic suggestiveness and the evidence presented in the preceding essay, we find occasional additional proof for this rhythmic disposition.

In example 8.4c, from the first movement of the Piano Sonata in D, the *fz* mark on the note following the little notes places the parent note clearly on the beat; the turn, in anticipation. In example 8.4d, from the Piano Trio in D Minor, the same motive is written in measure 35 with the three little notes, two measures later with the turn symbol written *after* the note ♪∞♪, a design that everybody, even C. P. E. Bach, recognized as calling for an interbeat ornament. This proves that the figurations of both measures 35 and 36 have the turn in anticipation.

In example 8.4e, from the Finale of the String Quartet, op. 64, no. 1, the staccato marks over the eighth notes call for anticipation of the turn, both to maintain the rhythmic integrity of the six even eighth notes, and to allow for the staccato rendition of the note following the turn. In example 8.4f, from the second movement of the Piano Trio in E♭, the crescendo-decrescendo forks peaking at the note following the main-note turn, written in four little notes, make musical sense only when anticipated. An on-beat start would undo the rhythmic parallelism of the two groups of eighth notes and would be irrational in its dynamics: starting on the beat a crescendo of the delayed principal note would make little sense.

That the wavy turn symbol on top of the note can call for anticipation is shown in example 8.4g, from the Piano Trio in F♯ Major, where the turn is written with the symbol for the violin, with—undoubtedly anticipated—three little notes for the unison piano.

Example 8.4a.   Piano Sonata in E♭ Major (Hob. XVI:49),
                second movement

Example 8.4b.   Alternative Notation of 8.4a

Example 8.4c.   Piano Sonata in D Major (Hob. XVI:42),
                first movement, m. 87

Example 8.4d.   Piano Trio in D Minor (Hob. XV:23),
second movement, mm. 35–37

Example 8.4e.   String Quartet, op. 64, no. 1 (Hob. III:65),
fourth movement, m. 31

Example 8.4f.   Piano Trio in E♭ Major (Hob. XV:29),
second movement

Example 8.4g.   Piano Trio in F♯ (Hob. XV:26),
third movement

   Although such anticipation of the turn, when written with three or four little
notes, would seem natural to most readers, simply because of its graphic suggestiveness, it has to be defended because it is predictably rejected by the believers
in the downbeat doctrine. Among these we find the eminent Haydn scholar

László Somfai, who lists Haydn's turn as notated with three little notes:
as one of Haydn's most common *on-beat position* ornaments and transcribes it

accordingly: .[1]
   Occasionally, however, when musical reasons speak overwhelmingly

against this dogmatic solution, Somfai has to make a concession, as for instance in this interpretation of the theme from the E♭ Sonata given in example 8.4a. He does not see it in the way sketched in example 8.4b; instead, as given in example 8.5a, he interrupts the first of these (underlying) double-dotted notes by making a strong phrasing break (marked by two dashes) on the second beat, on which he places the turn (with an implied accent on the upper note) and then breaks the phrase again after the third and fourth beats. He stops short of repeating this pattern for the start of the second measure: at the doubled motion of this motive, a similar interruption and accented downbeat rendition of the turn would border on the irrational. Somfai, in a silent compromise, departs from his principle and gives the only sensible pre-beat transcription of this figure. Yet his silence is disturbing; he ought to have explained why he antici-pated the second turn but would not allow the same treatment for the first, which, he insists, *has* to strike with the beat after being preceded by a caesura. That seems like unfair discrimination: should not all turns have the same rights and privileges?

As a rationale for his three phrasing breaks and the jolt of the brusque accented entry of the first turn, he speaks of having a dream that one day musicians will play a beautiful theme like this "with sufficient breathing, impor-tant graces, and vivid rhythmic action instead of the established stuffy legato style."[2] His illustration of the "stuffy legato style" is shown in example 8.5b.

The "sufficient breathing" manifests itself in no fewer than *four* breaths for that brief phrase. The "important grace" is no doubt the first turn that ought to be a connecting ornament, yet it interrupts the flow of the melody by its ac-cented on-beat start after a phrasing break; and the "vivid rhythmic action" is probably the splitting up of the brief subphrase into four parcels.

I believe this interpretation to be misconceived. The piece is marked "Ada-gio e cantabile," which means it is to be played in a songful style. If a singer were to take four breaths for such a theme fragment of only five beats, he would need either medical attention or musical reeducation. It is a misconception that the classical masters fractured their songful melodies by frequent articulation breaks and many interruptions of the breath.

Example 8.5.   Piano Sonata in E♭ (Hob. XVI:49),
                    second movement

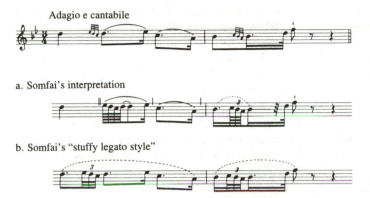

a. Somfai's interpretation

b. Somfai's "stuffy legato style"

Leopold Mozart may be innocently responsible for such an idea, when a passage in his treatise about the management of the bow was misinterpreted to signify interruptions for each stroke. That misinterpretation emerges from what he says about rendering a songful theme. He warns against the interruption of the melody unless required by phrasing or special expression. He favors the legato mode in emulation of the voice that "spontaneously flows from one pitch into another" ("Die menschliche Stimme ziehet sich ganz ungezwungen von einem Tone in den andern"). When, he continues, the nature of the melody does not call for a break in continuity, "one should not only keep the bow on the string and *when changing the stroke connect one tone smoothly with the next* [italics mine] but also try to fit many notes into the same bow stroke" ("Man bemühe sich also . . . nicht nur bei der Abänderung des Striches den Bogen auf der Violin zu lassen und folglich einen Strich mit dem andern wohl zu verbinden; sondern auch viele Noten in einem Bogenstrich . . . vorzutragen").[3] Clearly his ideal was a smooth legato style for songful melodies and not fractionalization. Nor do I know why "vivid rhythmic action" should be a vital ingredient of cantabile playing. If Somfai dreams of a fractured cantabile manner, I would find a dream about the "stuffy legato style" more pleasurable.

The Trill and the Evidence of Mechanical Clocks

"Conventional wisdom" has it that all trills of the seventeenth and eighteenth and the early nineteenth centuries (up to and including Beethoven and Schubert) have to start with the accented auxiliary on the beat, until Hummel "invented" the start with the main note. I believe I have proved that this is a myth in my two books on ornamentation. There I have shown that, among others, Bach's trills very often, and Mozart's trills almost always started with the main note.

Predictably, Haydn's trills are being included in that sweeping rule. Such sweeping rules are of course very convenient: they provide what I have called "instant authenticity." There is no need to think or to feel or to analyze. Whoever starts every ornament on the beat and every trill with the accented auxiliary, cannot fail to win the establishment's stamp of approval.

In his tabulation of Haydn's "on-beat position ornaments" quoted above, Somfai includes the trill along with the turn, the mordent, the slide, and the arpeggio. He accordingly illustrates the trill's execution like this: ┝•⎯•⎯•⎯ , etc.

On previous occasions I had pointed out that a trill starting with the accented auxiliary has the function of an appoggiatura, and I called it the "appoggiatura trill." Consequently, it makes musical sense only in spots where, on leaving out the trill, the improvised addition of an appoggiatura would be fitting. Where it would not, the built-in appoggiatura would be a disturbance and this kind of trill-start out of place. The trill should then either start with the main note, or may, depending on the circumstances, be preceded by an unaccented, prebeat grace note, slide, or turn. In a case like that of example 8.6, from the String Quartet in F, op. 74, no. 2, appoggiatura trills for the unison lower trills that descend stepwise over the interval of an eleventh would make no melodic sense and, besides, clash irrationally for the first three measures with the figurations of the first violin that are anchored in the key unison notes.

Example 8.6.   String Quartet, op. 74, no. 2 (Hob. III:73),
                first movement

Many more such contexts can be found, but the open-minded reader is bound to be impressed by the following evidence offered by three musical clocks for whose builder Haydn wrote, around 1790, a series of charming original pieces as well as a few arrangements of his earlier compositions. The recipient was Joseph Niemecz, a master builder of musical clocks who was librarian at Esterháza, the castle of Haydn's employer. Niemecz was a practicing musician who played several instruments and was reported to have studied composition with Haydn.

The new Haydn *Gesamtausgabe,* which is being published by Henle in Munich (*Joseph Haydn Werke*), brought out in 1984 as volume 21 a collection of "Stücke für das Laufwerk (Flötenuhrstücke)," edited by Sonja Gerlach and George R. Hill. The collection contains all those Haydn pieces for clocks whose authenticity is certified by autographs, along with some others where the editors consider Haydn's authorship likely but not certain. The edition presents the original text and above it, a transcription of the way the Niemecz clocks interpret the score. Only three of these clocks survived. One is from 1792, one from 1793, and the third is undated. This latter contains a piece from 1796, which is therefore the earliest possible date for its manufacture. For their transcription the editors have used both tape recordings and, for the 1793 and the undated clock, an impression of the cylinders that allowed an exact reconstruction of melody and rhythm.

The transcriptions are understandably of particular interest regarding the realization of ornaments. In this matter the clocks sometimes agree, and sometimes disagree, as will be shown presently.

There is no direct evidence that Haydn supervised the manufacture of the clocks or approved of their pinning. Haydn had left for Vienna and London in 1790, so the clocks of 1792 and 1793 were built during his absence. Haydn returned to his old position in 1795, this time to Eisenstadt and Vienna (Esterháza having been abandoned) and Niemecz too moved to Vienna in 1795. Considering the reported teacher-student relationship and the certain admiration of Niemecz for Haydn, it is hardly daring to assume that the master craftsman solicited Haydn's advice after his return for the building of the "undated" clock and that Haydn had a hand in its preparation. Supporting this theory is the fugue (No. II.7 in the Henle edition): the clock of 1792 either disregards or misinterprets a clear directive by Haydn in his autograph, whereas the undated clock rectifies the mistake. The probability is strong that this clock with its main note trills and its anticipated turns and mordents is a truly authoritative document.

The above-mentioned fugue, the first measures of which are reproduced in example 8.7, has several points of great interest. As to the mistake of the clock of 1792, Haydn did not write into the score the mordents that are shown on the line of Haydn's original text. Instead, he wrote a directive at the end of the piece that every time the theme occurs, the half note has to receive a mordent ("mus bey jedweder Halben Notte folgender Halbe Mordent kommen") and illustrates it thus: , adding that this theme occurs sixteen times. The clock of 1792, as seen on the top line of the example, has a *Nachschlag* instead of a mordent. The undated clock corrected the mistake and shows the mordent for every one of the sixteen entries of the fugue theme. Interestingly, this mordent is always *anticipated:* in the transcription an on-beat mordent, follow-

ing editorial procedure, would have been indicated not by small notes ![small notes figure]

but by regular ones ![regular notes figure] . Observe that on both clocks all the trills start with the main note. It is the more remarkable that they do so coming every time after the fall of a third, i.e., in a context conducive to the insertion of a note in the manner of *tierces coulées,* favoring an upper note start of the trill. Such a start, however, would have blurred the sharp contour of the fugue theme.

Example 8.7.   Fugue (Henle II.7)

In the piece numbered I.4 we see trills that on the clock of 1792 start with the auxiliary; on the undated clock, on the main note (ex. 8.8). A long sustained trill—the kind that Couperin called *tremblement continu*—starts in measure 9 and lasts for eight measures. On both clocks it not only starts with the main note but throughout emphasizes the latter by its rhythmic disposition.

Example 8.8.   Piece (Henle I.4)

Example 8.8   (continued)

In only one piece, No. II.4, do the trills in both clocks start on the upper note. The piece happens to be one for which Haydn's authorship is uncertain since no autograph survived, and dubious on stylistic grounds for its musical barrenness and simplemindedness.

As to the turn written with the three little notes, the clock of 1792 sets it *on,* the undated one, *before* the beat. The very first measure of the piece No. II.1, as given in example 8.9a, points up this difference. The prebeat interpretation of the undated clock is especially noteworthy in a recurring pattern of the piece No. II.2 (given in ex. 8.9b), where a minimal space (a fraction of a thirty-second note) barely permits the prebeat turn to be squeezed in. Again we see another main-note trill in measure 4 on which both clocks agree.

Example 8.9a.   Piece (Henle II.1)

Clock of 1793

Undated clock

Text of Haydn autograph

Example 8.9b.   Piece (Henle II.2) (Hob. XIX:12)

Clock of 1793

Undated clock

Text of Haydn autograph

In brief summary, these two chapters on Haydn's ornaments were meant to demonstrate that the convenient formula for "instant authenticity"—to render every ornament on the beat and start each trill with the auxiliary—is as wrong for Haydn as I had elsewhere shown it to be wrong for Bach and Mozart.

The first essay showed, in a compactness imposed by outward circumstances, that both the *Vorschlag* and the slide were often anticipated; and that the so-called Haydn ornament could take on a wide variety of designs, as turn, mordent, or trill in a wide range of rhythmic dispositions.

The second essay has supplemented these findings by showing rhythmic variants of the turn, the characteristic anticipation of the arpeggio, and the evidence of three musical clocks. Built in the 1790s by Joseph Niemecz, with whom Haydn had been closely associated in Esterháza, these clocks play a number of pieces that Haydn had written for them. One of these clocks (the undated one) proves to be closer to Haydn's intentions, since in the fugue (No.

II.7) it follows Haydn's instructions exactly, whereas the clock of 1792 misinterpreted them. The undated clock is more consistent in the main-note start of the trill, as well as in the anticipation of the turn and mordent. All in all, both clocks emphatically confirm the thesis of these two essays: the need to free Haydn's ornamentation from the rigorism of the traditional rules, the need to give up the convenient crutch of "instant authenticity," and the need to treat Haydn's ornaments with rhythmic and melodic flexibility that disregards the traditional ban on anticipation and favors the main-note start of his trills.

Notes

1. "How to Read and Understand Haydn's Notation in Its Chronologically Changing Concepts," *Proceedings of the International Joseph Haydn Congress*, Vienna, Hofburg, 5–12 September 1982 (Munich, 1986), pp. 23–34 (tabulation on p. 29).

2. Ibid., p. 34.

3. Leopold Mozart, *Versuch einer gründlichen Violinschule* (Augsburg, 1756), chap. 5, par. 14; facs. eds. Vienna, 1922; Frankfurt-am-Main, 1956. English trans. E. Knocker (London, 1948; 2nd ed., 1951).

9

Interpretation Problems of Ornament Symbols and Two Recent Case Histories: Hans Klotz on Bach, Faye Ferguson on Mozart

Among the many problems of performance practice for music of the seventeenth and eighteenth centuries ornamentation has always been, and continues to be one of the greatest challenges to musicians and scholars. It looms so large because it played such a huge and controversial role in that era. Though its role hardly dwindled after 1800, its problems—still considerable with Beethoven and Schubert—gradually diminished with the demise of improvisation, the decreasing use of symbols, and the ever-greater specificity of notation.

Notation is at the root of the difficulties we encounter here as it is at the root of all problems of performance practice. They all can indeed be identified with those elements of execution that are not or only inadequately expressed in the score.

Ornaments, which I am addressing here, were reflected in notation in three manners: they were either (1) indicated by symbols or (2) written out in regular notes, or (3) not notated at all. To these three alternatives corresponded three distinct types of performance problems. (1) For the symbols the problem is their proper interpretation. (2) For ornaments written out in regular notes, the problem is to identify certain such notes as ornamental and to render them accordingly with greater lightness and a measure of improvisatory freedom. (3) For ornaments not written at all, the problem is the double one, first to determine where additional embellishment is needed, and second, to devise an appropriate design.

The interpretation of the symbols has been the subject of the widest discussions in the literature old and modern. It is to this matter that the present article is addressed.

All ornaments are born of improvisation and as such they were born free,

This article originally appeared in *Performance Practice Review* 1 (Spring–Fall 1988): 71–106. Reprinted by permission of the publisher.

yet many modern writers have endeavored to deprive them of their freedom and put them into narrow cages. One is tempted to paraphrase Rousseau's famous opening sentence of his *Contrat social:* "Man is born free, and everywhere he is in chains" ("L'homme est né libre, et partout il est dans les fers") and substitute "ornament" for "man."

The Emergence of Symbols

The first ornaments were presumably pitches a singer added to the melody of a song so that he sang two or more pitches to one syllable, forming a melisma. To do so must respond to a fundamental human urge of embellishing what is simple and severe, because we find it at all times in all cultures. Such ornamentation was "melodic" in the sense that pitches were added *between* the regular, or structural, notes of the song. The original melody remained intact and in place and the embellishments wound around it like a garland between columns. This type of ornamentation remains alive to the present, except that its notation has changed. Today such ornaments in art music are written out by the composer in either regular or in small notes. Until nearly the end of the eighteenth century the improvisatory origin of these embellishments was made manifest when many of these melismatic ornaments (called *passaggi* or coloraturas) were not specified by the composer, but left to the impromptu skills of the performer. By then the era of free improvisation was drawing to a close, and the music of Haydn and Mozart, except for *Eingänge* and cadenzas, left hardly any room for improvisation. They wrote out their *passaggi* and so did all the later masters.

Up to about 1600 all ornaments were of this "melodic" kind; they decorated and enlivened the melody but did not have any effect on the harmony. By the turn of the century, with the emergence of recitative, monody, and the concomitant striving for passionate expression, musicians seem to have first seized on the potential of ornamental additions to create expressive dissonances: they displaced a note on a strong beat with another a step above or below, forming an appoggiatura that created a sigh effect with its resolution to the delayed principal note. Thus was born the first "harmonic" ornament. At first used only sporadically, it gradually found its favorite niche, preceding a final cadential trill. Even there it was far from holding a monopoly, and elsewhere "melodic" one-note graces that anticipated the beat, leaving the principal note in place, continued to flourish in Italy, Germany, and France and have done so to the present.

Meanwhile some ornamental figures from one to three or four pitches—few enough to allow only limited modes of arrangement—were used often enough to allow their being grouped into formulas. These formulas in turn lend themselves to representation by the shorthand device of a symbol. Symbols as such are age-old and go back to ornamental neumes in the early Middle Ages, but the direct ancestry of the Baroque ornaments and their symbols might go no further back than the early sixteenth century to symbols for trills, such as Vicenzo Capirola's red dots (1517) or Silvestro Ganassi's letters "V" and "S" for the whole-tone and half-tone trill respectively (1535). The first rich flourishing of symbols occurred at the hand of the French lutenists, English virginalists, and gambists. When the French clavecinists in mid-seventeenth century took over the inheritance of the passing lute school, it was they who developed ornamental symbols to a high degree of refinement and sophistication. Their growing numbers created problems for the performers, who could not guess any more what the various signs meant, and needed an explanation. Thus were born the first ornament tables and with them came into being the most fatal source of misconceptions as formed by modern ornament theory and practice.

The Role of Ornament Tables

Ornaments small enough (in the sense of number of pitches involved) to allow symbolization have lost some of the near-total freedom still enjoyed by the lengthy *passaggi* or coloraturas, yet, in spite of having been somewhat disciplined, tamed and domesticated, have retained enough of their innate freedom to fulfill the function that ornament is to play within a musical work. This function in music is to provide variety, to add grace and elegance, to soften hardness, to round angularity, to smooth, to liquefy. In order to do so they need to be rendered with flexibility and a touch of improvisatory freedom. It is most emphatically not the function of ornament to harden, to stiffen, to regularize the musical texture. An ornament that is rendered with military-drill precision is a contradiction in terms. Yet this is exactly what has been happening under the banner of would-be "authentic" performances, and it has been happening through the unlikely medium of ornament tables.

    An ornament is like an organic substance and as such is in constant flux. It has no rigid shape, and cannot have one if it is to do its work. Regular notes cannot do justice to the irregularity of a specific ornament in a specific context, because notation is too rigid with its mathematical ratios while the ornamental irregularities are too subtle and intangible to be rendered in such fixed terms. A symbol, on the other hand, is not only a convenient shorthand device, but is actually a superior notational device because it does not bind the ornament to exact ratios and allows it to assume, however subtly, ever-differing shapes. But how is the symbol to be explained to the uninitiated? The only way to do so is by offering an abstraction of the design, a reduction to its common denominator, to its Platonic idea as it were, that has countless diverging manifestations in reality. In turning to ornament tables for their answers, modern scholars and performers generally make two fatal mistakes. The first is that of misunderstanding the abstract nature of their design and taking the models on their literal, mathematical face value every time the symbol appears. As a consequence, they use them like prefabricated spare parts mechanically inserted. The result is the kind of machinelike ornament rendition that, in total contradiction to the nature and function of ornament, petrifies the musical texture and guarantees monotony through exact repetitions. The French organist and scholar Antoine Geoffroy-Dechaume hit on a felicitous formulation when he spoke of the "inanity of ornament tables" ("l'inanité des tables") that offer only a single transcription of any ornament while each is capable of a great variety of execution.[1] Ornament tables themselves are not the culprits; they were often written by eminent musicians and are an indispensable means of explaining the *basic* design of an ornament. The culprits are those modern scholars and musicians who misinterpret them by not realizing that the abstract idea has to be in each case adapted to an ever-changing environment while permitting the ornament to live, breathe, and change.

The second fatal mistake is the casual, unthinking, near-automatic way in which ornament tables by one master are "applied" to another who may be separated by time, style, region, nationality. The would-be rationale for such action is a widespread belief in a "common practice" for an age, even for a whole century, spanning all nationalities. It is a very convenient theory, because it yields all the answers, but the theory is fiction and therefore most of the answers are wrong. The very idea that, say, Bach performed in the same manner as Couperin or as Pergolesi, or Mozart in the manner of C. P. E. Bach, is almost on the face of it incongruous. It is bad enough to insist on applying with pedantic rigidity Bach's own brief ornament table, written as a child's introduction for the nine-year-old Wilhelm Friedemann, while not realizing that Bach's infinite variety of melodic designs had its counterpart in a comparable richness of ornamental designs. But to take somebody else's patterns, be it Philipp Emanuel, or Couperin or whoever, and apply them to Bach's music is a reckless gamble at best.

A strong sense that something had gone radically wrong with the modern "authentic" ornament interpretation prompted me, a quarter-century ago, to enter the field myself. I trust that several articles and two major books[2] made a strong case for the need of a thorough revision of ornamentation theory and practice. The most urgent need is to abandon the fundamentalist approach of going strictly by the book, of believing in the literal truth of every model in an ornament table and every rule in a tract. Theorists and tables need to be studied and considered, but the tables have to be understood as the abstractions they are, and rules have to be viewed as generalities with numerous exceptions; also both tables and tracts have to be most carefully screened as to their probable or improbable pertinence in a specific case. Most importantly, further insight is to be sought from the study of the music itself, which can yield important clues when properly analyzed. A systematic search for such evidence has already yielded a great deal of information that differs strongly from the inferences drawn from "the book" and proves that ornamentation during both the seventeenth and eighteenth centuries was much more flexible and varied than the fundamentalist scholars of the establishment believe to be the case.

Any major revision of a well-established idea or method has always, and will always meet with fierce resistance, the force of inertia being more powerful than any force of persuasion. Thus it might take a generation before the case for revision can get a sympathetic hearing. Meanwhile scholars and historically oriented performers continue in the old vein of relying on ornament tables, which they apply in the time-honored, automatic "spare part" fashion.

That such is the case can be heard in many performances and can be seen in several recent publications. The following two case histories are meant to illustrate this state of affairs with regard to scholarship. The first concerns an extensive monograph on Bach's ornamentation by Hans Klotz; the second refers to a review by Faye Ferguson in *Mozart Jahrbuch* 1986 of my recent book on Mozart's ornamentation and improvisation.

Case History 1: Hans Klotz on Bach

Hans Klotz, a composer of choral music, author of several books and numerous articles on organ playing, including a monograph of Bach's organ works, and collaborator on the *Neue Bach Ausgabe,* published in 1984 *Die Ornamentik der Klavier- und Orgelwerke von Johann Sebastian Bach,* a substantial book of 219 pages (Kassel: Bärenreiter, 1984). After previous writers, among them Putnam Aldrich and Robert Donington, imposed bonds of rigorism on Bach's keyboard ornaments, Klotz topped their efforts by consummating their ossification. This is strange if we consider that Klotz wrote one splendid paragraph about the freedom of ornaments, a freedom that defies rational fixation. "Ornaments," he writes, "are free-floating configurations ("freischwebende Gebilde"), which move within the meter of the principal notes, without changing it, yet are free from its laws. The real value of the ornamental notes is irrational, their rhythm incommensurable with our system of notation" (pp. 37–38). To this I can only say "amen." Unfortunately, this well-conceived credo remains suspended in a vacuum: the rest of the book cancels this declaration of freedom for ornaments with an incessant flow of dicta that establish rigid, ironclad rules for every single ornament. The "free-floating" ornaments, far from being allowed to float, are in the end nailed to the ground.

My *Ornamentation* attempted to dismantle the cages that modern scholarship had erected for the imprisonment of ornaments and did so by mustering a huge amount of evidence, theoretical as well as musical, pointing to a far greater freedom of ornament rendition than modern scholars have so far conceded. I do believe I can say without undue arrogance that anybody writing on ornaments in the period covered by my book (ca. 1600–1770) ought to come to terms with the evidence presented in it. I realize there are language barriers, but Klotz did read Putnam Aldrich, in whom he found a kindred spirit. He mentions my book in one paragraph (on p. 94) in which he cites *one* example of mine, but keeps total silence about its massive documentation, which undermines his every premise and his every thesis. I refuse to believe that he wished to bypass my documentation and reasoning by simply ignoring it. I can only assume that in writing his book he did not know mine and became aware of its existence too late for more than a cursory, last-minute mention.

The Klotz book has some unquestionable assets. One or the other ornament, for instance the turn, is well presented. Interesting as documentation is the presentation of twelve ornament tables in facsimile. But all in all the book is severely flawed in its structure: it is flawed in its basic theses and flawed in its method.

At the very outset (p. 2), Klotz presents his theses:

1. Bach's ornamentation is characterized by (a) the principle of the neighbor note ("Nebentonprinzip"), (b) the on-the-beat principle ("Initialcharacter"), (c) the dissonance, and (d) the détaché.

2. Bach's [symbol-indicated] ornamentation is unequivocally and unconfutably distinguished from improvised ornamentation.

3. Bach's keyboard ornamentation is identical with that of the French keyboard players.

All three of these theses are untenable.

Ad 1.a) The *principle of the neighbor note* is at best an exaggeration as it seems obviously meant to apply to the *Vorschlag,* the trill, the turn. It clearly does not apply to the mordent, the slide, the arpeggio.

b) The *on-beat principle* required that every ornament start exactly on the beat. Here Klotz, as others had done before, clamps down the iron gate of the "cage" that guarantees the regimentation of ornaments. Such a principle cannot be reconciled with Klotz's characterization of ornaments as "free-floating configurations" that are not bound by the meter. There is no greater bondage to the meter than being forcefully tied to each beat.

Now it is true that certain ornaments have to fall on the beat, but many others do not; some may take the beat when it is musically appropriate and avoid it otherwise; some again must shun the beat. A genuine appoggiatura has to fall on the beat because it forms a dissonance that needs the beat for emphasis before it is resolved. But there is no such need for any other ornament: not for a

Vorschlag that is not an appoggiatura, that does not form a dissonance and is not intended to be stressed; not for the trill, unless it is linked to an appoggiatura; not for the mordent, unless its principle function is to reinforce the meter; not for the slide that can fall on, before or between the beat; not for the turn, not for an arpeggio that is logically anticipated when, as is mostly the case, the melody note is at its end rather than at its start.

The on-beat principle is of course not new: it is the establishment doctrine, widely believed and widely practiced. Klotz simply reconfirmed and fortified its orthodoxy. Where did it come from? From ornament tables taken at face value. The tables, as stated earlier, show the design of an ornament in abstract simplifi- cation within the space of the principal note, hence starting on the beat. Yet Klotz, further supplementing his fine statement about the "free-floating" orna- ments, writes that "the old ornament tables render the ornamental designs metri- cally in gross simplification" ("die alten Ornamenttafeln die Verzierungsformeln im Metrischen oft grob vereinfacht wiedergeben") adding that the pertaining text often "strongly exaggerates their meaning" (p. 2). Moreover, Klotz approv- ingly cites Aldrich, saying that our ornament tables have to be understood in terms of melodic outline and not of metrical literalness (p. 75). Yet neither of the two scholars drew the proper inferences from these insights. Had they done so they would have realized that the downbeat start of the models might be precisely such a "gross simplification." Such realization would have cautioned them against elevating the onbeat start to a fundamental principle of ornament rendition and against committing, by this elevation what, with only moderate exaggeration, can be called the original sin of ornament performance practice.

c) *The dissonance principle.* Here Klotz has a point with the genuine appog- giatura and with the particular type of trill that has appoggiatura function, but other ornaments do not or do not have to form a dissonance: not a *Vorschlag* before a dissonant principal note, not a *Vorschlag* that is anticipated with purely connective function; not a trill whose function it is to add brilliance to a single note, or to keep the decaying sound of the harpsichord alive, or to reinforce and enliven the melody, not to enrich the harmony; not the mordent, not the turn before a dissonant note, not the turn after a note, not the slide, not the arpeggio, not a *Nachschlag,* that even Klotz admits does not take the beat and that, even if it happens to form a dissonance with the bass, is never perceived vertically as dissonance, but always melodically as a passing note or cambiata; not what I call a *Zwischenschlag,* a one-note grace that is slurred to both the preceding and the following note and belongs equally to both of them.

d) *The principle of detachment.* The note before an ornament, says Klotz, should be slightly shortened to permit the ornament to enter exactly on the beat. Again we have a vast overstatement. Certain ornaments, like the *Vorschlag* or the slide, will occasionally be slightly detached from the preceding note to clarify their bond to their following principal one. But a trill is more often than not slurred to the preceding note and so is the mordent; so always are the *Zwischenschlag* and the *Nachschlag*. We shall see how the adherence to this principle can have regrettable musical results.

Ad 2. *The strict separation of symbolized and improvised ornaments.* This separation is important for Klotz, who tries to maintain for Bach the integrity of the downbeat style by assigning any prebeat or interbeat ornamental forms to the realm of improvisation. The wall he erects between the two types is to ban any intercourse between them and to protect the symbol-indicated realm from being infected with subversive interbeat designs. Such a separation is arbitrary and unwarranted. It is unwarranted musically: there is no conceivable reason why any design that was acceptable as improvisation would not be acceptable as response to a symbol. The listener, after all, is unaware of the notation. The separation is unwarranted historically: no principles governed the choice of the three notational alternatives (written out, or symbolized, or omitted). Their selection was arbitrary and the relative incidence of these alternatives varied from nation to nation, from composer to composer, from work to work. Italians and all Germans who were indebted to the Italian style gave wide latitude to improvisation (Handel belonged in that group). French composers generally liked to keep a tighter control over their performers and were more explicit in using regular notes and symbols for their ornaments. Very few of these composers allowed no role for improvisation. Couperin was one of these very few; he marked all ornaments he desired and the great density of their occurrence leaves no room for sensible additions. In the preface to his third book of clavecin pieces he specifically demands that all his symbols be honored, that no ornaments be left out, none added. His attitude is by no means typical: the eminent theorist Saint Lambert, writing in 1702, stresses complete freedom for the *agréments* (i.e., the small ornaments that *can* be indicated by symbols) by claiming for the performer the right not only to add new ones but to leave out those that are prescribed or to substitute others in their stead. There is no better proof for the free intermingling, even among French clavecinists, of symbolized and improvised ornaments, and for the illogic of the attempt to erect a wall between the two. As a further testimony to this state of affairs, we find many French treatises throughout the whole of the eighteenth century not only explaining the symbols and their execution, but also pointing to contexts in which certain ornaments could, or should or should not be added.

As to Bach, he did write out in regular notes nearly all of the *passaggi* that German and Italian contemporaries would have left to improvisation, and in his keyboard music he did mark many of his *agréments* with symbols, but we have no reason to assume with Klotz that Bach would have "strenuously objected" to any additional ornamentation of his music (p. 43). He himself has shown by adding ornaments to later versions of keyboard pieces (inventions, organ chorales) that the original version was receptive to further embellishment. And, considering the near-universal inclination of the time to bring variety to a repeat, Bach almost certainly welcomed, and probably expected, on repeats in dance pieces discreet additions of ornaments. All in all, the "wall" is a fiction, and any inferences drawn by Klotz from its existence for the execution of ornaments are fallacious.

Ad 3: *Bach's keyboard ornamentation is identical with that of the French*. Here again we have a bold assertion that does not stand up to scrutiny. First, there was no unified French keyboard ornamentation. Even their ornament tables with their "gross simplifications" do not agree. The tables of Nivers, Raison, D'Anglebert, and Couperin certainly do not agree, and we have seen how diametrically opposed the opinions of Saint Lambert and Couperin are about the observance of the symbols. There are far wider differences if we consider musical evidence. Certainly, Bach studied French keyboard players: in his Arnstadt years, if not before, he copied D'Anglebert's ornament table, two suites by Dieupart, and an organ book by Grigny. And clearly he adopted several of D'Anglebert's symbols and basic designs. Yet in his music, D'Anglebert writes out several anticipated *ports de voix* in contradiction to his "grossly simplified" downbeat table models, and Grigny, in the very book that Bach had painstakingly and precisely copied, specifies a number of prebeat *Vorschläge*, anticipated trill auxiliaries and slides (by writing the little notes before the barline).

Now besides the French, Bach had studied German and Italian masters.[3] He transcribed Vivaldi, Marcello, Palestrina, Pergolesi, and Frescobaldi; he studied the music of Bruhns, Reinken, Froberger, Kerll, Pachelbel, Fischer, Strunck, and Boehm, and spent many months in Lübeck to study Buxtehude's art at its source. He drank from whatever source he felt could benefit him. In adopting models that seemed worthwhile to him he did not proceed by accumulation and assembly into neatly separable units, as would befit an eclectic. Bach was no eclectic: he absorbed what he learned from the multinational models and assimilated it into a higher, uniquely Bachian entity. It is simplistic to think that his keyboard works are all in the French style and used only French ornamentation; are we then to assume that, say, his vocal works are in the German style, chamber music and concertos in the Italian, and each used only the respective national ornamentation? This is absurd on the face of it. Various strands of Bach's musical inheritance show up in all of his works, some more in certain kinds, some more in others. Dense German polyphony and Italian concerto elements invade many a keyboard suite, we find French ornaments in very un-French organ chorales, Italian *passaggi* and trills everywhere. It is noteworthy that next to French symbols and designs, Bach used the Italian "t" symbol for the trill next to the French *chevron* ∿ and the German custos

⌐ for the slide. Bach did not adopt D'Anglebert's symbols for the mordent, the slide, and the various kinds of arpeggios.

Klotz is also wrong in saying that Bach addressed a public that was thoroughly acquainted with the [French] art of ornamentation and that it is "totally impossible to explain such behavior [of addressing the informed public] other than that Bach identified with this art" (p. 12). The logic of this argument escapes me: even if the German public had been "thoroughly acquainted" with French ornamentation, Bach would not have been compelled to completely identify with the latter. Yet, the German public in the early part of the eighteenth century was far from thoroughly acquainted with French practices. In the early decades of the eighteenth century French—far from unified—ornamentation only gradually began to filter into Germany, and many eminent masters, among them Mattheson, the Grauns, Heinichen, and Graupner, did not embrace it. It was indeed Bach himself who introduced some of D'Anglebert's symbols such

as: ⌐ ⌐ ⌐ to which he added variants of his own design, like

⌐ ⌐ ⌐ that were not used by any Frenchman. It is questionable that they were understood by many of his German contemporaries. Any way we look at that argument it does not hold water.

In the hope that this brief sketch may have sufficed to show that all three of Klotz's principal propositions are untenable, and why, we next have to look at his treatment of some of the individual ornaments.

Klotz on Individual Ornaments

The Vorschlag

Vorschlag is the generic term for a one-note grace that precedes its principal note and is slurred to it. I call an "appoggiatura" the kind of *Vorschlag* that takes the beat, is emphasized, and typically forms a dissonance that is resolved in legato to its principal note. Klotz admits for Bach solely the appoggiatura, since, in accord with his basic principles, a *Vorschlag,* as any other ornament, must fall on the beat. An anticipated *Vorschlag,* in his opinion, is illegal for Bach and therefore did not exist.[4] The way he argues this case is characteristic also of many subsequent statements: any evidence that contradicts his thesis is either withheld, belittled, dismissed as belonging on the other side of the "wall," as "having nothing to do with Bach," or explained as an oversight or a mistake.

He reproduces correctly (pp. 82–83) the appoggiatura patterns of D'Anglebert, Le Roux, Dieupart, and Rameau, but when he lists an identical pattern for Saint Lambert, he misleads the reader: Saint Lambert does show the pattern but does so in reporting the views of D'Anglebert, adding that these patterns may be fitting for *chansons* but only on few occasions for clavecin pieces; that for the latter anticipation is much more proper ("beaucoup plus convenable").[5] Klotz mentions later this preference of Saint Lambert's, wrongly claiming that he uses a special symbol for the anticipated type, then dismissing it by saying that "both sign and execution have nothing to do with Bach's ornamentation" (p. 94). There is no special sign for the anticipated *port de voix*.[6] That the execution has nothing to do with Bach is simply an arbitrary decree for which there can be no proof.

Saint Lambert does not stand alone among French masters. Klotz reproduces the ornament table of André Raison (1688), where the *only* pattern for the *port de voix* is anticipated, but fails to report on it when he lists the other French designs. Whereas Klotz reproduces in table 2 Nivers's rhythmically noncommittal trill and mordent designs (from the preface to his *Livre d'orgue* of 1665), he fails to report from the same document this master's anticipated *ports de voix* (see *Ornamentation,* ex. 10.6).

Had Klotz been acquainted with my book, he would have found a multitude of other French keyboard documents giving anticipated *ports de voix,* such as the table of the organist Chaumont (1696, ibid., ex. 10.7b), didactic illustrations by Gigault (1682 and 1685, ibid., exx. 10.8 and 10.9), documents by Grigny (from the organ book of 1699 copied by Bach [ibid., ex. 10.10]), by Louis Marchand (ibid., ex. 10.11) and many more from the whole of the eighteenth century in my chapters 9 through 12, too numerous to list here.

Klotz notes that Alfred Kreutz finds reason for the anticipation of Bach's *Vorschlag* in Saint Lambert, Loulié and Quantz,[7] and tries to dismiss both Loulié and Quantz with his "wall" argument, claiming that both these authors referred to improvised graces that had "nothing to do with Bach" (pp. 92, 93). This is again a misstatement: both Loulié and Quantz refer to symbolized graces.[8] And Quantz, who both had a French teacher and had spent six months in Paris studying French music and performance practices, stresses the French origin of the anticipated *Vorschläge*.

It is in this connection that Klotz makes the single reference to my book: he quotes *one* example of mine (his p. 94), one of many that strongly suggest the anticipation of a *Vorschlag*. It shows eight instances in which scribes from Bach's circle (three of them written by his devoted and reliable student Gerber) set the hook symbol for the *Vorschlag* before the barline, even when there was plenty of space between the barline and the following principal note. It also shows three examples of such clear prebar placement of the hook symbol in autograph suites by Gerber himself (*Ornamentation,* ex. 16.11). First Klotz tries to downgrade this external evidence by claiming that my (printed) example was imprecise in reproducing the original. Now in the double hook symbol that Bach often used: ⊃ what matters is the lower hook that stands for the *Vorschlag,* not the upper one which stands for the slur. And in spite of unavoidable small imprecisions when irregular graphic designs are rendered in print, my lower hooks in the three instances Klotz reproduces are quite precise, with one imprecision only for the irrelevant upper hook. Hence, this argument is invalid; the hooks in the other examples are precise enough to convey the intended evidence. Then Klotz admits that three *Vorschlag* symbols in a gigue *are* before the measure line, and one astride the latter. Klotz simply blames the writer for carelessness. It was forbidden, therefore it had to be a mistake!

In addition to external evidence, by no means limited to the fourteen specimens of my example 16.11 in *Ornamentation,* I present a great deal of internal evidence of various kinds for anticipation of the *Vorschlag.* One kind is derived from spots where a downbeat rendition would result in offensive forbidden parallels. The role of parallels in ornament rendition has been controversial over the last centuries. Some authors of old diminution treatises (among them Ortiz, Ganassi, and Finck) admitted parallels in *fast* diminutions where they could hardly be perceived, others admitted them in thickly set accompaniments (among them, Saint Lambert), others yet distinguished "ear fifths" from "eye fifths" with the clear meaning that only those parallels that are disturbing to the ear must be avoided. Others yet were adamant about the absolute prohibition (among them, Werckmeister). Of eighteenth-century theorists, C. P. E. Bach, Quantz, Agricola, and Türk, stress the need to avoid parallels in ornaments. On one matter everybody is agreed, that parallels that are blatant and offensive are unacceptable. It so happens that Klotz himself unequivocally adopts the prohibition for Bach: "Bach," he writes, "respected the prohibition of fifths and octaves also in his ornamentation" (p. 190). How then does he explain the many instances where obtrusive parallels would result from the downbeat rule (I listed no fewer than twenty-six such instances in *Ornamentation,* exx. 16.12–16.16, with no claim to completeness). Such instances, Klotz says, are simply "oversights" (p. 193), an explanation as convenient as it is unconvincing.

Here I shall present only one example (ex. 9.1) whose eloquence singlehandedly shatters the downbeat-only rule for Bach's *Vorschläge.* It is a passage (and its parallel spot) from the *Art of Fugue* autograph, "Canon per augmentationem in contrario motu," where on-beat rendition would result in a series of offensive parallels. Here no fewer than six reasons make the anticipation of the *Vorschläge* imperative: 1) this is not a rough compositional draft, where oversights could occur (though hardly six times in a row), but a calligraphic fair copy; 2) we have to do with the supreme manifesto of voice leading, where any mistake has yet to be discovered; 3) it is a two-part setting that is the most sensitive to faulty counterpoint; 4) in such a two-part setting the repeated sounding of the open (parallel) octave is particularly offensive; 5) we have to do with *Vorschläge* before written-out appoggiaturas, the very case for which

Quantz with musical logic and common sense requires anticipation (*Versuch,* chap. 8, par. 6); and 6) the *Vorschläge* are disregarded in the augmentation (mm. 48–51 and parallel spot), which proves that they are inconsequential to the melodic profile, hence have to be unobtrusive in the metrical shade of the measure.

Example 9.1.   J. S. Bach, *Art of Fugue* (BWV 1080.4), "Canon per augmentationem in contrario motu"

Concerning the real appoggiatura, I am glad to report that Klotz agrees with me about its basic shortness in Bach. Here his sole reliance on French designs kept him from following in the footsteps of most modern scholars, who "applied" to Bach, often with lamentable results, Philipp Emanuel's and his followers' *galant* long and overlong appoggiatura patterns.

The Trill

Klotz elevates the trill pattern in Bach's brief table (*Explication,* given in ex. 9.2) to the guiding principle for all that master's trills.

Example 9.2.   J. S. Bach, *Explication,* trill table

He dismisses Emery's and Kreutz's severe reservations about this table (my reservations he apparently has not seen) as being beside the point. On the contrary, the *Explication,* he says, is the most informative of all tables and offers us the proper solutions for all the listed situations. Thus Bach's trill "starts always with the auxiliary and stops after a few repercussions, to end with the unadorned sound of the main note." (The start on the beat is for Klotz a matter of course, not worth mentioning.) Almost apologetically, Klotz points to the need to replace the thirty-second notes of the model with sixteenths in alla breve, and with sixty-fourths in an adagio (p. 22). The only other—very minor—deviations from strict literalness that he allows are first, variants for the number of alternations: instead of the three in Bach's model, there can be two, four, or five (p. 65); second, for long trills, a gradual, imperceptible speeding of the alternations (following a quote from Couperin to that effect). These seem to be the only touches of non-literalness, the only faint echo of the idea of "free-floating" ornaments in the whole book.

Again, the documentation meant to prove the upper-note-on-the-beat as sole design, is egregiously inadequate. It is rooted entirely in a number of table patterns (Chambonnières, Le Bègue, Raison, D'Anglebert, Le Roux, Saint Lambert, Rameau, and Dieupart). Their number seems impressive, but here we certainly have to do with, in Klotz's words quoted above, "coarse metrical simplifications of ornament tables." Klotz must have forgotten his own words in extracting from these very tables the immutable rule about the on-beat start of the auxiliary. Yet even if we were to forget about the need to qualify the metrical disposition of the tables, they still are far from telling the whole story. What the agreement of the tables (including Bach's own) really shows is the start with the auxiliary, the alternations, and the end with the main note, a melodic design that, in view of the "coarse metrical simplifications," can assume an infinity of rhythmic shapes, including the start with the auxiliary before the beat (a "grace note trill" in my terminology) and the partial or full anticipation of the whole trill. Klotz quotes several authors who stress the start with the auxiliary, but short of the Berlin school of C. P. E. Bach, Marpurg and their circle, where such a start is implied, he has not found a single French source that verbally specifies the start with the auxiliary on the beat. And that is more than coincidence. Whereas Couperin specifies for the extended mordent (*pincé continu*) the start on the beat, he omits such mention for the extended trill (*tremblement continu*); and his pattern (its facsimile in Klotz table 11; see also *Ornamentation*, ex. 25.1) indicates the prebeat start of the auxiliary. In an exact metrical disposition the main note hits every beat, and the auxiliary is an extra note preceding the first on-beat main note:

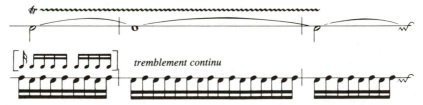

This anticipated design is fully confirmed in a passage from the Allemande *La majestueuse,* where a dotted half note, preceded by an anticipated three-note turn figure written before the barline in little notes, is replaced on a *petite reprise* by a *tremblement continu* preceded by only two notes, because the third is the anticipated auxiliary of the trill:

Couperin's *tremblement lié sans être appuyé* (a) as well as his *tremblement détaché* (b) is fully anticipated, as any unprejudiced reader can infer from the painstakingly exact line-up in the model:

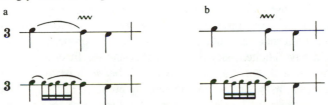

Such full anticipation is confirmed by Père Engramelle who spelled the anticipation out in regular notes.[9]

In addition I was able to trace a rich heritage of French main-note and grace-note trills from the early seventeenth century through the eighteenth. For the voice and melody instruments these designs were particularly widespread, but strongly touched the keyboard as well. My chapter 24 has many examples of vocal and instrumental main-note and grace-note trills side by side with trills starting with an appoggiatura. There the reader will find also specimens of grace-note trills for the keyboard (*Ornamentation*, exx. 24.29 Chaumont; 24.30 Grigny; 24.32 J. B. Loeillet). In chapter 26 see among others the main-note trills for the keyboard by Dandrieu (1724) and Van Helmont (1739) (ibid., ex. 26.8), for the voice by Lacassagne (1766) (ibid., ex. 26.11), for the violin by L'Abbé le Fils (1761) (also grace-note trills, ibid., ex. 26.25) and Brijon (1780) (ibid., ex. 26.16), and too many others to enumerate here. But I believe I have made the point that Klotz's belief in French unanimity about the rigid auxiliary-on-the-beat start of every trill is a chimera.

If we add to this that the Italian trill was overwhelmingly of the main-note type throughout the eighteenth century and beyond (see *Ornamentation*, chaps. 27 and 30) and so was the German trill well into Bach's time (ibid., chaps. 28 and 31) then we have to conclude that the whole edifice of Klotz's monolithic Bach trill is based on nothing more solid than wishful thinking.

Klotz does show, though not in his trill chapter, Murschhauser's main-note pattern of 1703 (p. 20) and dismisses it as following sixteenth-century (!) Italian designs. Murschhauser was not alone. Praetorius in 1619, Bernhard around 1650, Mylius in 1685, Falck in 1688, Stierlein in 1695, Printz in 1696, Feyertag in 1695, Fuhrmann in 1706 and 1715, and Beyer in 1705 and 1730 all show the main-note trill *exclusively* in their tables.[10] Surely these theorists were not all bogged down in sixteenth-century Italian procedures.

Klotz does show Buxtehude's and Lübeck's written-out main-note trills (we can find many more in masters like Froberger, Kerll, Pachelbel, Boehm, Speth, Scherer and many others whose music Bach had studied), and mentions cases where Bach wrote similar patterns "in works of stylistic affinity to the north German masters" (p. 201), but dismisses this important evidence by peremptorily declaring that these trills "have nothing to do" with those that Bach indicates by symbols. Why? They are trills after all, simply another manifestation of the many-faceted trill idea that, weren't we told, is supposed to be "free-floating." Those main-note trills by German keyboard composers (derived from Italian masters like Frescobaldi) were written out not because they were another species of ornament, but simply to insure their proper length whereas a symbol might have elicited only the briefest response. In order to defend his monolithic trill model, Klotz again erects a wall between written out and symbolized ornaments, as he had before between symbolized and improvised ones. This wall is no more real or logical than the first; here too, the notational difference cannot be heard by the listener and what cannot be heard is musically irrelevant. Again Klotz fabricated a fiction in order to dismiss an inconvenient piece of evidence.

This piece of fiction does not go very far to protect the monopoly of Klotz's model. There is a great deal of evidence not only for Bach's use of the main-note but of the grace-note trill and of full or partial anticipation. For this material I have to refer the reader to chapter 29 in my book.

In winding up the discussion of the trill, one illustration can show how literally Klotz applies the pattern from the table and how this intransigent literalness yields musically incongruous results. In the passage of example 9.3a from the organ choral *O Mensch, bewein' dein Sünde gross* (from the *Orgelbüchlein*), Klotz gives the solution of 9.3b. Here the melody that is being ornamented is the soothing, caressing wavy line of example 9.3c that cries out for legatissimo treatment.

Example 9.3a.   J. S. Bach, Organ Choral, *O Mensch bewein' dein Sünde gross* (BWV 622), main outline, middle parts omitted

Example 9.3b.   Klotz's Interpretation of 9.3a

Example 9.3c.   Melodic Line Only of 9.3a

Klotz certainly knew that Bach, as well as many other composers of the time, wrote hardly any articulation marks in his keyboard scores and that the lack of slur marks did not by itself imply detached articulation; further, he must have known that the first A♭ in the example is a written-out appoggiatura that resolves its dissonance on the trilled G; and he knew that an appoggiatura by its nature has to be slurred to its note of resolution since he said so himself: "[Bach's *Vorschlag*] is played in the time of the principal note, more strongly than the latter, to which it is slurred 'legatissimo'" (p. 80). Thus for the first trill Klotz's solution is wrong by his own lights: instead of a legatissimo resolution, calling for main-note start of the repercussions, there is a sharp interruption as a consequence of which any sense of resolution is obliterated. The second trill, so differently notated from the first, could for that very reason not be meant to be a near-replica and here, too, there is hardly a musically satisfactory alternative to a main-note start. The Klotz solution that disfigures the soothing melody by cutting it in two spots and stutteringly repeating the A♭ four times is thus not only provably wrong, but musically objectionable.

The Slide

As a matter of course, the Bach slide is for Klotz a pure downbeat ornament ("ein reines Initialornament") that starts in the time of the principal note and leads to the latter in strict legatissimo (p. 108).

Of the French clavecinists that supposedly determined Bach's clavier ornamentation, Klotz lists only two: D'Anglebert and Saint Lambert. Of D'Anglebert, who displays two downbeat models and one upbeat model, Klotz picked predictably a downbeat model and failed to mention the upbeat variant. Saint Lambert's model is rhythmically noncommittal:

and more suggestive of upbeat than downbeat style, since the little notes are not presented as symbol but as the resolution of the symbol; and a resolution is not supposed to present puzzles; also in view of this master's decided advocacy of the prebeat style for all the *ports de voix,* Saint Lambert's model can hardly give support to Klotz's thesis. Klotz was apparently not aware that L'Affilard in 1694 and Loulié in 1696 spelled out the prebeat nature of the slide (see *Ornamentation,* exx. 19.4 and 19.5); that Villeneuve in 1733, La Chapelle in 1737, and Denis in 1747 did the same (see ibid., exx. 12.10, 19.12b and c), that Grigny in the very organ book of 1690 that Bach copied repeatedly wrote the two little slide notes before the barline (see ibid., exx. 19.6a–d, f–i); and that Siret in 1716, d'Agincourt in 1733, Villeneuve in 1733, Luc Marchand in 1749, and Azaïs in 1776 did the same (ibid., exx. 19.11, and 19.12).

Had he read my book he would have also known that in several instances Couperin's slide would produce blatant parallels if taken on the beat. Furthermore he would have known thirteen of my examples where Bach's slide would produce unacceptable parallels (ibid., exx. 21.5 and 21.6). Klotz does mention that J. G. Walther, in his *Praecepta der Musikalischen Composition* of 1708 recommends anticipation of the slide (p. 112). He believes he can dismiss this piece of evidence by saying that it is not confirmed by the "classical" explanations, and that Walther did not return to it in his *Lexicon* of 1732. But neither did he show an on-beat pattern: he did not discuss the ornament in his *Lexicon* and the failure to do so does not imply a revocation of his earlier statement.

Klotz may have also been interested in seeing my documentation about the apparently general anticipation in Italy of the slide written with two equal little notes (*Ornamentation,* chap. 22). That C. P. E. Bach and his circle favored the downbeat slide was to be expected, but Klotz himself had very sensibly eliminated Philipp Emanuel as a reliable source for his father's ornamentation.

All other ornaments are similarly treated, similarly regimented, and there is no need to review them singly and in detail. The discussion so far should suffice to show that, all in all, the book is severely flawed to the point where it is not only misleading, but indeed harmful with its dogmatic rigidity. There are the faulty premises that served as fundamental theses (as discussed at the outset); there is egregiously inadequate research that kept from the author and his public a vast amount of evidence that contradicts both theses and conclusions; and there is a method that, oblivious of beautiful statements about "free-floating figurations," crystallizes the pure abstractions of several select ornament tables into rigid shapes that become the law of execution. The combination of all these factors results in prescriptions that totally subvert the very function of embellishment by creating, instead of variety, monotony through the insertion of ornaments like the mentioned prefabricated spare parts, and the limitation of every ornament to the vertical role of reinforcing the beat and depriving it of the horizontal potential of embellishing the melody; and worst of all, by hardening through rigorism, instead of softening through flexibility.

Case History 2: Faye Ferguson on Mozart

The second case history differs from the first in several ways. First, it refers not to a book, but to a review of a book.[11] Second, it exhibits in parts at least, different aspects of the interpretation problem for ornament symbols. Next to injudicious applications of ornament tables, which overlap with the case of Klotz, we find a variety of other arguments in a handful of cases where Ferguson tries to condemn my performance suggestions and to advance alternate solutions. I shall attempt a critical analysis of her line of reasoning with a view to shed some light on what arguments are legitimate in favoring a certain solution and which are not.

Ferguson's review starts inauspiciously by questioning my competence. This is somewhat strange in view of the fact that she is a newcomer in the field, not having, to my knowledge, so far published a single line on matters of ornamentation, whereas I have written on this subject two major books and numerous articles. She quotes me as writing "whatever weight we may ascribe to the theorists, we have to resort to musical evidence to get a direct bearing on Mozart's music. . . . We can gather important information from internal evidence that is based on musical logic (or just plain *musical common sense*)." To this she answers: "While the proposition itself is attractive, it presupposes a high level of competence on the part of the musical analyst. *Where this competence is lacking* [italics mine], the analyst is likely to arrive at solutions that fly in the face of both theory and *musical common sense*." Here we have two distinct types of "musical common sense": the first that guided some of my judgments and that, owing to my incompetence, is defective and flies in the face of the second, superior "musical common sense" as possessed by Ferguson, that is to serve as a valid yardstick for condemning my suggestions and solutions. I submit that the questioning of my competence and of my musical common sense is an *argumentum ad hominem* that, as all arguments of this type—considered indefensible infractions of scholarly mores—cannot be disproved and can only be pilloried.

Ferguson then criticizes a few of my ornament analyses (four appoggiaturas and one turn) on the basis of which she feels entitled to condemn the whole book (that deals of course with many more subjects and with hundreds of examples). It will be instructive to look at her comments for the variety and the types of arguments presented.

Many German theorists after 1750 formulate the rule that an appoggiatura lasts one-half of a binary, two-thirds of a ternary note. A few of them, among them Quantz, C. P. E. Bach and Leopold Mozart, supplement this principle by another rule about an "overlong" appoggiatura that takes the *whole* value of the principal note if the latter is followed by either a tie or a rest. Ferguson quotes me listing this rule and the pattern:

"overlong"

She comments: "A dozen pages later he has forgotten this pattern in connection with an example he quotes from *Die Zauberflöte*." Far from forgotten, I had disproved the use of this pattern for Mozart. In his vocal music Mozart frequently wrote an appoggiatura symbol for the voice, but spelled the grace out in regular notes for an attending unison instrument. In this manner he provided in very numerous cases a clear solution to the intended rendition. In a very extensive search I found out, and have documented in the book, that Mozart followed the "half-a-binary" rule only for appoggiaturas before relatively short (a quarter note or less) principal notes; that he did *not* honor the "two-thirds of a ternary" rule; that with regard to the "overlong" pattern I had found only two instances out of countless thousands that would apply to a rest (after a principal note of a quarter-note length) and *not a single one* that would apply to a tie. This is the kind of internal evidence that tells us what Mozart used and thereby qualifies and often nullifies the rules of the theorists.

As to the illustration from *Die Zauberflöte* (given here in ex. 9.4a), where I supposedly "forgot" the overlong rule of some theorists, Ferguson quotes me as saying that "the *Neue Mozart-Ausgabe* [hereafter: *NMA*] gives the interpretation of b, to honor the 'Vorschlag' denomination, but since the rest suggests a breathing spot for the singer, the rendition of c seems more likely [p. 19]."

Example 9.4.   W. A. Mozart, *Die Zauberflöte* (K. 620), Act 1, Scene 3
a = as written; b = *NMA* interpretation; c = Neumann
suggested interpretation

Ferguson, who wishes to vindicate the *NMA* solution, counters that my suggestion not only "bypasses the theorists, it bypasses clear musical evidence." Her argument that is to provide the "clear evidence" is unusual. She points to the orchestral strings that hold a chord through the third eighth note. "If," she writes, "the voice abides by the theorists' [overlong] rule, it fills the measure along with the accompanying instruments; if it clips the phrase, it permits the orchestra to have, so to speak, the last word. The version of the *NMA* is therefore not only historically correct, it also makes good musical sense." Ferguson seems to have discovered a law that voice and accompaniment have to be synchronized, or else either the orchestra or the voice would have "the last word," and that her "musical sense" apparently judges to be unacceptable. If such a law existed we would have to rewrite all of Mozart's operas and other vocal works. Moreover, she has a problem with the first violin part: the same kind of appoggiatura precedes for the voice a quarter note; for the violin, a dotted quarter note, and when the voice sings again on the fourth eighth note, the violin is silent. When Mozart wrote different rhythms for two parts, he obviously intended a different execution, but Ferguson's argument calls for equalization of the two parts, and to achieve the latter she resorts to an extraordinary device: she applies one rule for the voice, another for the violins: the vocal appoggiatura goes by the "overlong" rule; the violin appoggiatura goes (with full citation of C. P. E. Bach's precept) by the two-thirds of a ternary note rule (though the violin appoggiatura, too, being followed by a rest, would be eligible for the "overlong" rule). No greater tribute can be paid to the authority of the "theorists" than that of applying two of their—conflicting—rules simultaneously. It so happens that neither rule is pertinent to Mozart.

Ferguson's next argument is also unusual. Concerning a passage from the same aria (ex. 9.5a), she quotes me as saying that the first appoggiatura should have about a sixteenth-note length, and that for the second one "the intensification inherent in the repeat on a higher pitch level would, independently of denomination, entitle the singer to lengthen the appoggiatura at his discretion beyond a sixteenth-note value."

Ferguson then points to a parallel spot in the aria (mm. 53 and 56) where the appoggiaturas (here written as sixteenth notes) are set to the syllable "wä[re]." Mozart was often casual about the denomination of the little notes, and often mingled indiscriminately quarters with eighths or eighths with sixteenths (as in our case). Thus, in measure 27 of this aria, as shown in example 9.5b, he wrote the downward-leaping appoggiatura as an eighth note for the voice, and as a sixteenth for the unison first violins; in the second Finale, as shown in example 9.5c, Pamina has a quarter-note, and the unison violins an eighth-note appoggiatura; in the first measures of "Das Veilchen" he wrote the *Vorschläge* as eighth notes; in the autograph Index of his works[12] he wrote them as sixteenths. Clearly, their meaning could be, and often was, the same. But Ferguson sees significance in the difference and speculates that in the first of the two parallel phrases in Tamino's aria (see ex. 9.5a) the "more open syllable 'neu-'" calls for a long appoggiatura, whereas in the second phrase the "more closed syllable 'wä-[re]'" should not be prolonged. Here she ran afoul of elementary German diction: the syllable "wä-[re]" is not short and closed, but long and open! As such it is rather more suitable to support a long appoggiatura than the syllable "neu-" (pronounced "noy"), where the sound that matters for the appoggiatura is not the diphthong but the *short* "o" sound. However, guided by *her* idea of German diction she concludes that "the prolongation of the former ["neu-"], of course, supports the theorists' *overlong* [italics mine] prescription." Here she manages to confuse the rules of her much-flaunted "theorists": what she had in mind is not the "overlong" prescription but the "two-thirds-of-a-ternary-note" rule. First with the help of faulty diction she postulates the extended appoggiatura, which, in a neat circle, is in turn to prove, alas, the *wrong* rule. It is indeed a comedy of errors.

Example 9.5a.   W. A. Mozart, *Die Zauberflöte* (K. 620), Act 1, Scene 3,

Example 9.5b.   Ibid., Act 1, Scene 3, m. 27

Example 9.5c.   Ibid., Act 1, Scene 3, Second Finale

Macht ___ froh   durch   des   To-[des]

Her next argument is still more remarkable. It deals with the String Quartet in D, K. 575, and Ferguson quotes me as writing:

> An interesting document shows Mozart's flexibility regarding the denominations [of *Vorschläge*]. In the autograph of the String Quartet in D, K. 575, the first theme, in its many appearances, is always notated as shown in example [9.6a]. In the autograph "Index [*Verzeichnüss*] of all my works," Mozart wrote, almost certainly from memory, the "incipit" as shown in example [9.6b]. In the third measure he made a mistake. Probably he wrote a half note instead of a whole note for the first violin, but with all notes stemmed upward, it is barely possible that the quarter-note a″ was not a symbol but a regular note, in which case he forgot to dot the half note. In either case we have a discrepancy with the regular notation with longer values for the appoggiaturas, which in turn confirms the idea that we need not feel confined by the symbols' denominations.
>
> In this particular case [the quote from my book continues] the solution suggested by the *NMA* follows the value of the symbols, but it seems to me that more flexibility is desirable. I would suggest dwelling a little longer on the first, rather strongly affective appoggiatura, whereas the second and third *Vorschläge* have more the nature of passing notes with a linking function of *tierces coulées* that does not call for emphasis. One of several possibilities is shown in example [9.6c], which in turn can always be varied slightly within the same general character [p. 33].

Example 9.6a.   W. A. Mozart, String Quartet in D Major (K. 575),
                first movement

Example 9.6b.   Ibid., first movement as in the autograph
                Verzeichnüss, incipit

Example 9.6c.   Possible Interpretation of 9.6b

To this Ferguson first remarks: "Neumann fails either to notice or to report that
the incipit in Mozart's *Verzeichnüss* differs in many details from the version of
the autograph score." This reproach is most peculiar inasmuch as the whole
paragraph she quoted is focused on the difference between autograph and Index.
But this is only a needle prick; the sword thrust is directed at my suggestion to
play the first appoggiatura "a little longer" as roughly intimated by a dotted
eighth note in example 9.6c ("perhaps" I wrote there). Ferguson writes: "By
'dwelling a little longer' on the first appoggiatura in measure 3, *one runs the
risk* [italics mine] of introducing covered octaves between the two violins,
should they land at the same time on the octave g' + g" . . . a solution which
would be rejected by performers of even limited experience." Not that my
suggested solution would create the octaves, but *if* a violinist were to play the
appoggiatura for the exact length of a quarter note (something I have never
proposed), *then* octaves would result; they would be offensive even to begin-
ners, but, so she hints, not to me. This convoluted thought process, meant to
condemn my performance suggestion is, I submit, not an argument, but a deceit:
by distorting a directive, almost any suggestion can be twisted into irrationality.

   This exercise in demagoguery has a worthy sequel in an extraordinary
statement. Mozart's autograph Index is on a few occasions inexact about the
date and is often inexact in the rendition of the incipits. On that basis Ferguson

proclaims that "in no case can it [the Index] be used as a [my words:] 'document [which] shows Mozart's flexibility regarding the denominations [of *Vorschläge*].'" What Mozart writes, she decrees, is irrelevant, indeed unusable. If we want to appreciate the profundity of this nonsense, we should consider what exactly we are after when we search for historically correct, or as it is now fashionable to say, "authentic" performances. What matters, or what ought to matter above everything is the composer's idea of the work. Everything else is only peripheral. Now it is precisely the discrepancies of the index entries from the original that provide us a priceless glimpse at the way Mozart thought of his work when, after finishing it, he recalled its start. Painstaking precision would have provided no new performance clues. But the discrepancies do, because they add, as it were, a new triangulation point for getting better bearings on Mozart's ideas. Thus, when he gives the tempo of the *Figaro* overture as Allegro vivace instead of Presto we have a further reason—in addition to the mostly overlooked C meter—to find fault with the breakneck speed favored by most conductors. When in the String Quartet in F, K. 590, the Index has in the second measure a *sforzando* instead of a *forte*, while the *forte* starts in mid-measure with the descending scale; and when furthermore a ¢ replaces the C of the original, we get a more vivid picture of Mozart's idea of this opening than the autograph provided. We gather that, on second thought, Mozart conceived of a more ingeniously differentiated dynamic shading for the initial motive; and moreover that he wished the tempo to be felt not in four but in two beats. When in "Das Veilchen," as noted before, the Index has sixteenth-note instead of eighth-note *Vorschläge* and when, by contrast, in our example of the String Quartet, K. 575, it has eighth notes instead of sixteenth notes, we have a right to infer that the denominations can be interchangeable and that an insistence (like Ferguson's with her "ä" and "eu" argument) on their literal meaning can be misleading. The Index is a treasure trove of fascinating glimpses into Mozart's thought processes and notational habits.[13] The statement that "in no case" must the Index be used for such a purpose, is at best grossly misguided.

To provide some respite from appoggiatura agonies, Ferguson takes me to task for misinterpreting two of Mozart's turn symbols from the Violin-Piano Sonata in B♭, K. 454, shown in example 9.7 in the facsimile of the autograph (giving the violin part on the top staff and the piano on the two lower staves).[14]

Example 9.7.   W. A. Mozart, Sonata for Violin and Piano in B♭
                (K. 454), first movement (autograph)

(violin)

(piano)

In this passage the *NMA* had mistakenly placed the turn symbol above the first
of the thirty-second notes instead of after the dotted eighth note. Anybody who
has seen just a few of Mozart's autographs and who has an open mind will agree
that certainly the first of these signs belongs between the notes, and hence has
the well-known meaning of a turn that follows the more or less extended sound
of the principal note. And if the first of these turns conveys this unmistakable
graphic message, the second turn, as a sequential figure, has to follow suit.
Here is a very good reason why the symbol might give the impression of being
placed above the first thirty-second note. In his excellent preface to the facsimile
edition,[15] Eduard Melkus recounts the famous story of this sonata, which
Mozart wrote literally in the last minute for a concert he gave with the violinist
Strinasacchi. Pressed for time, he wrote in the score first the complete violin
part (both performers played from the same music) and sketched in fragments
of the piano part, which, as suggested by different ink, he finished at a later
date. Since the violin part determined the disposition of the barlines, the piano
part had to be fitted in, occasionally forcing extraordinary cramping, and in our
case the degree of such cramping did not allow enough space for the second
turn symbol to be clearly written between the dot and the following thirty-second
note. I believe the meaning of a "turn after the note" is incontestable and I
proposed the solution given in example 9.8a.

Ferguson disagrees: "Neumann falls into error by taking Mozart's notation
too literally." Here she obviously admits that "literally" my reading of the
notation is correct. But she adds: "While he is aware that Mozart often placed

his dynamic marks slightly ahead of the note to which they should first apply, he seems to be unaware that Mozart often did the same with his signs for turns, trills, and mordents." I am very definitely unaware of what simply did not exist. As to the mordent symbol, Mozart did not use it; as to the trill sign and those turn symbols that were meant to be placed above or below a note, Mozart wrote them overwhelmingly, say in 99 out of 100 cases, straight where they belong, though naturally, in fast writing small inaccuracies occur once in a while.[16] There is no analogy to the dynamic marks that are often written slightly ahead, because Mozart wrote them mostly, as the ductus of his pen indicates, before he wrote the note to which they belonged, whereas he wrote the trill and turn signs for rather obvious reasons after the principal note was already on paper.

For her reading of the two turns, which Ferguson insists belong on top of the first thirty-second note, she turns to Türk for support and proposes the solution of example 9.8b.

Now even *if* the symbols belonged, as she decrees they do, above the first of the thirty-second notes, and even *if* Türk's rule were applicable—two fictional assumptions—her solution would be wrong and ought to read as shown in example 9.8c, because surely the turn must not infringe the value of the preceding dotted eighth note; to do so would be the privilege only of a turn *after the (dotted eighth) note,* the reading rejected by Ferguson. The corrected solution à la Türk-Ferguson, with its frantic one-hundred-twenty-eighth notes would sound not like an ornament, but recall a nervous tic. Viewed from every angle the picture is the same: the Ferguson solution is indefensible.

Example 9.8.   Possible Interpretations of 9.7 a = Neumann;
b = Ferguson; c = Ferguson corrected

Ferguson's next argument is still more curious. In example 9.9 from the G-Major Piano Concerto, K. 453, she quotes me as recommending a fairly precise sixteenth-note length for the downward-leaping appoggiatura.

Ferguson determines that the appoggiatura should have an exact eighth-note length. This is surprising since it conflicts with both her previous ideas and with her revered "theorists." Before, in her memorable "ä" and "eu" argument, she had pleaded for literal interpretation of the *Vorschlag* symbols, which would in this case support my suggestion of an approximate sixteenth-note length. By contrast, according to the "theorists," it ought to be a quarter note (the one-half of a binary note rule). Her argument for the eighth note is highly original and runs like this. The first measure starts with a quarter note, the second with a dotted eighth, therefore the third (with the appoggiatura) ought to start with an eighth note to make for a logical sequence. She seems to refer to a so-far unknown law of regularly diminishing note values: a correlation between a straight-line mathematical progression and melodic beauty. Even if such a law existed it would not apply to our example: the first quarter note is *nominally* longer than the dotted eighth that starts the second measure, but actually it is not. Being a detached note, its length is undetermined and lies most likely between an eighth and dotted eighth; and whatever its exact length, the listener will perceive the first note of the second measure as being longer because of its melodic emphasis, at the height of a spontaneous, if subtle, crescendo, and because of its legato connection with its short companion that is a *Nachschlag* (type of *anticipazione della nota*) and as such should be rendered lightly and somewhat shorter than its written value. These considerations alone destroy the argument along with the neat mathematical progression.

Example 9.9.   W. A. Mozart, Piano Concerto in G Major (K. 453),
              second movement

That is not all. Of all the possible alternatives for the length of the falling appoggiatura, an exact eighth note is the least satisfactory: the squareness with which the principal note coincides with the start of the accompaniment is singularly stiff and unattractive.

Furthermore, had an exact eighth-note value been of importance to Mozart, he would have specified it, since the prospect was minimal that a performer would so interpret the sixteenth-note symbol. Again, as viewed from various angles, Ferguson's theory may be original but it makes no sense.

Ferguson's pursuit of mathematical orderliness has tripped her up also in the last of her exhibits. It presents a passage from the second movement of the F-Major Piano Concerto, K. 459 (ex. 9.10). It starts with woodwinds alone (mm. 66–70), in a witty descending passage where each group of three identical notes is preceded by a *Vorschlag*. While this sequential figure is taken over by the strings, the solo piano winds around them gracefully, as if decking them with garlands (mm. 70–74).

Example 9.10.   W. A. Mozart, Piano Concerto in F Major (K. 459), second movement

Example 9.10   (continued)

In their edition of the work for the *NMA* Eva and Paul Badura-Skoda have suggested grace-note (i.e., unaccented prebeat) renditions of the *Vorschlag* symbols. I wholeheartedly agreed because there are several reasons (to be listed presently) that more than suggest, that urge, such a solution. Yet Ferguson disagrees: she wants all the symbols resolved as sixteenth-note, on-the-beat appoggiaturas, so as to have the first violins coincide with the series of written-out piano appoggiaturas and their resolutions. This seems very neat and orderly. Besides, Ferguson objects to parallel seconds and sevenths and, supposedly, even to one solitary fifth (I have not discovered it yet) that would result from that grace-note rendition. Also, her "ear" decides in favor of the appoggiatura solution.

First, there is nothing wrong with parallel seconds and sevenths and nothing even with a parallel fifth, if it cannot be heard. As mentioned before, theorists as far back as Finck and Ortiz in the mid-sixteenth century found parallels created by ornamentation acceptable if they passed so quickly as to be de facto inaudible, and theorists of the seventeenth and eighteenth centuries made the distinction between "eye fifths" and "ear fifths," of which only the latter had to be avoided. If I should find the guilty fifth, it is certain to be an "eye fifth," since I have gratifyingly heard the passage performed with grace notes and in the process received no parallel shock.

Ferguson's appoggiatura solution deprives the passage of its Mozartian sparkle and humor in favor of a plodding, philistine version that is in the true spirit of Türk. It further deprives the passage of the "garland" effect in favor of some rather unpleasant "ear unisons."

In my book I have pointed out, and given reasons, why *Vorschläge* before groups of two, three, or more even notes have the strong presumption of grace note meaning. This being the case, Mozart would have run a grave risk of such interpretation had he, as Ferguson believes, intended appoggiatura treatment. He writes with total consistency, about 120 times, the *Vorschlag* as sixteenth-note symbol; not once did he write it out as he did for the piano part. This sharp contrast alone suggests different intent, and the more so, as Mozart often writes in cases of appoggiaturas a symbol for the soloist, regular notes for the shadowing instruments, but *never* the reverse. All things considered, Ferguson's elaborately presented solution has neither theoretical merit with regard to notation, nor musical merit with regard to the character and spirit of the passage; her objections to voice leading are illusory, while her version is flawed in this very respect. There is no musically reasonable alternative to the Badura-Skoda solution.

This completes the full account of Ferguson's exhibits. The lessons to be learned from them are as varied as are her freewheeling arguments. In part they reinforce the lesson learned from Klotz about "applying" ornament tables. If, as was shown, it was often improper to "apply" even Bach's own ornament table to some of his symbols, how much more dangerous is it to "apply" C. P. E. Bach and Türk to Mozart. The danger is magnified if, as happened to Ferguson, one confuses the rules and refers to two contrasting ones as if they were one and the same.

We learn that it is dangerous, if, according to what fits best one's ideas, one follows certain theorists here, ignores them there; if one insists on the literal meaning of *Vorschlag* denominations here, but rejects them there; if one interprets a graphic sign (the turn symbol) not by what it clearly says but by what one would like it to say, claiming à la Klotz, that Mozart made a mistake; then trying to explain what would be a gross notational irregularity with first a false analogy (dynamic marks), then with a misstatement of fact (the alleged high incidence of such irregularities). And where such devices do not suffice, simply invent laws whose only purpose is to provide a—fictional—underpinning to the proclaimed solution (synchronism between voice and accompaniment, the mathematical progression of initial note values). The greatest danger of all that seems to have bedeviled the whole undertaking is to first postulate the answers, then to search for anything that would seem to give them support. It is reminiscent of Alice's court case: "Verdict first, trial later"—an idea delightful in Wonderland but disastrous in a scholarly enterprise.

Notes

1. "L'Appoggiature ancienne," in *L'Interprétation de la musique française aux XVIIème et XVIIIème siècles* (Paris, 1974).

2. *Ornamentation in Baroque and Post-Baroque Music: With Special Emphasis on J. S. Bach* (Princeton, N.J., 1978) (hereafter: *Ornamentation*); *Ornamentation and Improvisation in Mozart* (Princeton, N.J., 1986).

3. For a more detailed presentation of the formation and use of Bach's ornamental style see my *Ornamentation*, chap. 7.

4. Klotz's thought process here and throughout the book is reminiscent of a satirical poem by Christian Morgenstern about a man who, hit on the head by a falling brick, concludes with logic "razor-sharp" that the accident did not happen, could not have happened, because it was illegal: " . . . denn, so schließt er messerscharf / weil nicht sein kann, was nicht sein darf."

5. *Les principes du clavecin* (Paris, 1702), pp. 49–50.

6. There are special signs for two variants, the descending *port de voix appuyé*, where the pitch of the grace note is sounded three times (all in anticipation), and for the *demy port de voix*, where it is sounded only once.

7. *Die Ornamentik in J. S. Bachs Klavierwerken* (Frankfurt, 1950); a fine brief study written as annex to the Peters Urtext edition of the English Suites.

8. Etienne Loulié, *Eléments ou principes de musique* (Paris, 1696), p. 66; Johann Joachim Quantz, *Versuch einer Anweisung die Flöte traversiere zu spielen* (Berlin, 1752), chap. 17, section 2, p. 20. See also exx. 9.19 and 12.25 in my *Ornamentation*.

9. Engramelle wrote the section on the mechanical organ in Bédos de Celle's *L'Art du facteur d'orgues* (Paris, 1778). See pls. 106 and 107 for the anticipated patterns (my ex. 25.10).

10. See *Ornamentation*, chap. 28 and exx. 28.1,2,4,5,6,7,9,10,11,12,13,14.

11. Faye Ferguson, "Frederick Neumann: *Ornamentation and Improvisation in Mozart*, Princeton, 1986," *Mozart-Jahrbuch 1986* (Kassel, 1987), pp. 243–49.

12. *Verzeichnüss aller meiner Werke vom Monath Febrario 1784 bis Monath* . . . [November 1791]. MS at British Library; facs. eds. Vienna, 1938; New York, 1956.

13. In an article (on Handel) in *Early Music* (August 1986), I listed in n. 3 (p. 406) a number of discrepancies in the Index that provide important performance clues. Far more needs to be done in this matter.

14. This example is reprinted by kind permission of the Stiftelsen Musikkulturens Fraemjande, Stockholm, and of the Kungl. Musikaliska Akademien, also in Stockholm.

15. *Sonat för cembalo och violin av W. A. Mozart* (facs. ed. Stockholm, 1982).

16. In support of her claim of Mozart's anticipative notation of turn, trill, and mordent (!) symbols, Ferguson asserts that in the first Allegro of the Violin Sonata in G, K. 379 (373a), "at least one-third of the turn symbols well precede the note they are intended to embellish." This simply is not so. Of the sixteen turns in this movement not a single one "precedes"—let alone

"well"—the note head to which it belongs in the way the symbol of the first turn in ex. 9.7 lies in its totality to the left of the note head. Fourteen of the sixteen symbols are where they belong and only two are somewhat shifted to the left while still clearly overlapping with the note head. Most importantly, in neither of these two cases can there be the slightest ambiguity about the symbol's meaning: both times it is under a note (the first note of the theme) that is preceded by rests.

10

Some Problems of Mozart Ornamentation:
A Response to Robert Levin

Performance practice is today both highly topical and highly controversial. My own attempts to revise a number of traditional views of performance practice theory may perhaps have contributed to the rise in the intensity and temperature of controversy in the field. Thus when I challenge orthodoxy or take issue with a colleague's view, I fully expect to meet with more or less sharp rejoinders. That is the way the game is played and often knowledge is advanced in such spirited give-and-take. On the other hand, it is questionable whether it is appropriate for a scholar to write the review of a book in which his own ideas have been strongly criticized. The reviewer after all ought to be a disinterested, not an interested, party.

I had in this respect a sobering experience with my book *Ornamentation and Improvisation in Mozart* (Princeton University Press, 1986). In it I had taken issue with Robert Levin's ideas on two important matters regarding improvisation (pp. 256 and 258 of my book).

First, I objected to the, in my mind, exaggerated scope he assigns to the improvisatory intrusions into Mozart's text. Speaking of his piano concertos, he writes: "[I]f modern performers tried to adopt the posture of performers as *composer* Mozart's music would be played more profoundly, more expressively and above all more spontaneously—for spontaneity is an essential element of his art."[1] To approach the music as "composer" can only mean a recomposing by free improvisatory additions apparently anywhere in a concerto, and that, I felt, is far too high a price to exact from Mozart for whatever spontaneity could be gained by such a "posture."

Second, Levin discussed the question of whether genuine Mozart cadenzas are "sacrosanct" or whether others can or should be substituted.[2] Levin's performer-composer, as could be expected, opts for new cadenzas since, he argues, improvisation and the uncertainty that promises surprises are of the cadenza's essence. I disagreed, in the firm conviction that the vast majority of an audience would prefer a Mozart cadenza to the "surprise" of a new one that is bound to be inferior in invention, style, and form. These criticisms may have contributed to Levin's adversarial tone in his review of my Mozart book written for the *Journal of the American Musicological Society* (12 [August 1988]: 335–68).

In the following I should like to deal with some of the more important censorious items Levin found in my work and to take exception to his statements.

Item: Misrepresentation (1). "Spotchecks," Levin says, have turned up some fifty cases of mistakes in the music examples, implying that a thorough check would have turned up many more. That is at best an exaggeration. Clearly, there are mistakes and so far, with the help of friends, I have found about ten, which will be corrected when the book is reprinted in paperback. The printing of both text and music was full of mistakes and the proofreading was all left to me. Some mistakes slipped by but the implication of scholarly slovenliness is inappropriate. As an example of the charge Levin writes (n. 15) that for the Rondo in F, K. 494, discussed on pages 61 and 62, both texts, musical (m. 98) and verbal (p. 62, second line) are "garbled." This is a misstatement. I have just rechecked the musical text several times, especially measure 98, against the autograph (the facsimile is reprinted in the *Music Forum* 1: 6–8) and found it to be absolutely accurate. If it deviates from Levin's source, it is the latter that must be garbled. As to the text, there is no mistake in the wording itself, only the line of type is ever so slightly bent—hardly a matter of overwhelming importance.

Item: Misrepresentation (2). Levin attributes to me the thought that on recapitulations in solo works "no improvised embellishments are necessary (and thus, appropriate)" (p. 366). However, I never said that such ornamental additions are inappropriate. Speaking of repeat marks, I wrote, "It is possible, perhaps even likely, that in performance Mozart made small additions in the repeat of a passage or a section" (*Ornamentation*, p. 278). As to recapitulations, I pointed to a number of cases in symphonies and chamber music where (among others in the last three symphonies) Mozart, departing from his frequent habit of directing the copyist to insert a number of measures "dal segno," wrote out note by note an exact repeat with no additions whatsoever. From that evidence I deduced "that we are under no stylistic obligation to ornament any recapitulation." There is a great difference between saying that there is no obligation to do something and that it is inappropriate to do it.

Item: "Solecism" (1). Levin charges me with several "solecisms" in the suggestion of improvised ornaments. Now I had at the outset emphasized "that all my performance suggestions for cadenzas and related ornaments aim to show form rather than content: to indicate the approximate length and character of the embellishments in the hope that others with more inventive talent will improve on their musical substance" (*Ornamentation,* p. 218). I did not pretend to approach Mozart performance "as composer," as Levin does, and compose authoritative models, but saw my role simply as that of a coach who tries to steer performers in the right direction.

In a fermata embellishment that I suggested for Despina's aria "In uomini" from *Così fan tutte* (*Ornamentation,* ex. 10.1), Levin criticizes parallel octaves with the bass. I believe that, within the frame of an improvised ornament—accorded in this respect much tolerance by the old theorists—the octaves are innocuous, well hidden as they are by the contrary motion of the B♮. Also, I believe that alone the just-quoted statement of purpose for my improvisatory suggestions ought to have exempted me from petty quibbling about orthodox rules of counterpoint. Mozart himself did not observe them: in the very same measure he writes open, not hidden, parallel unisons with the first violins (B♮–C).

Example 10.1.   W. A. Mozart, *Così fan tutte,* "In uomini" (Despina)

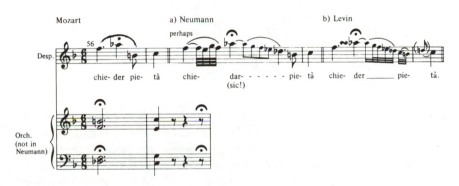

For a still better perspective on my "solecism" let us look at example 10.2 with the blatant octaves—notated, not improvised—G♯–B in highly sensitive two-part writing. Had *I* written them, Levin would have found me incompetent, but *I* did not write them; Mozart did: it is straight and ungarbled from the second movement of the A-Major Piano Sonata, K. 331(300i).

Example 10.2.   W. A. Mozart, Piano Sonata in A Major (K. 331 [300i]),
second movement, m. 13

Item: "Solecism" (2). My suggested coloratura insert for Despina's second aria "Una donna a quindici anni" (act 2, no. 19), shown in example 10.3, implies, so Levin says, "a V–i progression in A," which is improper. Quite the contrary, it implies, as extension of the written enharmonic equivalent of the diminished triad, the ever-useful and versatile diminished seventh chord, never mind the spelling according to a theory book. An improvised coloratura is heard not read—and by definition not even written!—and the listener could not care less whether a note—if it were written—would have been spelled as F♮ or as E♯.

Example 10.3.   W. A. Mozart, *Così fan tutte*, "Una donna a quindici anni"
(Despina)

Item: "Solecism" (3). Among a large sampling of lead-in formulas by Mozart, I listed the one shown in example 10.4, as typical a lead-in as can be found anywhere. It prepares a "cadenza in tempo" that sounds like nothing more than a development section in a sonata-rondo form. Levin finds it "astonishing" that I called the passage a "lead-in . . . thereby implying that what follows is part of the formal structure of the movement." It is, he says not a "lead-in" but a "springboard." This is pedantic-semantic hairsplitting: what is the difference between a springboard and a lead-in? Maybe one leaps, the other runs into a new section? Now whether one considers the "cadenza in tempo" to be structural as I do or not, as Levin does, is quite irrelevant. There is no justification for Levin's arbitrary claim that a "lead-in" (Mozart's *Eingang*) deserves this name only when it prepares a structural part of a composition. This assumption finds no support in any dictionary or encyclopedia and with good reason: on many an occasion lead-ins occur in the very middle of a structural part. I have shown in my book (p. 273) twelve lead-ins from each variation in K. 359 (374a), all of which prepare a four-measure final subphrase—hardly a structural part of the composition. Eva and Paul Badura-Skoda, in their book *Interpreting Mozart on the Keyboard* (London, 1962), show similar examples from the Variations, K. 613, "in which each variation contains a different version of the original lead-in contained in the theme" (p. 236). Levin had no reason to be "astonished"; I have reason and the reader has.

Example 10.4.   W. A. Mozart, Piano Sonata in B♭ Major
                (K. 333[315c]), third movement

Item: "Solecism" (4). Levin criticizes a suggested lead-in for the Finale of the Piano Concerto in C, K. 467 (p. 265 of my book) for touching momentarily the tonic (on the sixth chord) too early. Granted that most lead-ins that move from dominant to tonic do not anticipate the latter; granted, too, that this was not one of my better examples. But there are some precedents: for instance, in Mozart's variations on "Come un agnello" by Sarti (K. 460) a lengthy lead-in at the end of variation 7 not only touches but dwells on the tonic (its six-four chord) shortly before its end. If my example was a solecism, I am in good company.

Item: Subjectivity vs. objectivity. Levin criticizes my "subjective" recourse to musical sense and judgment. The reader, he writes (p. 358), "deserves theoretically grounded arguments" not *"ipse dixits"* based on my musical instinct. The "theoretically grounded arguments" are no doubt those based on rules found in old treatises. Now, as I discussed in the preceding essay, the routine application of these very rules has begotten the unmusical rigorism of ornament rendition that contradicts the very nature and function of ornament. Any discussion of desirable performance that relies solely on "theoretically grounded arguments" and fails to engage the "subjective" elements of musical logic, judgment, and common sense, is bound to be at best limiting, at worst misleading and distorting. The very purpose of my two major books on ornamentation was to free the music of the great masters of the past from the dire consequences of this kind of "objectivity."

Here we also meet one of several self-contradictions found in the review. Whereas from me Levin demands "objectivity," for himself he claims the right to approach Mozart interpretation in the "posture" of a composer. To assume such "posture" is to embrace the ultimate in subjectivity.

Item: Wide fermatas. Mozart used small and wide fermatas. The common, small fermata over a single note or a single rest, as is well known, means release from the meter and extension at the discretion of the performer. Sometimes, however, such fermatas will call for the insertion of an embellishment that can range from a few pitches to whole cadenzas.

A fermata is "wide" when it extends over two or more notes or rests or over a whole measure. Not infrequently, and especially in instrumental music, we find a wide fermata placed over the barline indicating the need for an ornamental addition such as a lead-in, shown in example 10.5a, from the Finale of the D-Minor Piano Concerto, K. 466, or a cadenza-like flourish (I called it an "end-embellishment"), shown in example 10.5b, from the Finale of the Violin Concerto in D, K. 218. In this latter case the ornamental implication is clear beyond any possible doubt: a wide fermata that encompasses the a″ and crosses the barline is followed by a single note an eleventh higher on d⁗, a leap that, if understood literally, would be irrational both musically and technically. Mozart simply indicated that he wanted the insertion of an ornamental passage that ends on the high D.

Example 10.5a.   W. A. Mozart, Piano Concerto in D Minor (K. 466), Finale

Example 10.5b.   W. A. Mozart, Violin Concerto No. 4 in D Major (K. 218), Finale

In vocal music too, ornamental intention is indicated when a wide fermata encompasses two or more notes or rests or a whole measure. Mozart used the wide fermata from his early youth, and we find it invariably in da capo arias (which he gave up in his maturity) for the final cadence, where an embellishment was a stylistic requirement, as well as often for the cadence of the B

section. In the vast majority of these cases, Mozart writes it like this: with occasional minor variants. Few editions reproduce correctly the wide fermata, and even the *NMA* is often imprecise in this matter. A model of precision is, among others, the volume of *Mitridate* (*NMA* II, 5/4), edited by Luigi Ferdinando Tagliavini, where twenty-six wide, measure-length fermatas are reproduced and suggestions for their embellishment offered in the preface (p. xiv). Wide fermatas and their cue for embellishment also occur, of course, outside of da capo arias. We have just encountered such a fermata in example 10.3, covering a whole measure in Despina's aria, and here Levin obviously agreed that a coloratura insert was required.

Then we have the extraordinary case of Fiordiligi's aria "Come scoglio immoto resta" in *Così fan tutte* (act 1, no. 14), where there are no fewer than eight wide fermatas, as shown in example 10.6; the first in the introductory Andante maestoso, the other seven in the main Allegro section. I expressed my conviction that these eight wide fermatas in Fiordiligi's aria call for embellishments and I made simple suggestions for their possible execution. The exceptional density of their occurrence in that aria finds an explanation in the singer for whom it was written. Mozart once wrote his father that he always had his singers in mind and tried to make his arias fit them "like a glove." Here the singer was Adriana Ferrarese del Bene. She was a virtuoso singer who prided herself on her improvisatory skills. Though Mozart did not greatly esteem her, he still, as was his wont, set out to please her. He had done so earlier when she sang Susanna for the 1789 revival of *Le nozze di Figaro*. She did not care for the heavenly "Deh vieni" and asked for a brilliant showpiece instead. Mozart gave in and wrote for her "Al desio di chi t'adora," K. 577, that is totally out of character for Susanna. So we must not be surprised that he tried to humor her again for Fiordiligi, whose aria "Come scoglio" offered, in addition to some written-out virtuosic passages, eight opportunities for added coloraturas.

Example 10.6.   W. A. Mozart, *Così fan tutte*, "Come scoglio immoto resta" (Fiordiligi)

Example 10.6.   (continued)

co- me sco-glio im- mo——— to re- sta con-   tra-i ven-ti, e

la   tem-   pe-sta

e nell- - a- mor

Levin disagrees and criticizes me for not considering "the possibility that Mozart's four [*sic*] fermatas, each over a whole measure, might imply a return to the original, slower tempo in which this text and its melodic motive were first presented." I did not consider it, because the idea is illogical. First, Levin has the facts wrong: 1) there are not four but eight fermatas; 2) the first fermata (a) occurs still in the introductory Andante maestoso part and therefore cannot refer to an earlier, slower tempo; 3) the second and third fermatas (b) have a text and a melody that have not been presented in the first part, and the same is true of the eighth fermata (d); the fourth, fifth, sixth and seventh fermatas (c) do repeat the text of the introduction but have an entirely different melody. So much for the facts. Further, if Levin were right, measure 57 would be allegro, 58 maestoso, 59 allegro, 60 maestoso, 61 allegro, 62 maestoso, and 63 allegro again! That makes little sense, yet Levin tries hard to gain credibility for it by referring (n. 10) to Constanze's aria "Ach, ich liebte" from *Die Entführung* (act 1, no. 6), where "Mozart resorts to doubled note values to convey the *tempo primo* when the original (slower) theme is cited within the ensuing *allegro*." Here too Levin has the facts wrong. Only a small fraction of the adagio theme is recalled in the allegro and for six measures only, whereas the first two are quadrupled in note value, the third and fourth doubled, the next two again quadrupled. Also the melody, not just the rhythm, is slightly modified. How this should clarify the meaning of the fermatas in Fiordiligi's aria is beyond my capacity to speculate. Surely had Mozart wanted a measure-by-measure alternation of slower and shorter note values he would have spelled them out.

What is the most ironic about Levin's charge is his inconsistency on matters of improvisation. He criticizes me for pleading ornamental restraint in recapitulations and other kinds of repeats because he wants to approach Mozart performance "as composer." Then, where Mozart gave a virtuoso singer his most explicit cue for embellishments, Levin faults me for suggesting a modest embroidery when, taking leave of the posture of "composer," he wants the austerity of the line intensified by drastically slowing the tempo!

He wonders why I did not suggest similar embellishments for the slow introductory part of the aria and the answer is simple: first, there are no fermatas (except at the very end where I did suggest an embellishment); second, the string accompaniment would interfere with any added embellishments; third, I do not pretend to approach Mozart performance "as composer."

Item: "Rubato" (or caesura?). Türk, the zealous guardian of the downbeat principle for ornaments, tries to prove his case for Mozart by pointing to the passage (shown in ex. 10.7a) from the Violin Sonata in G where, so Türk argues, the thirty-seconds leading to the measure line do not leave any space for anticipating the arpeggio and thereby prove that the latter has to start on the beat (ex. 10.7b). I answered that here the downbeat start is musically unacceptable: it cripples the characteristic four-measure rhythm of the melody ♩ ♩ ♫♫ the first time it appears, and also, since the five-note arpeggio cannot possibly be accommodated within the thirty-second rest in the bass, it would become chaotically enmeshed in the broken chord figuration of the bass. The only possible solution is that of a caesura-like minimal delay, the insertion of a microrhythm that would permit the a″, the goal-note of the arpeggio, to function as the downbeat, and therewith insure both the integrity of the melodic rhythm and the integrity of the interplay of melody and bass. I gave, as shown in example 10.7c, an approximate solution as it might look in modern notation.

Example 10.7a.   W. A. Mozart, Violin Sonata in G Major
            (K. 379[373a]), second movement

Example 10.7b.   Türk, Interpretation of 10.7a

Example 10.7c.   Neumann, Possible Modern Interpretive Notation of 10.7a

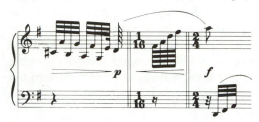

Levin disagrees and sides with Türk. By calling the caesura-microrhythm a "rubato," he says it conflicts with Mozart's oft-quoted letter to his father on the playing of the piano maker Stein's daughter. To Mozart's annoyance she got slower and slower with every return of a theme. Mozart adds: "Everyone is amazed that I can always keep strict time. What these people cannot grasp is that in tempo rubato in an Adagio, the left hand should go on playing in strict time. With them the left hand always follows suit." The inserted microrhythm does not conflict with Mozart's keeping strict time. Surely Levin knows the difference between a caesura and a tempo fluctuation to which Levin's "rubato" refers (as contrasted with Mozart's "tempo rubato" of right-hand flexibility versus left-hand steadiness). Does he believe that Mozart's "keeping strict time" meant that he played with an unyielding machine-like rhythm without ever permitting the music to breathe? A caesura, a *Luftpause* in German, where it means literally a moment's delay to allow for a breath, is an indispensable device for artistic performance in all media. In any case, Levin would need to show us how he would solve the unavoidable entanglement of the symbolized arpeggio in the right hand with the written-out arpeggio in the left if the former is to start on the downbeat.

Item: Why not? Levin charges that in suggesting executions of certain ornaments I omit "plausible solutions without giving a reason." He documents the charge with the illustrations of example 10.8. Of these, example 10.8a shows a turn "before the note" that is usually indicated with the symbol

placed on top of the note. This kind of turn usually implies a touch of piquancy in the form of a nippy accent. I gave three alternate solutions that do fulfill this need. I did not list Levin's "why not," which is one of many more possibilities, because it is bland and does not add that dash of spice that I consider desirable here. In example 10.8b the "why not" is my rhythmic preference for 10.8c, and the "why not" of 10.8c is my preference for 10.8b. There is a reason for the difference since these two examples are not interchangeable. In 10.8b, the turn ("after the note") is embedded in a light upbeat, and Levin's solution adds a heaviness to this upbeat that I consider undesirable. I believe my solution is leaner, more elegant and more logical in leading the unburdened upbeat into the warm, appoggiatura-like downbeat. By contrast, in example 10.8c, the turn is part of an emphasized downbeat where my proposed rhythmic solution appropriately adds to the emphasis on the principal note, whereas Levin's solutions, fitting for an unaccented beat, are less well chosen. Clearly these matters cannot be decided *objectively* by rules or mathematics, but only *subjectively* by musical insight and intelligence. For ornaments, and especially for turns, there are always a number of possible solutions, and one needs to select the one that seems to be the most satisfactory in a given context. It is unreasonable to expect for every case a complete scrutiny of all the possible alternatives.

Example 10.8a.   W. A. Mozart, String Quartet in D Major (K. 499),
             first movement

Example 10.8b.   W. A. Mozart, String Quartet in D Major (K. 575),
             second movement

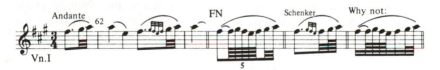

Example 10.8c.   W. A. Mozart, Quintet for Piano and Winds (K. 452),
             second movement

Item: Grace notes vs. appoggiaturas. One case of this alternative refers to a passage in the slow movement of the Piano Concerto in F, K. 459, where I, in agreement with the Badura-Skodas (who edited the respective volume for the *NMA*) suggest grace notes, whereas Levin opts for appoggiaturas. It is the same spot that Faye Ferguson had singled out with practically identical arguments. I refer the reader to my discussion of this case in the preceding essay (pp. 148–51).

Then there is the case of example 10.9 from *Eine kleine Nachtmusik,* where I suggested grace notes while pointing to the "almost always heard" appoggiaturas. Several reasons favor grace notes. One is that, true to their name, they impart more grace to the passage; another is the clear contrast of the notation in example 10.9a with that of 10.9b, where two measures later, in a varied form, long appoggiaturas are written out; third, as already Tartini had noted, a *Vorschlag* before two or more even notes ought to be a grace note ("appoggiatura breve ossia di passaggio").[3] Levin, who takes me to task for often using the words "clearly" and "obviously," asks: "If the contrast was 'clearly' intended, why is it 'almost always' ignored in performance?" If my interpretation "is not axiomatic to every reader" then my use of the terms "clear" and "obvious" implies "that virtually all practicing musicians throughout the world are benighted." First, I neither said nor implied that my *interpretation* is obvious; I said the sharp contrast in notation is obvious, and obvious it certainly is. And I would think that Mozart, in using a sharply discrepant notation made it clear that he wanted a contrasting execution. That a majority of players worldwide disagree with me does not prove that they are right and I am wrong. They disagree because they have been thoroughly indoctrinated with the dogma that every ornament has to take the beat. Their numbers do not protect them from being "benighted." They have company in that huge majority that follows the principles of the French overture style and the one that insists on starting every trill from Corelli and Lully to Mozart and Beethoven with the auxiliary on the beat. It so happens that *historical facts are not determined by majority vote,* no matter how large the majority may be.

Example 10.9a.   W. A. Mozart, *Eine kleine Nachtmusik* (K. 575), first movement

Example 10.9b.   Ibid., first movement, mm. 15–17

I believe I should spare the reader the tedium of analyzing the few remaining criticisms, all of which, like the ones discussed, are similarly lacking in substance, balance, and constructiveness.

There is one exception that I should note in all fairness. In his thirteen-page review Levin does make one valid point, and I gladly acknowledge that I might have done better to put a period after the "K" of the Köchel numbers.

Notes

1. Robert D. Levin, "Improvisation and Embellishment in Mozart's Piano Concertos," *Musical Newsletter* 5, no. 2 (Spring 1975): 3–14.

2. Ibid., p. 11.

3. Giuseppe Tartini, "Regole per arrivare a saper ben sonare il violino . . . ," MS Bologna, facs. as supplement to German-French-English publication, *Traité des agréments*, ed. Erwin R. Jacobi (Celle and New York, 1961), pp. 7–8.

11

Authenticity and the Vocal Vibrato

The following essay deals critically with the belief held by many authenticists that "early music" should be sung and played without vibrato. In its introductory section a few sentences overlap with chapter 2, for which the reader's indulgence is requested.

The performance of "early music" by organizations exclusively devoted to this specialty has in the last decades more and more assumed the nature of a cultist ritual. Under the banner of authenticity members of the cult present us with performances that are occasionally boring and dull because their aim is not, or at least not primarily, to give aesthetic pleasure, to elate and enchant, but to demonstrate, educate, and provide spiritual purification. For the audience it is an ascetic exercise in moral uplift comparable to the dutiful absorption of a long, uninspiring sermon.

"Authenticity" has become a powerful slogan and, provided we can explain it as the idea of restoring old music to the spirit in which it was conceived, its aim is noble. Unfortunately the aim defies realization. What does authenticity mean in actual practice? It would seem to involve the matching of an historical model. But which model and how can we match it? A composer's solo performance? A performance directed by the composer? Any contemporary performance even without the composer's participation? The composer's mental concept? Whatever alternative or combination of alternatives we choose, the lacunae in our knowledge are so great that any attempt at reconstruction has to rely heavily on guesswork. For this reason many scholars and musicians have taken a dim view of authenticity. In a discussion on "the limits of authenticity" in *Early Music* of February 1984, all three participants—Nicholas Temperley, Richard Taruskin, and Daniel Leech-Wilkinson—with various degrees of force-

This article originally appeared in *American Choral Review* 29 (Spring 1987): 13–17. Reprinted by permission of the publisher.

fulness rejected the notion of authenticity. More surprisingly still, Nikolaus Harnoncourt, one of the leading prophets and practitioners of historically oriented performance, joined the ranks of the skeptics and declared that authenticity "does not exist" and is indeed a "swindle."[1]

In view of such formidable objections, how do the advocates of authenticity proceed in trying to justify their far-reaching claims? First, the use of historical instruments becomes the *sine qua non* of any performance. This stricture, however, does not lead far towards the presumable goal: a work may be rendered in the historically purest tone color, yet in a wretched account of the composition so far as expression, tempo, dynamics, articulation, phrasing, ornamentation, rhythms and, yes, vibrato are concerned; we are easily deceived about the shortcomings of such a performance because the old instruments may play tricks on our critical abilities. Their archaic sound may conjure up an aura of historicity that hypnotizes us into believing we are privy to the revelation of the true, original spirit of a composition, when in fact we might be witnessing a musical travesty.

Putting tone color at the top of their list means, in fact, getting the priorities mixed up. In pre-1800 music the importance of tone color may range from fairly substantive in, say, Mozart, to fairly indifferent in, say, Bach. It never was the dominant factor but always subordinate to other elements of interpretation in re-creating the spirit of a work. Modern strings and winds do not injure a Mozart opera, but wrong tempi, expressions, and ornaments do. What matters to Bach is line, not color. Had he been concerned about color, he would have prescribed the registrations for his organ works, yet he never did; and he would not have transcribed so casually from any medium to just about any other medium.

Next on the priority list is the number of performers, of which we are often informed through documents, such as pay records. The numbers can be significant when they were the free artistic choice of the composer. This, however, was rarely the case. Mostly composers had to be satisfied with what the circumstances offered. Mozart was enchanted when for once he had a large orchestra at his disposal. In a letter to his father of 11 April 1781, he writes: "I recently forgot to tell you that my symphony went magnificently and had great success— forty violins played—the woodwinds all doubled—ten violas—ten basses— eight violoncelli, and six bassoons." It would seem that there is no need to miniaturize his orchestras; there is only a need to balance them.

We have no reason to assume that Bach was averse to having more than twelve singers for his chorus (or no more than four, if we accept Joshua Rifkin's arguments). The historically correct numbers, even more so than the historically correct instruments, have a very limited value in ensuring the proper spirit of a work—provided the numbers used are within reason and balance the orchestra.

Aside from instruments and numbers, the other previously listed and far more important elements of performance confront us with lacunae in our knowledge in all degrees of magnitude. The attempt to fill these usually results in turning to the canon of rules that modern research has established for historical performances. Unfortunately, many of the research procedures involved are defective; as a consequence some of the proclaimed principles are questionable, others provably false. It is by following such faulty leads that "authentic" performances often disfigure the music they claim to restore.

In previous studies I have tried to show that the principal rules of "authentic" performance are partly in need of revision, partly in need of repeal. I refer to such issues as ornament rendition, *notes inégales,* rhythmic contraction, and synchronization. Here I shall discuss another of the tenets of authenticity, one that often contributes to the dullness of performances: the ban on the vocal vibrato, which usually goes hand in hand with an analogous ban, or at least a restriction, of the string vibrato.

Vibrato is a complex phenomenon. It consists of fast, regular oscillations of either pitch or loudness, or of their combination. These oscillations have a critical speed, a threshold, of approximately seven pulsations per second, above which they—heretofore clearly, and often unpleasantly, audible—fuse into the sensation of a richer sound while the perception of the oscillations is minimized or disappears altogether. This phenomenon, called "sonance," is comparable to the way the rainbow colors on a rotating disc turn white at a certain speed, or else to the stereophonic merger of slightly different sound impressions into a single one with added depth. Where intensity pulsation is present, there is often a concomitant oscillation of timbre. Such is always the case with strings whenever the horizontal shaking motion producing pitch fluctuations is attended by a vertical up-and-down movement of the finger that produces both intensity and timbre fluctuations. It is the specific combination of these elements, together with the speed and range of the pulsations, that in each case makes for the individual character and highly personal nature of an artist's vibrato.

Applied to strings, the vibrato mechanism is visible and therefore better understood, whereas the mechanism of the vocal vibrato is hidden and more mysterious. Here, the aural deception inherent in the phenomenon of "sonance" has deluded many early theorists into believing that the oscillations are strictly intensity fluctuations like those of the *tremulant* stop on the organ. Yet as revealed by electronic sound analysis, the intensity fluctuations are practically always supplemented by oscillations of pitch and often of timbre as well.[2] The ability of the vibrato to enliven and enrich the musical sound has been known throughout the ages, and vibrato has quite certainly been used on instruments in imitation of the voice.

Vocal vibrato must be ageless because it develops spontaneously in most mature and in all artistically trained voices. For such a voice to sing non-vibrato involves a special effort and means fighting nature. Often the effort is unsuccessful, especially in some aging voices where the weakening of the involved musculature produces a "tremolo," the obtrusively audible wavering of the voice.

The ban on vocal vibrato seems to have two roots. One is the generally vibratoless nature of boys' voices; the other, the seeming silence of old treatises on the vibrato as part of vocal tone production. As such, it was simply there, taken for granted as a fact of life, not artificially induced like the string vibrato and therefore not calling for special theoretical attention. Matters were different with certain vibrato-related devices that were willfully and artfully produced for the sake of specific effects. Among them was the seventeenth-century ornament called *trillo,* a fast tone repetition that could have both staccato and legato character and was one of Monteverdi's favorite devices; others were the very deliberate and fairly slow intensity fluctuations, often done in an exact rhythm. They were known in Italy, France, and Germany, and were given various names such as *tremolo* in Italy, *Schwärmer* in Germany, and *balancement* in France.[3]

Two important documents—from the seventeenth and eighteenth centuries, respectively—attest to the fact that unimpeachable authorities considered the vibrato a natural component of the human voice and a requisite for artistic singing. In 1619 Praetorius devoted a chapter of his great theoretical work *Syntagma Musicum* to the way boys ought to be instructed in the Italian manner of singing. They have to have, he wrote, a good voice to begin with, and as one of three requisites he listed the possession of a vibrato. "These are the requisites: that a singer possess a beautiful, lovely, trembling and wavering voice."[4] Praetorius anticipated this when he criticized singers who, "gifted by God and nature with a singularly lovely trembling, and fluctuating or wavering voice," indulge in excesses of embellishments that obscure the text.[5] His remarks are all the more significant since they were made in the context of instructions for boys and would apply with greater force to adult singers.

The other witness is Mozart. In a letter to his father from Paris of 12 June 1778, he wrote:

> Meissner, as you know, has the bad habit of purposefully pulsating the voice, marking on a long-held note all the quarters and sometimes even the eights—and that manner of his I have never been able to tolerate. It is truly abominable and such singing runs counter to nature. The human voice vibrates by itself, but in a way and to a degree that is beautiful—this is the nature of the voice, and one imitates it not only on wind instruments, but also on strings, and even on the clavichord, but as soon as one carries it too far, it ceases to be beautiful, because it is unnatural.

This passage is remarkable on several counts. It confirms the presence of vibrato as being in "the nature of the voice" and it stresses its beauty, which prompted an imitation on string and wind instruments that Mozart clearly approved of; it characterizes the vibrato as a natural, spontaneous component of the voice, setting it apart from willful pulsating manipulations of the voice which Mozart found objectionable when carried too far, and outright "abominable" when done in the bad taste of Meissner's rhythmic emphases. One thing emerges clearly: Mozart desired the vocal vibrato as well as its—discreet—instrumental imitation.

String vibrato was not as all-pervasive as it is today but was used selectively and with discrimination.[6] In particular the over-rich, voluptuous variety practiced by many of today's virtuosi is inappropriate for eighteenth-century music. But to ban the vibrato altogether or reduce it to an almost imperceptible minimum is due to historical misunderstanding and a musical aberration; and this applies to an even greater degree to the artificial elimination of its vocal counterpart. Such procedures dull the luster, diminish the intensity, and weaken the expressiveness of any phrase that calls for warmth of sound. A performance should indeed be an act of artistic communion and not one of historical demonstration, least of all when the history that is being demonstrated is unhistorical.

Notes

1. *Bericht über das Bachfest-Symposium*, Congress Report (Marburg, 1978), p. 78.

2. The pitch fluctuations are often surprisingly large. In electronic analyses of Caruso records it was found that in moments of great intensity the fluctuations reached the width of a whole tone! On strings they hardly ever exceed a quarter tone.

3. For further documentation see my *Ornamentation in Baroque and Post-Baroque Music* (Princeton, 1978), chap. 45.

4. *Syntagma musicum*, vol. 3 (1619); facsimile reprint (Kassel, 1958), p. 231.

5. Ibid., pp. 229–30.

6. See the reference cited in n. 3 for details about the nature and use of the string vibrato.

12

Ornamentation in the Bassoon Music of Vivaldi and Mozart

The following essay was presented at the Miller/Skinner Bassoon Symposium in 1985 at Towson State University. Though limited to certain bassoon works, it is included here because its ideas are applicable to all media.

Musical ornamentation has been with us from time immemorial. It is only one among many manifestations of an urge to embellish which must respond to a basic human need, since we find it in a wide variety of pursuits in all cultures and all periods. There is ornamentation in the figurative arts, in architecture, in fashion, in jewelry, in make-up, in hairdos, in landscaping, even in rhetoric, and of course in the decorative arts, which are totally dedicated to embellishing the environment. I mention these facts not as an ornamental prelude, but to explain the vast role that ornamentation plays in music of all times.

The extent of this role is not generally recognized. When we speak of musical ornamentation we think of the seventeenth and eighteenth centuries, of strange symbols and little notes, and maybe of cadenzas. The reason for this limited view resides in changed habits of notation and performance conventions that obscure the still-considerable role of ornamentation in the nineteenth and twentieth centuries. Symbols gradually vanished and the role of improvisation, except in jazz, was suppressed. Because of these changes, ornamentation is more of a performance problem in the music of the seventeenth and eighteenth centuries, where symbols are often ambiguous and the role of improvisation uncertain, than in later years when composers exerted more control over the performer.

During this period of the Baroque and Classical styles, we have to distinguish ornaments that are fully written out in regular notes, those that are indi-

This article originally appeared in *The Double Reed* 9 (Fall 1986): 26–31; (Winter 1986): 40–48. Reprinted by permission of the publisher.

cated by symbols, be they abstract signs or little unmetrical notes, and those that do not appear in the score but are expected to be improvised by the performer.

Those that are written out in regular notes solve the hardest problem, that of design, but they still challenge us to recognize their ornamental nature and to render them therefore with a certain amount of rhythmic freedom that reflects the improvisatory origin of musical embellishments.

In the second category, the symbol-indicated ornaments, we face the problem of their proper interpretation.

The third and hardest category confronts us with the need first to diagnose where ornamental additions are needed, desirable, or optional, and then to invent their proper design.

All three categories are applicable to both Vivaldi and Mozart but in a different manner, as might be expected from their different nationalities, different styles, and different dates: Vivaldi (1675–1741) died almost fifteen years before Mozart (1756–91) was born.

Vivaldi

I shall turn first to problems of ornamentation in Vivaldi's music with special regard to the bassoon and start with ornaments that are not indicated in the score.

The Italian masters in Vivaldi's time played their slow movements in an ornate style, with florid embellishments. Generally, they did not specify these *passaggi,* as the ornamented figurations were called. They wrote down only the structural keynotes of the melody and expected the performer to flesh out the skeleton with ornamental designs. Some masters, Vivaldi among them, were inconsistent about the way they handled the *passaggi.* Sometimes they wrote out the desired embellishments in full, although on other occasions they resorted to the skeletal notation.

Then we find works that occupy a middle ground: the ornamentation is sketched in but not fully executed. Here it is usually advisable to add a few more decorations to those indicated. A rule of thumb to apply here would be that a slow movement whose fastest notes are eighths with only occasional sixteenths is skeletal and needs to be embellished; a movement that contains many passages in thirty-second notes is likely to be fully ornamented; one whose fastest notes are sixteenths might not need but will often be receptive to some additional animation with thirty-seconds.

Bassoonists are lucky since the adagios of their concertos seem to be sufficiently ornamented in the score, lightening our problem of interpretation.*

---

*To aid the identification of the concertos, they are listed by Fanna (F), Pincherle (P), and Ryom (RV) numbers. The measure numbers are listed as they are in the collected edition, *Le opere di Antonio Vivaldi,* ed. G. F. Malipiero (Rome, 1947–).

It means that generally no additional embellishment is needed, but it does not mean that occasionally some such additions are not acceptable or even desirable, as can be the case when the orchestral accompaniment is static and the solo part becomes "sleepy." In example 12.1b from the Concerto in D Minor, the lively figures of the violins provide enough interest to justify the slow-moving phrase of the bassoon. Yet if a player felt the need for more animation he could not be faulted if he were to add some embellishment, maybe of the kind shown in example 12.1c. Generally, it is wiser to use discretion and err on the side of too little rather than too much: if a melody is beautiful, it can stand on its own even unadorned, whereas an excess of ornament can make it impossible to recognize the melody's shape through the thicket of luxuriant overgrowth.

Example 12.1.   A. Vivaldi, Concerto in D Minor (F. VIII, No. 5;
P. 282; RV 481), second movement a = solo bassoon,
as written; b = first violins; c = a possible
ornamentation of a

It is important to identify the ornamental character of written-out passage work in fast notes because such character has implications for rhythm and tempo. A musical passage which is ornamental should be rendered with the lightness and elegance that befits its surface character of a decoration. It should not be rendered with heaviness and slowness as if it were the melody proper, where each of its notes calls for expressiveness. Such interpretation is wrongly focused on the single trees instead of on the forest. To get the right focus, it is helpful to search for the melodic core under the decorative cloak, and then add the written passage as if it were a free improvisation.

Consider example 12.2(a) from the Concerto in B♭. Its melodic core may be something like (b) or any of many similar solutions. When we then add the written notes of the passage we realize that its notated rhythm is not of the thematic essence, but can and ought to be flexibly treated in a way that notation cannot indicate. Here, I think, it is unnecessary to make a clear contrast between the thirty-second and sixty-fourth notes, but to treat them as ten roughly equivalent notes that start slowly and then get slightly faster. When taking such rhythmic rubato freedoms we have to be alert to a possibly desired exact rhythmic coordination with another voice in the ensemble. However, for ornamental passages this will only rarely be the case.

Example 12.2.   A. Vivaldi, Concerto in B♭ (F. VIII, No. 36; P. 386; RV 504), second movement

Regarding tempo, the suggested dismantling of the ornamental passages will alone mostly suggest a more flowing pace than we might otherwise be inclined to take. Generally I would caution against taking slow movements in Vivaldi and other masters of the period too slowly. As far as I can ascertain, a subdividing of the beat was not practiced in the seventeenth and eighteenth centuries and may not have been used until the early nineteenth century. An adagio in C meter has to be conceived of as being in four, not in eight slow beats.

By and large, the problem of improvised *passaggi,* or coloraturas, is limited to the slow movements. But because of the easygoing ways of the Italians with embellishments in general, we should feel free to add occasional passage work even in fast movements where the accompaniment is without melodic interest and the solo part appears lean.

"Small" ornaments such as appoggiaturas, grace notes, slides, mordents, and trills, can be added anywhere where they seem to fit without creating fussiness or overcharging a line.

Let us turn now to those of the small ornaments that are indicated by symbol. Because of the laxness of the Italians with unmarked additions of small as well as extended ornaments mentioned above, they were slow in adopting symbols other than those for the trill. The French, who liked to curb the Italian-type freedom of improvisatory additions, had pioneered the use of symbols for the small ornaments. These little notes were without metrical value and were to be played between the regular notes, taking their value from either the preceding or the following notes. The Italians adopted their use some thirty to forty years after the French. Vivaldi himself was slow in adopting them. They are absent from his early concertos and make their appearance in operas and concertos of the mid-1720s. Since the bassoon concertos I have seen all make use of the little unmetrical notes, I would assume that they date at least from the time after ca. 1725.

According to the *New Grove Dictionary of Music,* Vivaldi wrote some thirty-nine bassoon concertos, including two that are incomplete and four whose thematic materials and accompaniment are shared with concertos for other instruments. If I may extrapolate from the roughly ten I have examined, the only small ornaments we need to be concerned about are the trill, the *Vorschlag* (i.e., either the appoggiatura or the grace note), and the slide.

First let us consider the trill. We must rid ourselves of the widespread belief that each trill is to start with the upper auxiliary on the beat. This principle does not apply to the Italian trill, which, as a rule, started with the main note. In examples 12.3(a) and (b) from the Concerto in A Minor, nothing else makes sense: in (a) the descending scale has to land on A, the written note of the trill; in (b) the same melodic logic demands the trill's start on F to complete the triadic figuration. Similarly, the trill chains of (c) from the same concerto call for main-note start to bring out, rather than obscure, the ascending scale.

Example 12.3. A. Vivaldi, Concerto in A Minor (F. VIII, No. 2; P. 70; RV 498)

a = first movement; b = second movement; c = third movement

As always, there are exceptions. The Italians were fond of the appoggiatura, and, notably at cadences, they often liked to precede a trill with an appoggiatura. See for an illustration example 12.4a from the Concerto in C Major, or 12.4b from the Concerto in A Minor.

Example 12.4a.   A. Vivaldi, Concerto in C Major (F. VIII, No. 13;
             P. 46; RV 477), second movement

Example 12.4b.   A. Vivaldi, Concerto in A Minor (F. VIII, No. 2;
             P. 70; RV 498), second movement

Every so often we find a trill is preceded by a little note on the upper auxiliary indicating the trill's start on the latter. It is not necessarily played on the beat and, indeed, is often played before the beat. We find this notation mainly on a trill that follows the leap of an augmented or diminished interval where the auxiliary smoothens the melodic line. See examples 12.5a and 12.5b.

Example 12.5a.   A. Vivaldi, Concerto in E Minor (F. VIII, No. 6;
             P. 137; RV 484), third movement

Example 12.5b.   A. Vivaldi, Concerto in B♭ (F. VIII, No. 36; P. 386;
             RV 504), second movement

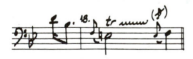

There are other cases of little notes before trills not involving such leaps, which indicated that the trill was to start on the upper auxiliary, since this practice was otherwise not understood in Vivaldi's time. I have the strong feeling that these little notes preceding trills were, as a rule, meant to be short and either before or on the beat according to the given situation. I don't believe that they ever indicate a long appoggiatura like those of example 12.4a or 12.4b above, since we don't seem to find them in front of cadential trills.

On the other hand, for trills that are not preceded by the little note and are not cadential trills, the first choice should be the start with the main note.

Turning now to the appoggiaturas and grace notes, we see that Vivaldi uses exclusively the sign of a little eighth note and never varies its denomination. Rules of a later period, such as those of Giuseppe Tartini (1692–1770), that an appoggiatura indicated by a small note-symbol takes one-half of a binary and two-thirds of a dotted note, do not seem to apply to Vivaldi.

For Vivaldi, and more specifically for the bassoon works, it seems that the little note always stands for a short note that might fall either before (grace note) or on the beat (appoggiatura). Although it is written as an eighth note, this grace note is seldom played that length, let alone a longer value. Such meaning is clear in example 12.6 from the Concerto in E Minor, where the juxtaposition, many times consistently repeated, of Vivaldi's symbols and written-out Lombard rhythms, admits only the grace-note (i.e., anticipated) meaning of the symbols.

Such meaning is also obvious in the formula  which I have called the "Italian mordent," found in the same concerto, or in the related phrase of example 12.7 from Concerto in D Minor. Other *tierces coulées,* the filling in of descending thirds, like those of example 12.6, are also most likely candidates for grace-note use such as example 12.8a, from the Concerto in F Major, or 12.8b from the Concerto in D Minor.

Example 12.6.   A. Vivaldi, Concerto in E Minor (F. VIII, No. 6; P. 137; RV 484), first movement

Example 12.7.   A. Vivaldi, Concerto in D Minor (F. VIII, No. 5; P. 282; RV 481), first movement

Example 12.8a.   A. Vivaldi, Concerto in F Major (F. VIII, No. 20;
P. 305; RV 498), first movement

Example 12.8b.   A. Vivaldi, Concerto in D Minor (F. VIII, No. 5;
P. 282; RV 481), first movement

The frequent grace-note meaning of the symbol is certain. It is really possible that this was the basic meaning for Vivaldi since there is no musical evidence that would contradict such a meaning. Considering the latitude conceded to the performer, it is, however, probable that short downbeat rendition is often equally justified. If both styles are legitimate transcriptions for the symbol, we can often achieve attractive results by mixing them. Example 12.9a, from the Concerto in F Major might be done as in example 12.9b.

Example 12.9a.   A. Vivaldi, Concerto in F Major (F. VIII, No. 20;
P. 305; RV 498), first movement, as written

Example 12.9b.   Possible Realization of 12.9a

In example 12.10 from the same concerto, I would recommend grace notes throughout. We must not be misled by the figure at the start of each measure which, in the time of Haydn and Mozart, became a formula that was routinely resolved into four equal notes. In the mid-eighteenth century when the formula first emerged, the four notes were not yet equalized, but the first note was played shorter. In Vivaldi, it is no formula yet, but a chance occurrence. I am as certain as one can be in these matters that the Mozart solution is not fitting here, and that a grace note treatment should be the first choice.

Example 12.10.   A. Vivaldi, Concerto in F Major (F. VIII, No. 20;
                 P. 305; RV 498), first movement

An interpretation using the small note on the downbeat will probably be more likely to be fitting when the grace repeats the preceding pitch. In example 12.11, from the Concerto in E♭ Major, a short appoggiatura treatment would seem in order. In example 12.12, from the Concerto in D Minor, either a grace note or a brief, but unaccented, appoggiatura would make sense. Incidentally, when a brief appoggiatura is unaccented, the difference between it and a grace note will often blur.

Example 12.11.   A. Vivaldi, Concerto in E♭ Major, second movement

Example 12.12.   A. Vivaldi, Concerto in D Minor (F. VIII, No. 5;
                 P. 282; RV 481), third movement

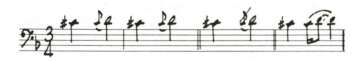

To sum up, the single little note in Vivaldi, in general, is short, either as a grace note or as a short appoggiatura. Long appoggiaturas occur, of course, but are either written out in regular notes, or, as in cadential trills, not indicated and left to the discretion of the performer.

Mozart

Let us turn now to Mozart and his two surviving bassoon works, the Concerto in B♭, K. 191(186e), and the Sonata in B♭, K. 292(196c). Mozart's ornamentation is of course different from Vivaldi's, but in some features it is closer to Vivaldi than to, say, C. P. E. Bach, who is still, unfortunately, considered by too many as the chief authority for all masters of the eighteenth century.

Mozart is among many masters whose performances have suffered, and continue to suffer, from his subjection to C. P. E.'s rigid rules. Many of us forget that in musical matters Austria in the eighteenth century was looking to Italy and not to northern Germany.

On the subject of ornamentation, it seems that in the two works cited above the problems are essentially limited to the following: the *Vorschlag,* in its two forms of grace note and appoggiatura, the trill, the *Eingang,* and the cadenza.

Eingang, meaning "lead-in," is Mozart's own term for an introductory passage that leads into a theme. Often written out, but also often left to the performer's improvisation, as is the case in both the concerto and the sonata, the *Eingang* is signified by a fermata on the dominant chord of the prevailing key or on a rest following the dominant. The *Eingang*'s most characteristic occurrence is in Rondo movements connecting the end of a section with the re-entry of the refrain. Mozart's spelled-out *Eingänge* are occasionally long, but for the most part they consist of only a few notes such as a scale or similar figuration. I think it is wise to look to Mozart's short specimens for our models by doing only what is necessary without getting too loquacious. There are several such *Eingänge* in both the concerto and the sonata that need to be added and I shall have some suggestions.

Cadenzas are introduced by a $^6_4$ chord on the tonic with fermata, and end typically with a trill on the dominant seventh. They are more substantial, should preferably quote and elaborate on themes or motives from the movement, and should contain some brilliant passage work. Cadenzas should not be too long, should not markedly exceed the technical level of the piece, should not modulate too far afield, and should not jump outside the stylistic framework. In other words, they should neither technically nor stylistically flaunt their character as a foreign implant, one that disturbs the organic unity of the movement.

For symbol-indicated ornaments, here notably the trill and the *Vorschlag,* there are no pat solutions. There are cases where the solution seems obvious, and others where there is more than one possible way.

Let me emphasize that the textbook solutions whereby each ornament, including the *Vorschlag,* has to fall accented on the beat, and every trill has to start with the upper note, also on the beat, are simply not applicable to Mozart. Furthermore, the much-repeated rule that an appoggiatura before a binary note takes one half of the latter does apply occasionally, but by no means always, even though endorsed by Leopold Mozart. The companion rule, whereby an appoggiatura before a dotted note takes two-thirds of the value, rarely applies to Mozart, and if so, only before short notes.

Mozart's trill, following a long-standing Italian tradition, is essentially a main-note trill. This is true to the point where one can say that the first choice for Mozart's trill should be the start with the main note. There is even much incontrovertible evidence that many of Mozart's cadential trills were of the main-note variety.

There are, however, contexts that favor the start with the upper auxiliary. The upper note could be placed unaccented before the beat as a grace note, or accented on the beat as a short appoggiatura. I refer to these types as grace-note trill and appoggiatura trill respectively. As a guideline to solving this problem, I suggest leaving out the trill and asking yourself if a short appoggiatura or a grace note could be profitably added to the unornamented note. If so, then the trill could be sensibly rendered accordingly. If neither of these additions is convincing then the start with the main note is indicated.

Regarding the *Vorschlag,* there are again no hard and fast rules. In contrast to Vivaldi, Mozart uses a variety of denominations to mark the little note, ranging from quarter notes to thirty-seconds. There is meaning in the various forms, and it is a pity we do not have the autographs of the two bassoon works, because publishers or copyists were often lackadaisical in rendering Mozart's original denominations. But, in general, the ones found in the first edition, which is our main source, do make sense, and André, the publisher, was generally reliable.

The denominations give only approximate clues, with the longer values standing mainly for appoggiaturas and the smaller values standing for either appoggiaturas or grace notes. There are, of course, exceptions in both cases, especially in the music of the young Mozart.

Since a bassoonist's main interest focuses on the concerto, I shall now go through it and make suggestions. Please note that the following are suggestions, *not* prescriptions.**

The main note of the trill in example 12.13, measure 38, is an appoggiatura. It makes little sense to place a second appoggiatura on the first. An anticipated auxiliary is both more logical and more graceful.

In measure 39, the repeat of the same pitch on a stressed beat favors an appoggiatura.

** Key: gn = grace note ♪ ; app = appoggiatura ♫. or ♩♪ ; mn tr = main note trill; gn tr = grace note trill ♪ ; app tr = appoggiatura trill ; the figure is always . The measures are numbered as they are in the collected edition, *Neue Ausgabe sämtlicher Werke* (Kassel, 1955–).

Example 12.13.   W. A. Mozart, Concerto in B♭ Major (K. 191[186e]),
first movement, mm. 38–39

The first trill could be either a grace-note or main-note trill. All other trills in this passage begin on the main note in measure 50 (ex. 12.14) because the repetition of the B♭ or C is thematic.

Example 12.14.   Ibid., first movement,
mm. 50–54

In measure 64 (ex. 12.15), short appoggiaturas are indicated although a grace-note treatment is also possible (*tierces coulées*). In measure 65 the trill could either start with the main note or with a brief appoggiatura. In measure 66 a main-note trill seems fitting.

Example 12.15.   Ibid., first movement,
mm. 64–66

Since the trill in measure 70 (ex. 12.16) is cadential, it can be introduced either by an appoggiatura or a slide.

Example 12.16.   Ibid., first movement,
              m. 70

In measure 88 I would suggest a grace note on the third beat, followed by a main-note trill. In measure 95 (ex. 12.17), the upward-leaping *Vorschlag* should be anticipated and treated as a stylized form of singer's *portamento*.

Example 12.17.   Ibid., first movement,
              mm. 88 and 95

Measure 97 (ex. 12.18) presents the first opportunity for an *Eingang*. A possible model is provided.

Example 12.18.   Ibid., first movement,
              m. 97

In measure 117, the main note of the trill is already an appoggiatura, so a main-note or grace-note trill is indicated (ex. 12.19).

Example 12.19.   Ibid., first movement,
              m. 117

The trill in measure 136 (ex. 12.20) is tied to the preceding appoggiatura indicating a main-note trill.

Example 12.20.   Ibid., first movement,
              m. 136

Using short appoggiaturas in measure 143 (ex. 12.21) is more vigorous than a grace-note treatment.

Example 12.21.   Ibid., first movement,
              m. 143

Because of the large leap between measures 150 and 151 (ex. 12.22), a slide trill, one of Mozart's favorite cadential formulas, seems preferable to an appoggiatura trill.

Example 12.22.   Ibid., first movement,
              mm. 150–51

In measures 7 and 8 of the second movement (ex. 12.23), the first two *Vorschläge* occur before written out appoggiaturas, indicating a grace note treatment. In addition, an on-the-beat appoggiatura would result in parallel

octaves with the accompaniment. The third *Vorschlag* should be performed as
an appoggiatura.

Example 12.23. Ibid., second movement,
mm. 7–8

In measure 11 (ex. 12.24), a short appoggiatura is more expressive than a
grace note. In measure 12, the main note of the trill is a written-out appoggiatura, suggesting the use of an anticipated grace note.

Example 12.24. Ibid., second movement,
mm. 11–12

In measures 41 and 42 (ex. 12.25), a main-note treatment brings out the
characteristic interval of a minor seventh between C and the B♭ above it.

Example 12.25. Ibid., second movement,
mm. 41–42

The trill in measure 45 (ex. 12.26) works equally well as either a main
note, grace note, or appoggiatura trill.

Example 12.26.   Ibid., second movement,
                 m. 45

The cadential trill of measure 47 could be preceded by either a long or a short appoggiatura or by a slide (ex. 12.27).

Example 12.27.   Ibid., second movement,
                 m. 47

Because of the leap of the trill in measure 27 of the third movement (ex. 12.28), a main-note trill is preferable:

Example 12.28.   Ibid., third movement,
                 m. 27

The little note in measure 32 will best be played as a long appoggiatura (ex. 12.29):

Example 12.29.   Ibid., third movement,
                 mm. 31–32

The little notes in measure 59 could be grace notes (ex. 12.30):

Example 12.30.   Ibid., third movement,
                 m. 59

Measure 106 (ex. 12.31) presents another opportunity for an *Eingang*. A longer *Eingang* than the one shown in the example may be justified here because it is a substitute for a cadenza.

Example 12.31.   Ibid., third movement,
                 m. 106

Turning now to the Sonata in B♭ , the little notes in measures 63 and 64 will be played as grace notes (ex. 12.32):

Example 12.32.   Sonata in B♭ Major (K. 292[196c]), first movement,
                 mm. 63–65

Measure 130 calls for an *Eingang* perhaps of the kind suggested (ex. 12.33):

Example 12.33.   Ibid., second movement,
                 mm. 29–30

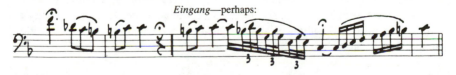

In the third movement Rondo, *Eingänge* are needed in measures 36, 62, and 91, as sketched in the following (examples 12.34a, b, and c):

Example 12.34a.   Ibid., third movement,
                  mm. 35–36

Eingang

Example 12.34b.   Ibid., third movement,
                  mm. 61–62

Eingang

Example 12.34c.   Ibid., third movement,
                  mm. 90–91

Eingang

The ambiguity of some of the symbols, notably for the *Vorschlag,* is at the same time a hardship, a challenge, and an opportunity for the performer. The hardship is due to the occasional agony of choice, the challenge stems from the need to exert one's judgment and musicianship, and the opportunity lies in the possibility of varying one's performance from one time to the next.

Ornaments are born of improvisation and must always retain a measure of flexibility to be true to their function. They must never be calcified. Mozart, like all great masters who discussed performance, never spoke of rules, but always of what he called "Gusto," which, like the French *goût,* is a combination of musicianship and intelligence. As mature performers, you ought to know what the style permits or requires, but you cannot abdicate the responsibility of using your taste and judgment, your "Gusto," in all matters of interpretation including, of course, the rendition of ornaments.

Part Four

Varia

13

Bach: Progressive or Conservative and the Authorship of the Goldberg Aria

The following essay was published as part of the tercentennial Bach-Handel-Scarlatti series of the Musical Quarterly *in 1985. Heavily edited at the time, it is presented here in a revised version that restores some of its original text.*

Bach's tercentennial will give rise to a flood of new studies on the master's life, personality, and works. Wishing to add a droplet to this flood of celebratory essays, I am venturing into the controversial field of his style. More specifically, I am taking issue with a recent attempt by the well-known Bach scholar Robert L. Marshall for his provocative reevaluation of Bach's style during the years 1730–45, when he was between the ages of forty-five and sixty.[1]

In the course of the discussion I shall also give reasons why the Aria of the Goldberg Variations that plays a prominent role in Marshall's arguments is quite certainly not by Bach, but by a so-far unknown Frenchman.

Traditional opinion regards Bach's music (along with Handel's) as the supreme embodiment of what is commonly called the late Baroque. Yet, in the early years of the eighteenth century, long before the death of these two masters, the late Baroque began to crumble under the powerful and soon-to-be-victorious assault of the new *galant*—or Pre-Classical style, which received its strongest impulse from the Italian *opera buffa*. Because Bach remained faithful to the older style, he was considered a conservative who consummated the developments of the past and did not embrace the new musical fashion.

In contrast to these ideas, Marshall's thesis postulates that in those years of Bach's late middle age he did show a strong inclination to follow the modern *galant* orientation, hence the epithet of being "progressive." I will try to show

This article originally appeared in *Musical Quarterly* 71 (1985): 281–94. Reprinted by permission of the publisher.

that Marshall did not succeed in demonstrating his point and that the earlier picture of Bach's conservatism is more fitting.

Salient features of the Bachian late Baroque are polyphony, a strong thoroughbass, a linear thrust of melody that spins out in often complex figurations and irregular phrases, rich harmony, and fast harmonic rhythm. Salient features of the *galant* style are homophony, and simple, often folklike, songful melodies of immediate appeal, with regular phrases, simple harmonies, and slow harmonic rhythm.

Those are prototypes and as such oversimplifications; therefore, it is dangerous to take them too literally. It is also dangerous to overlook the fact that some of the "salient features" are not limited to the style for which they are listed. For instance, in the *style galant* simple folklike melodies of immediate appeal, chordal texture, and regular phrase structure cannot *per se* be labeled as *galant*. The same traits occur, for instance, in the Renaissance in *villanelle, balletti* and *canzonette,* written by masters such as Josquin, Lasso, Marenzio, Palestrina, and Gastoldi; to call such songs *galant* would reduce the term to absurdity. (In popular music the same and similar traits have recurred up until the present day.)

Bach had no formal teacher to guide the shaping of his style. He taught himself through the study of famous composers. His obituary (prepared by Philipp Emanuel and his former student J. F. Agricola) mentions Bruhns, Reinken, Buxtehude, and "several good French organists" as musicians whose music he studied. On a later occasion, Philipp Emanuel added the names of Froberger, Strungk, and Boehm. All of these are seventeenth-century polyphonic masters. With their study Bach laid the foundation of his lifelong commitment to the polyphonic art.

From the age of fifteen to eighteen Bach frequently heard the French musical establishment from Celle. Through this acquaintance he became familiar with, and assimilated, the French style with its overtures, dances, and suites. During the same period he probably also had his first personal contact in Hamburg with the aged Reinken, who loomed large as one of his mentors of the North German organ school.

In his early twenties, an extended visit to Lübeck with Buxtehude made a deep impression on him. In Bach's Weimar years (age twenty-three to thirty-two), he experienced one of the most portentous influences on the formation of his style: the encounter with the Italian concerto in its Vivaldian form. He was fascinated by its rhythmic drive and incisiveness, its fiery energy, its Latin clarity, and its splendid structure in which the ritornello pillars sustain a logical modulation scheme. The concerto style left deep traces in Bach's work to the end of his life.

After having thoroughly assimilated this latest powerful influence, the main elements of his mature style were by and large fully assembled in a synthesis of solid German polyphonic workmanship, French splendor and grace, and the brilliance of the Italian concerto transformed and adapted to his artistic ideals and to the needs of individual compositions.

This style, developed by the age of thirty, so fully satisfied his artistic aspirations that he felt no urge to depart from it for the sake of the modern, popular, *galant* fashion. There is reason to assume that he looked at the latter with the kind of benign amusement that many classical music lovers often feel toward popular music today. He spoke, perhaps even fondly, of the "pretty ditties" of the Dresden Italian opera but was reported to have referred to the Berlin *galant* music as "Berlin blue"—a washable color.

Yet the new style was the rage of the time and its representatives and admirers attacked the masters of the late Baroque as old-fashioned pedants who indulged in sterile constructivism and neglected the true aim of music of flattering the ear and moving the heart. Thus in 1737 Bach became the target of an attack by his former student Scheibe, who accused him of being turgid and bombastic and of having deprived music of naturalness by an excess of artificiality. Bach was deeply hurt, but the attack did not prompt him to mend his old-fashioned ways and join the modern crowd.

In fact, with advancing years, Bach distanced himself even further from modern trends by reaching back into the past with his studies of Frescobaldi, Palestrina, and other early masters. The fruit of these labors includes a number of works in the *stile antico,* a pseudo-Palestrinian style: the second Kyrie, the Gratias agimus, and the Credo of the B-Minor Mass; the E-Major Fugue of *The Well-Tempered Clavier* II, the first three chorales of *Clavierübung* III, and a few others. Christoph Wolff has clarified these stylistic developments in a splendid study.[2]

In his final years, Bach endeavored to sum up the art of Baroque polyphony in a series of compositions that consecrated his communion with the vanishing world of his past: the *Canonic Variations, The Musical Offering, The Art of Fugue.* All of these works contain elements of pure theoretical speculation, the kind of "brain music" that was anathema to the "moderns." Wolff sees a penchant in Bach's late work to emphasize more the *docere* than the *movere* or *delectare* (p. 157). These late works were militantly anti-*galant*, antimodern, archconservative. The works in the *stile antico,* when viewed from a similar perspective, could be called not just conservative, but reactionary or regressive. Even the Goldberg Variations, written to entertain an aristocratic patron, contain nine canons amidst a variety of other Baroque forms. And, as if to make up for the playful nature of a few of the variations, Bach entered in his personal copy of the work fourteen puzzle canons on the first eight bass notes of the Aria.

Now let us look at Marshall's case for Bach's modern leanings. Marshall's thesis is that, about 1730, Bach was disaffected with Leipzig and prompted by this disaffection and by his heightened awareness of the excellent and varied musical life in Dresden, with its splendid Italian opera, he increasingly expanded his musical horizons. As a result of this experience, much of the music written during the period 1730–45 would have absorbed elements of the latest Italian Pre-Classical (*galant*) style, principally operatic elements with predominantly homophonic textures, regular periodic phrase structure, and ingratiating melodies. To the extent that he allowed himself to be so influenced by the latest developments of musical fashion, Marshall considers it justified to characterize him as "progressive."

Before examining Marshall's evidence, we must realize how dangerous it is to postulate for any genius of the first order a close connection between his life's events, his joys or sorrows, and the type of art he produced at that time. Mozart wrote some of his most scintillating and joyful music in times of personal despondency. Bach's first wife and eleven of his children died during his lifetime and no one has yet found reflections of these heart-breaking tragedies in his works. With this in mind, are we really to believe that his disillusionment with his Leipzig position, the Scheibe attack, and a few other external events (listed by Marshall, p. 354, n. 78) would have had such a powerful impact on Bach's style? His professional unhappiness affected his working habits and apparently caused the "laziness" of which he was accused by his superiors; but it left no visible or audible mark on his style.

It is conceivable that Bach was so enchanted by the Hasse-style Italian opera that he set out to adopt some of its features, but the evidence for this is very slight. We may hear some distant echoes of Italian opera in occasional turns of melody (for example, some passages in the second duet, "Mein Freund ist mein," from Cantata No. 140). But whereas his acquaintance with the Vivaldian concerto led to a passionate embrace and lifelong love affair, the meeting with Italian *galant* opera led at best to a passing flirtation too superficial to be regarded as a major new aesthetic orientation.

Marshall sees another motive: Bach had applied for a court position and wanted to ingratiate himself with the Dresden establishment by a turn to the *galant*. If that were true, the presentation of the Kyrie and Gloria of the B-Minor Mass, which accompanied his application, would have been singularly inept. Even Marshall admits that the Mass is not a *galant* work, but he labors hard and, I believe, unsuccessfully to extract some *galant* particles from the Baroque monumentality of the dedicatory composition.

Marshall presents Cantata No. 51, *Jauchzet Gott in allen Landen,* of ca. 1730 as the entrance gate to Bach's "progressive" period. The work, which has virtuoso trumpet and soprano parts, is, Marshall says, an outright showpiece, written in an unabashedly (for Bach) unprecedented flamboyant style. With this characterization he seems to imply that virtuosity and flamboyance were *galant* characteristics. Are they really? Did not trumpet, horn, or organ virtuosity blossom in the Baroque and wither in the *galant* period? Cantata No. 172 of 1714 or the second Brandenburg Concerto of ca. 1720 have similar virtuoso trumpet parts; the virtuosity of the violin solo sonatas of 1720 was not equaled until Paganini. We even find virtuoso choral parts in early cantatas such as No. 21 of 1714. What could be more flamboyant than the early *Chromatic Fantasy* or the Weimar and pre-Weimar organ and harpsichord toccatas?

Marshall cites immediacy of appeal, fanfare melodies, and syncopations, again implying that they too are hallmarks of the *galant* style. Immediacy of appeal was not a *galant* preserve, and such an appeal graces many of Bach's and other Baroque masters' works. In fact it is more prevalent in works of Bach's younger years than in those of his middle and late age. Fanfare melodies abound in Italian concertos, and syncopation was hardly a *galant* innovation. (One of the various functions of blackening in mensural notation was to mark syncopations.)

Yet, in Marshall's mind, all these stylistic traits, as well as the vocal writing, would have been "associated at the time with nothing so much as the Italian opera—of the kind cultivated at Dresden." He finds the temptation "irresistible" (p. 325) to propose that Bach wrote the cantata for one of the Italian sopranos at the Dresden court. I can resist the temptation and find the suggestion unlikely. It seems inconceivable to me that an Italian singer of that time would have considered singing a Lutheran cantata in German. If Bach had wanted to ingratiate himself with an influential singer of the Dresden court, the obvious thing for him to compose would have been a cantata in Italian or a Catholic sacred piece in Latin.

Cantata No. 51 was written for the Leipzig church service, where the performance parts were located. Bach had at his disposal a virtuoso trumpeter (Gottfried Reiche) and must have had a talented youngster or falsettist for the vocal part. But even if, against all odds, Bach had an Italian singer in mind, that still would not prove the *galant* nature of the work. Neither can such an inference be drawn from what Marshall calls the handsome appearance of a score that, he says, could pass for a presentation copy (though, he hastens to add, it does not seem to have been presented to anyone). The argument is irrelevant. Even an intended presentation, if proved, has no value as evidence for the style of the work. Only on its own merits, and not by external circumstances, can we evaluate the style.

And nowhere do we find in this work the signature of the *galant* style. The first movement is orchestrally an Italian concerto, complicated in its texture by the addition of vocal counterpoint. The following recitative is of Bach's traditional slow-moving, nonoperatic type and leads into an arioso of very complex melodic structure and irregular phrase design. The following continuo aria also contains elaborate, typically Baroque melodies in free varied rhythms, set against a quasi ostinato in the bass. The fourth movement presents the chorale in rich elaboration: the chorale melody in the soprano is enveloped in a violin double concerto, reminiscent of the famous one in D minor with consistently imitative parts and a very lively bass that shares in the thematic elaboration. The final movement is a fugue whose anti-*galant* stance is implicit in its form. It is difficult to find a more representative array of stylistic features typical of the late Baroque.

Another exhibit, Cantata No. 201, known as the *Contest between Phoebus and Pan,* was written in 1729–30. As Marshall himself writes, it uses a mythological singing contest to embody "Bach's own aesthetic credo: his unwavering commitment to solid musical craftsmanship and his emphatic repudiation of the easy, light, and merely pleasing in music." Marshall finds the usual interpretation of the allegory "compelling," seeing in Pan's song "Zu Tanze, zu Sprunge," a parodistic caricature of the *galant* style and in Apollo's "Mit Verlangen" the "representative of Bach's traditionalistic values of high quality." Bach actually intensifies the ridicule of Pan with a dose of scatological humor by setting the word *wackelt* ("tottering") as wack-ack-ack-ack-ack-ack-ak-kelt (evoking inevitably the vulgar word *kacken,* meaning "to defecate"); we see that Bach's humor had an earthy quality.

Instead of scoring a point, Marshall wounds his thesis by conceding Bach's ridicule of the *galant* style and by his "unwavering commitment" to the contrasting style of his preference.

Marshall's case is stronger with the "Coffee" and the "Peasant" Cantatas, both unquestionably "modern" and *galant,* but marginal to Bach's work, as Marshall himself admits. (Their place in Bach's oeuvre is comparable to that of *Ein musikalischer Spass* in Mozart's.) Bach was clearly ill at ease in the idiom: both works are musically inferior and the fish-out-of-water feeling they convey reinforces the case against, not for, Bach's *galant* sympathies. Some sections of the "Peasant" Cantata (e.g., the introductory number) would be embarrassing if they were not so obviously intended as caricatures of village music and, by inference, of music that appeals to the masses. Neither work has evidential value for Marshall's thesis; we have to judge a master's style by the core, not the periphery.

Another of Marshall's examples is the Christe eleison from the B-Minor Mass. Sandwiched between the grandiose fugue of the first Kyrie, and the *stile antico* fugue of the second one, is a lovely duet for two sopranos that provides the kind of contrast that is a structural requisite between units of a composite work. Marshall admits that it is "not a *galant* piece, the harmony and counterpoint are both too rich." But he finds *galant* elements in the means that Bach uses to portray the "gentle affections": (1) unison violins, (2) "sweet parallel thirds and sixths," (3) mixtures of duplets and triplets, and (4) the feminine cadence with its subdivided downbeat and appoggiatura embellishment (ex. 13.1).

Let us examine these points one by one:

Example 13.1.   J. S. Bach, B-Minor Mass, Christe eleison

(1) Why unison violins should be a *galant* feature, I do not know and cannot guess. Bach used them in the very early Cantata No. 4 (before 1708), in Cantata No. 80 of 1715, and in a few other pre-1730 works. Here they are simply one voice in a complex four-part polyphony and that voice, carried

forward by a powerful linear drive, spins out an initial impulse in typical Baroque fashion; its obbligato pervades the whole movement.

(2) Tender affections expressed by sweet thirds and sixths were by no means introduced with the *galant* style. For a few random early examples, see Monteverdi's madrigal "Ohimè se tanto amato" from the fourth book of 1603 (ex. 13.2a), the Pastorale from Corelli's Christmas Concerto (ex. 13.2b), or Bach's "Cappriccio sopra la lontananza . . ." of 1704, its sixths and thirds further sweetened by the kind of feminine cadences, subdivided downbeats, and the appoggiatura embellishments that Marshall listed as *galant* attributes (ex. 13.2c). Moreover, George Buelow has strikingly shown that the parallel thirds and sixths are used as symbols of the duality of Christ and God the Father in a group of movements that contains much medieval number symbolism.[3]

(3) Mixture of duplets and triplets goes back at least to the sixteenth century with its blackened semibreves and minims in triplet value and was used by Bach from his earliest datable works on.

(4) Regarding feminine cadences, etc., see example 13.2c.

Example 13.2a.   C. Monteverdi, Madrigal "Ohimè se tanto amato" (1603)

Example 13.2b.   A. Corelli, Christmas Concerto, Pastorale

Example 13.2c.   J. S. Bach, "Cappriccio sopra la lontananza . . ." (BWV 992)

Marshall speculates that the soprano aria "Laudamus te" from the Mass was intended for the famous Faustina, Hasse's wife. This is certainly possible—if she were humble enough to accept the role of second soprano for which the aria is written—but does not prove anything about the style. Its melody, harmony, phrase structure, and interplay of the voices are as rich as those of the Christe eleison. Nothing could be more typically Baroque than the violin obbligato with its ornate *Fortspinnungs Melodik* (see ex. 13.3), its Baroque nature intensified by its being set against the counterpoint of the vocal solo.

Example 13.3.   J. S. Bach, B-Minor Mass, "Laudamus te"

Marshall then refers to the "popular 'Lombard' rhythms of the *style galant*" with which he assumes (wrongly, I am convinced) the many slurred binary figures in the Domine Deus were intended to be rendered. Even if they were so intended, the attribution of the "Lombard" rhythms to the *galant* style is unjustified, since their ancestry can be traced for centuries back. We find them, for example, in Ganassi (1535), in Caccini, in Frescobaldi, in Francesco Rognioni's diminution treatise of 1620, and in Biber in the 1680s, to name a few among many.

Finally, Marshall summons the Aria from the Goldberg Variations as, perhaps, the main pillar of his thesis. The Variations date from ca. 1742. The Aria is a *galant* piece, but is quite certainly not by Bach. I have for a long time, and at first purely instinctively, suspected the attribution. The un-Bachian flavor, the flimsiness of its substance, and the shallowness of its melodic content aroused my suspicion.[4] Then there is the sudden stylistic break of the last six measures, where the *galant* fractionalized melody suddenly turns into a Baroque-type *Fortspinnung* figuration (musically the best part of the piece). Such breaks do not occur in Bach's dances or related pieces.

So great is the power of suggestion that, as long as Bach's hand was assumed, everybody accepted the Aria as masterly, when in fact, it is only a cut or two above Diabelli's Waltz of Beethoven's variations.

I was delighted when I discovered that the Bach scholar Arnold Schering had previously rejected the traditional attribution, regarding the modulation scheme and ornamentation as un-Bachian.[5]

I will not discuss Schering's point of the modulatory scheme, but the ornamentation is certainly un-Bachian. Apart from the excess of embellishments, strewn over the music as in a shower of confetti, many of the ornaments are highly suspect (ex. 13.4). There are, above all, several collisions of different ornaments in the left and right hands in a manner used by French keyboard players but rarely by Bach. See, for example, the combination of a compound trill (*Doppelt Cadence*) with a mordent in measure 17 (a); of appoggiatura with trill in measure 21, of *port de voix* with trill in measure 22 (b); and, perhaps most damning, the combination of two appoggiaturas in parallel fourths in measure 26 (c),[6] an offense which can be slightly mitigated, but not cured, only by an intricate balancing act. At the end of the first part, the use of the same *port de voix* on the identical pitch on two successive beats (d) is clumsy and redundant.

Example 13.4.   J. S. Bach, Goldberg Variations, Aria

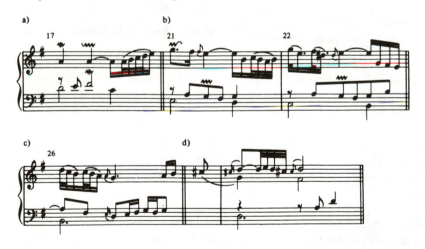

It is significant that none of the cited objectionable ornaments or ornament combinations recur in their respective spots in any of the thirty variations. The use of these ornaments alone is sufficient to question Bach's authorship.

There are other reasons. Until the end of the eighteenth century, independent sets of variations—as contrasted with movements in a larger work—were normally based on a preexisting composition. (This tendency carried over into the nineteenth and even the twentieth centuries.)[7] Before the mid-eighteenth century such variations were written mostly on a bass, or on a sequence of harmonies. Melody variations existed but were rare.

According to Warren Kirkendale (in a letter written to me), the word "aria" had in the late sixteenth and seventeenth centuries the meaning of a "standardized, pre-existent bass or harmonic progression" such as Aria di Ruggiero, Aria di Romanesca, etc.

Nino Pirrotta (also in correspondence with me) relates the word "aria" in the Renaissance to the idea of expected musical behavior: "bass patterns like those of Ruggiero, Romanesca, or passamezzo were called 'arie' because they conferred an expected behavior (i.e., an expected succession of harmonic steps) on whatever melody was built on them." By Bach's time the word "aria" had the modern meaning of a vocal set piece, but the "Renaissance concept was still present, for instance in Corelli's *Folia* or Bach's Passacaglia." Pirrotta is uncertain about the Goldberg Variations but sees a link to the old type in "their insistence on bass formulae featuring a descending tetrachord." I think there is little doubt that in this case, too, where the bass of the first eight measures is of a standard type, the term "aria" is used in the old meaning of a preexisting piece. It is certainly not an aria in the modern sense, and had it been his own composition, Bach might have more logically called the work "Sarabande with Thirty Variations."

There is another reason. The untitled and unattributed Aria was entered by Anna Magdalena in her Note Book of 1725 in the company of several single works by other composers. The entry must have been made many years before the composition of the Variations; and as far as I know, Bach practically never wrote a sarabande or any other dance piece by itself, outside of a cycle (except for a couple of minuets written as teaching pieces for Friedemann's Note Book). Because this fact alone suggests a foreign origin, Georg von Dadelsen, who wants to maintain Bach's authorship, resorts to two explanations of far-fetched complexity.[8]

In entering the previous piece, "Bist du bei mir," Anna Magdalena skipped two pages in its middle, and it is on those two pages that the Aria is written. Dadelsen speculates that Anna Magdalena left these two pages blank for maybe ten to fifteen years and did not fill them in with the Aria until the Variations were printed or readied for print around 1742. This assumption strains credibility: is it not far more plausible that she discovered the oversight soon after it happened and used the empty space as soon as she had an item that easily fitted in? By contrast, the theory of the entry of the piece after the variations were printed or being readied for print is triply implausible: 1) because of the improbable delay in filling the space; 2) because once the piece was already available to the Bach household in print, or about to be available, there was no conceivable reason for entering it into the Note Book; and 3) because there are no fewer than thirty-four deviations of the written and printed versions (listed in KB v/4, p. 95), and this huge number cannot be brushed off as carelessness in copying. Granted, most discrepancies are minor, but a few are substantial, such as the changed rhythm in measure 24, changed ornament types in measures 3 and 12; also the change of the treble clef in print to the soprano clef is improbable in the case of an alleged mechanical copy from either print or *Stichvorlage*. Even more improbable under the circumstances is the omission of the title "Aria." All these difficulties and implausibilities disappear if we assume an earlier entry into the Note Book, perhaps a copy from some Frenchman's manuscript.[9]

Dadelsen, sensing his labored construction was insecure, tried to bolster his case with a second argument. He contended that, had ten or more years elapsed between the Note Book entry and variations, Bach surely would have revised the piece. This argument, too, is unconvincing. Had it been his own composition, he might well have revised it. He left it intact precisely because it was somebody else's work; Bach's interest centered on the bass and not on other compositional details.

One more point can be made. The variations are built according to a carefully thought-out symmetrical plan with every third variation in canonic form, proceeding stepwise from the unison to the ninth. The second part starts with an overture; the last variation, a quodlibet using two folk songs, completes the symmetry in that the ending as well as the beginning uses preexisting material.

I believe it is time to reaffirm Schering's judgment and unburden Bach of the responsibility for this inferior composition. This means, of course, that we have to discard the Aria as a proof of Bach's progressiveness.

The Variations themselves contain, apart from the nine canons, a whole compendium of Baroque forms: inventions, fuguetta, overture, concerto and sonata movements, preludes, toccatas, but no *galant* operatic aria.

Finally, Christoph Wolff, in discussing Bach's most severe and abstract period, points to *galant* elements in *The Musical Offering* of 1747, specifically in the three-part Ricercar and in the third movement of the Trio Sonata. He assumed that Bach wanted to please the king by alluding to the style favored at the court. This theory was invalidated by Ursula Kirkendale, who, in an essay of dazzling brilliance, solved the mystery that had thus far surrounded the whole work. She uncovered the fact that, far from a haphazard collection of disparate pieces, *The Musical Offering* is patterned after Quintilian's *Institutio oratoria* which it follows with incredible literalness, piece by piece, and often measure by measure.[10] This astonishingly consistent and intimate correlation between Quintilian's text and Bach's music suggests that the *galant* episodes have nothing to do with a desire to flatter the king but instead to follow the text of Quintilian, which summons this exact type of musical expression in the passages in question. (Even *if* Bach had tried to please the king, the artificial effort involved would not reflect a change of his basic style.)

Marshall's analysis, it seems to me, overlooks the fact that Bach's late Baroque style could vary within a wide range without thereby breaking out of its stylistic frame. Polyphony can turn to simpler shades, even to homophony; harmony can become plain, and harmonic rhythm can slow down; and irregularity of phrase structure disappears in dances and dance-derived works. A continuo aria, a recitative, a homophonic toccata, and a prelude are no less Baroque than a five-part fugue just because their texture is simpler.

Marshall built his thesis largely by wrongly equating such lighter shades of the prototype with the intrusion of the *galant* style.

Marshall himself admits that we must view Bach's progressiveness "within the context of his basically unshakable late-Baroque idiom." This tell-tale phrase by itself contradicts the concept of "progressiveness" as an indication of *galant* leanings. If Bach's late-Baroque idiom was "unshakable," then he did not succumb to the ravishing siren songs of the Italian melodists. If we do find, once in a long while, echos of Italian *galant* operatic melody in his works, it is significant that they are so few and so ephemeral. Marshall himself speaks of Bach's last creative period and its series of increasingly severe instrumental cycles as "these retrospective, monumental surveys of the venerable skill of strict counterpoint, canon and fugue."

By having shown, I trust, that Marshall's evidence and arguments for major *galant* inroads into Bach's style are unconvincing, Bach's stylistic evolution achieves a unity of direction and purpose, and the abstract, retrospective works of his last years appear, not as an about-face after a period of *galant* leanings, but as the ultimate logical conclusion and emphatic reaffirmation of an unerring aesthetic creed.

Viewed in this light, Bach's stylistic evolution also reflects on his character. He did not compromise his aesthetic conviction to curry favor with the Dresden establishment; and the *galant* elements in *The Musical Offering* were not a courtier's compliment to the king's musical taste. Bach's unwillingness to make concessions to the prevailing fashion hurt his worldly career but is a telling tribute to the towering integrity of the artist and the man.

Notes

1. The theory was embodied in an article entitled "Bach the Progressive: Observations on His Later Works," *The Musical Quarterly* 62 (July 1976): 313–57.

2. *Der Stile antico in der Musik Johann Sebastian Bachs* (Wiesbaden, 1968).

3. "Symbol and Structure in the 'Kyrie' of Bach's B-Minor Mass," *Essays on the Music of J. S. Bach and Other Divers Subjects: A Tribute to Gerhard Herz* (New York, 1981), pp. 21–42.

4. See, for instance, the banality of mm. 13–16. Bach is occasionally academic and dry, but never banal.

5. I once told my mentor and friend, the late Arthur Mendel, dean of American Bach scholars, that I was convinced the aria was not by Bach. He expressed great surprise and then withdrew to his office. When he came out he said, and these were his exact words: "You are absolutely right, it is a piece of French fluff."

6. In the printed version, as shown in ex. 13.4c, the grace in the right hand is written in eighth notes, in the left, in sixteenth-note denominations. In the earlier version in Anna Magdalena's Note Book both have the same eighth-note value, which suggests identical rhythmic disposition.

7. Where variations as part of a composite work were in the form of a chaconne or passacaglia, the thematic bass was often of a standard type. In the Classical era independent variation cycles were still overwhelmingly written on another composer's song or dance piece. All of Mozart's fifteen sets of variations for the piano and two for violin and piano had a preexisting theme. Beethoven wrote a few variations on original themes, but many more on existing ones, including popular tunes ("Nel cor più non mi sento"), *God Save the King*, themes from *The Magic Flute*, *Don Giovanni*, *Figaro*, themes by Dressler, Righini, Dittersdorf, Salieri, Süssmayr, Winter, Waldstein, Müller, Handel, and, of course, Diabelli.

    Consider also Chopin's variations on *Don Giovanni*, Brahms's on Paganini, Haydn, and Handel, Reger's on Mozart, Britten's on Purcell, modern jazz practice, etc.

    The great nineteenth-century vogue of "paraphrases" and "fantasies" on well-known arias or songs of the day follows the same tradition that had its roots in what seems to be a timeless musical impulse of elaborating on known melodies.

8. *Neue Bach Ausgabe*, V/4, *Kritischer Bericht*, ed. Georg von Dadelsen (Kassel, 1957), pp. 93–94.

9. The missing title "Aria," for instance, becomes a matter of course: the piece was not yet an "aria" at that time and became one only after being used as borrowed theme for the variations.

10. "The Source for Bach's *Musical Offering*," *Journal of the American Musicological Society* 33 (1980): 88–141. Peter Williams, with a regrettable lapse of taste and judgment, referred to Kirkendale's analysis as "idiotic" (*Music & Letters* 65 [1984]: 391). The use of this unscholarly adjective is unfortunate.

14

Mattheson on Performance Practice

Apart from being a prolific composer, singer, keyboard player, conductor, and diplomat, Johann Mattheson was an indefatigable writer whose literary output exceeded 130 items. Even if we allow for some overlapping and repetition, the sheer quantity of that production is awe-inspiring. Reflecting his wide-ranging interests, his erudition and knowledge, his topics ranged well beyond music, though that remained his principal concern.

His theoretical works on music were greatly admired in his time and his forward-looking ideas on composition, style, and aesthetics strongly affected German musical thought and development in the eighteenth century and beyond. Today they are, for his epoch, a treasure trove of information on music theory, on the sociology of music, and on the life and works of the composers, while his incisive criticisms of his contemporaries are invariably revealing and arresting even if today we should not subscribe to all of his views.

Unfortunately, his otherwise encyclopedic coverage of the musical scene has, in the light of today's concerns, one weak spot: His writings deal, if at all, only peripherally with questions of performance practice. True, he wrote two books on the thorough-bass (the second an elaboration on the first,) but this topic is confined to one specialized skill, however important. The lamented meager pickings concern the wide spectrum of elements that enter into the interpretation of any piece that we attempt to perform according to the composer's conception. Some of these elements are tempo, dynamics, rhythm, phrasing, articulation, and ornamentation. Having examined a considerable number of tracts by Mattheson, I found only two chapters that focus on such problems. Both are in *Der vollkommene Capellmeister* (1739), his most important theoretical work. The chapters, to be discussed later, concern ornamentation and conducting. Apart from these two chapters we have to resort to garnering chance remarks that bear on performance and to scanning the remarks addressed to the composer for their possible implications for interpreters. I shall

This article originally appeared in *New Mattheson Studies*, ed. George J. Buelow and Hans Joachim Marx (Cambridge, 1983), pp. 257–68. Reprinted by permission of the publishers.

start by registering some of these scattered observations, a number of which contain striking statements, and reserve for the end a report on the two chapters mentioned.

One of Mattheson's most original, forceful, and important pronouncements expresses his low opinion of rules—a theme to which he returns on various occasions. He ridicules the pedants who look to rules as supreme authority: "Concerning such would-be luminaries who believe that music has to follow their rules, when in truth their rules have to follow the music, one can rightly say 'Faciunt intelligendo ut nihil intelligant'" (roughly: They manage in their thinking to understand nothing). Elsewhere he says: "Rules are valid as long as I consider it well and sensible to abide by them. They are valid no longer than that," and later: "The rule of nature, in music, is nothing but the ear" (*Critica musica* 1, p. 338, n.Z). It seems self-evident that such sentiment about the supremacy of the ear has validity for the performer as well as for the composer. Mattheson sees another reason for the relativity of rules in changing taste. Rules are based on aural perceptions ("observationes aurium") of what produces euphony and what discordancy, and he notes that the ideas of what sounds well, and what not, differ with time and taste. In this connection he cites Werckmeister, who allows ornaments an average time span of only twenty to thirty years before their appeal fades and they become outdated (*Orchestre* 2 [1717], p. 98).

Another of his general principles, insistently repeated, is the primacy of the voice over instruments: "The former is so to speak the mother, the latter the daughter." Instrumental music, he says, should emulate the voice in aiming at songfulness and smoothness ("alles fein singbar und fließend zu machen"; *Capellmeister,* p. 206, par. 4). Yet, aware of the vast difference between the two media, Mattheson in his methodical way lists no fewer than seventeen points of contrast between the two. The most interesting is perhaps the observation that vocal melody does not admit the same sharp and dotted character as does instrumental writing (*Capellmeister,* p. 206, par. 20). This tells us clearly that composers who wrote a voice part in a milder, a unison melody part in a sharper, rhythm did so not as a shorthand device that calls for rhythmic assimilation, but in acknowledgment of the difference between the idiomatic characteristics of the two media.

Another point he makes refers to balance. When voices are combined with instruments, the latter must not dominate; instead they should lower their dynamics by one degree in order to let the voices be properly heard (*Capellmeister,* p. 207, par. 28).

Mattheson admires the performance of the Italians, who owe much of their excellence to their singers. The Italians, he says, cultivate their best voices with the greatest care, in monasteries, churches, and hospices. By contrast, the Germans, with the exception of a few courts, do not train such voices when they happen to have them. They treat their singers as nonentities ("en bagatelle") and let them perish like animals ("crepiren," *Orchestre* 1 [1713], pp. 205–6). He has a comparable admiration for French instrumental and choral performance and is particularly impressed by their overtures and orchestral suites. The execution of the latter is "so admirable, so unified ['unie']. and so compact ['fermé']" that nothing surpasses it. They learn the music by heart and are not ashamed, as the Germans are, to rehearse a piece a hundred times to achieve perfection (*Orchestre* 1, p. 226). The Germans, he writes, try to combine Italian and French styles; the English look only to Italy for guidance.

Mattheson's discussion of the various meters and different musical forms is, as usual, addressed to the composer, but yields here and there some items of interest to the performer. The thorough cataloging of the meters and their use is notable by its failure to mention *notes inégales,* though he was familiar with French treatises, which never failed to include *inégalité* in a discussion of meter.

A remark in a later tract illuminates the still-prevailing link between meter. denominations, and absolute note values. Mattheson asks why a $\frac{9}{16}$ meter is needed, since one could write $\frac{9}{8}$ and "allegro." The answer is that in order properly to express fast pieces, we need fast meters and fast notes so that there shall be agreement between symbols and their meaning (*General-Baß-Schule* 1, pp. 374–75).

Of the various instrumental forms the French overture is his unquestioned favorite: Beautiful as are the Italian symphonies and concertos, he says, "A fresh French overture is preferable to all of them. . . . [O]ne can hear nothing more exhilarating than a fine overture" (*Orchestre* 1, pp. 226–27). Its first part, he writes earlier (ibid., p. 171), "has a fresh, gay, but also uplifting character" ("ein etwas frisches, ermunterndes und auch zugleich elevirtes Wesen"). It is interesting to compare this characterization to the widely held modern idea of the overture's "majestic" pomp.

Another interesting vignette concerns dynamics and the newly invented fortepiano. Mattheson translates an Italian essay by Marchese Scipio Maffei about this innovative instrument, and does so with obvious approval of its contents (*Critica musica* 2, pp. 335–38). Its author extols the joys of dynamic shading in music. He speaks of the gradual swelling and tapering of the sound, occasionally mixed with sudden dynamic contrasts—"a feat much in use in the great concerts in Rome"—that gives connoisseurs "incredible and wondrous delight." Then he proceeds to praise the great advance of the new invention in matters of dynamics and defends it against its critics, who find its sound dull and too weak.

In *Capellmeister* (pt. 2, chap. 13) Mattheson reviews, extends and elaborates on the description given in *Orchestre* 1 of the various musical forms in a survey that yields some points of interest for our subject. In a note about Italian, and Italian-style German recitative, Mattheson remarks that it has a meter but that the singer must not be bound by it. In the accompanied type that involves the whole orchestra more attention has to be paid to the beat in order to hold the instrumentalists together, but the vocal delivery should not betray such dependence.

In his review of the various dance forms Mattheson makes a clear distinction, notably for the minuet, gavotte, rigaudon, sarabande, and courante, between those that were meant to be played and those intended to be sung or danced. In order to distinguish these three types, Mattheson advises, one should look at a minuet by Kuhnau, Handel, or Graupner and ponder whether the piece is suitable for dancing or singing. A first glance, he says, will elicit a negative answer (*Capellmeister* p. 225, par. 85). The differentiation he makes is significant because some scholars have tried to establish the tempo of instrumental "play" dances by gathering clues from dance treatises and other dance-derived evidence. Mattheson's typology should discourage this line of research. Concerning the much-debated differences between the chaconne and the passacaglia, Mattheson declares the tempo of the chaconne to be more deliberate than that of the passacaglia and not, as some maintain, the other way around (ibid., p. 233, par. 135). He ends this section on musical forms with a new tribute to his favorite one, the overture, "whose character expresses nobility" (par. 141).

The two chapters mentioned above, which alone seem to focus specifically on performance, do give us some enlightening information. Mattheson attaches much importance to the discussion of conducting in the very last chapter of *Capellmeister* (pt. 3, chap 26; the paragraph numbers in the following section refer to this chapter, entitled "Von der Regierung, An- Auf- und Ausführung einer Musik"). Nobody, he says, has so far written anything useful on the subject.

In a previous chapter Mattheson had quoted Jean Rousseau about both the need to search for, and the difficulty of clarifying, the composer's intentions when performing his works (p. 173, par. 26). Now, in the closing paragraph of the whole book, he returns to the same idea and stresses the need for a judiciousness that will lead to correct interpretation of the composer's thoughts concerning his works.

His own experience in directing a vocal work has taught him that it is best to do so from the harpsichord while playing and singing, rather than just standing about and beating time (par. 16). He castigates as mischievous the habits of some conductors of beating loudly with a stick or with keys, or by stamping their feet. Provided the performers keep their eyes on the director, a small wave of the hand or a wink can achieve the best results without resort to ostentatious display ("ohne großes Federfechten," par. 14). This remark is noteworthy because it reveals that the good directors of the time used some of the subtlest of modern conducting techniques, and that the "Tact-Prügler" (time-threshers) mocked by Mattheson may have been numerous but were not the norm.

For the chorus he considers women's voices indispensable. Boys are of little use, he says: before they have achieved a tolerable skill their soprano voices are gone (par. 19–20). As early as *Orchestre* 1 (p. 206) he wrote that it was "ridiculous" to prevent women from singing in church. In Hamburg he had great difficulty introducing them into the cathedral: first he had to hide them from view, but in the end everybody wanted to see and hear them.

The best arrangement of the performers is different in church, chamber, theater, and orchestra and has often to be adapted to the locale. If the bass voices are weak, they should be placed in the middle; if strong and at least six in number, they may be divided, and half placed on either side (par. 28). A harpsichord is far preferable to the "rattling, annoying regale." In churches one can use a clean and quickly responding positive without a *Schnarrwerk* (a rattling stop that Mattheson despises) or, when the chorus is strong, two harpsichords (par. 29). Singers must always be in front except in operas, where the orchestra is closer to the public but on a lower level. Here the director has to see to it that the instruments do not overpower the voices (par. 30).

Mattheson gives some psychological advice that many a tyrant-conductor of today would do well to take to heart. The director of a chorus, he says, should be generous with praise as often as he finds occasion for it. Whenever he has to criticize he should do so with seriousness, but as gently and politely as possible. He gives an interesting account of J. S. Kusser (or Cousser), a well-known composer who was for a few years director of the Hamburg Opera. He was indefatigable in instruction; he let everybody under his supervision, from the highest to the lowest, come to his house, where he sang and played every note just as he wanted it to sound. He did so with gentleness and grace. In public rehearsals and performances, however, he was a tyrant and everybody trembled before him, but afterwards he unfailingly made up for his severity by extraordinary politeness. By these methods he accomplished things as no one had before. "He can serve as a model" (par. 8).

In performance the main responsibility of the director is the establishment of the proper tempo. It should be steady but also flexible enough to accommodate by slight slowing down a soloist's tastefully executed ornament, or by slight speeding up (and presumably also by slowing down) to respond to the demands of expression (par. 13).

Finally, an amusing piece of practical advice is worth recording. Since accidents can happen in any performance, the director of the choir will do well to prearrange spots where, at an agreed sign, everybody can meet and continue without obvious interruption (par. 32).

The penultimate chapter (pt. 3, chap. 25) addresses itself mainly to the organist's art of improvising for the church service the necessary preludes, fugues, chorale accompaniments, and postludes, with emphasis on the compositional aspects of these pieces. Preceding this discussion, however, are a few remarks more directly pertinent to performance practice. Mattheson distinguishes the role of the organist when playing with the trained singers of the church from his role when accompanying the congregation. In the former case the organist should use the powers of his instrument with modesty and always adapt the loudness of his playing to the number of singers so that the voices predominate (p. 471, par. 10). Only in a work involving two or three choruses may he play with full power; in such cases there will have to be a special conductor whose direction and tempo the organist has to adopt without resentment. By contrast, when playing with the congregation the organist must play loudly (more or less so according to the numbers present) so as to carry the lay singers along. It will then be best to place one lead singer ("Vorsänger") next to him who acts as liaison, carefully listening to the congregation and helping the organist to keep pace with it (p. 471, par. 15).

Turning now to the chapter on graceful singing and playing ("Von der Kunst zierlich zu singen und zu spielen," pt. 2, chap. 3; paragraph numbers in the following refer to this chapter), we encounter again at its outset the proposition that the voice is the fountainhead of music making, hence should serve as a model for instrumental performance. But to serve properly as model, the voice has to be treated correctly. We gain insight into some objectionable vocal practices of the day from Mattheson's listing of common faults (par. 10–16). He sees as the worst offense incorrect breathing; breathing either too frequently or in the wrong places will ruin proper phrasing. Reprehensible too are slurring what should be detached, and vice versa; poor intonation and poor diction; singing through the nose or with closed teeth or too widely opened mouth; using wrong dynamics; and failing to heed the old, wise principle of easing the sound with rising pitch and reinforcing it when descending to the lower register. The florid, improvised ornamentation, be it for voice or instruments, can create confusion if it does not fit in with the other parts or if it is, "in corrupt Italian manner," so extravagant as to demolish the melody.

At various points Mattheson expresses his disapproval of immoderate ornamentation. "One has to add some embellishments to a melody, but by no means too much. . . . The so-called *Manieren* [meaning here coloraturas] spoil many a good aria and I can't forgive the French when they embroider their *doubles* excessively and embellish, or rather disfigure, them with a thousand little curlicues that prevent us from perceiving anything of the original melody."[1] He then proceeds with the interesting but surprising statement that his day's Italian singers, in contrast to their recent predecessors, preferred a simple style to the highly embellished one, and left the decorations to the instruments "as is only fitting." He quotes in this connection Bononcini's operas and concludes that the florid embellishments ("decorationes") belong more to instrumental than to vocal music (par. 11).

A few years earlier, in *Orchestre* 1 (p. 229), he wrote differently and, it would seem, with more pertinence that the French singers used few coloraturas because their voices were not suited to them; exceptions occur for words such as "gloire" or "victoire" which they often dragged in by force. The Italians, he then wrote, used coloraturas almost to excess. It would seem that he must have heard different styles of both French and Italian vocal performance to give, within about eight years, such contradictory accounts.

Concerning the "small" graces—those that are often indicated by symbol—Mattheson, with his aversion to strict rules, quotes approvingly Hermann Finck and Heinichen who, over a gap of one hundred eighty years, agree that what matters for questions of ornaments are not rules but usage, much practice, and experience (par. 18–19). Mattheson recommends following the best Italians but without exaggeration or rigor. Though ornaments change with taste and style, a few have managed, he says, to maintain their hold on musical practice, and they are the ones that he deals with in the following pages of the chapter.

First he lists the *Accent* (otherwise *Vorschlag* or *port de voix*), which is done by touching very gently and "quasi-twice" the upper or lower neighbor pitch before sounding the principal tone (par. 20). A "single" *Accent* is very short and takes up only very little, a "double" *Accent* one-half, of the length of the following tone. The vocal *Accent* must be so gently executed and slurred that the two pitches seem to blend into one (par. 22). This explanation does not seem to favor a distinct, accented-downbeat execution since in that case the two pitches would be clearly distinguishable. For such a stepwise-moving *Accent* Mattheson refers to plentiful examples in textbooks, but he offers "approximate" models for leaping ones. Thus in example 14.1, (a) may be rendered as in (b), and (c) as in (d), but only approximately ("ungefehr") since ornaments "can hardly be expressed by notation." He then gives a specimen of a *Nachschlag* that he calls *Überschlag,* (ex. 14.2) where the written example (a) is sung as (b).

Example 14.1.   J. Mattheson, *Der vollkommene Capellmeister*,
    examples of *Accent*

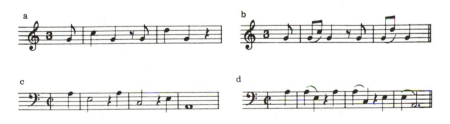

Example 14.2.   J. Mattheson, *Der vollkommene Capellmeister,*
example of *Überschlag*

In discussing vibrato, Mattheson mistakenly believes that it involves oscillations only of intensity (par. 27–29). Such is certainly the case with the tremulant stop of the organ, which he cites as proof, and with bow vibrato of strings and *Bebung* on the clavichord; but the string vibrato produced by shaking the finger of the left hand on the string, and the common vocal vibrato, are (as is easily verified today by electronic means) primarily oscillations of pitch.

Mattheson defines the trill (*trillo* for the long, *trilletto* for the short type) in the usual way as fast alternations of two neighbor tones (par. 30). He gives no model because, he says, the grace is well known (par. 41).[2] French singers, he tells us, use slow alternations, the Italians, very fast ones (par. 30). Either will occasionally start the trill with a long held tone on either pitch (a *tenuta* or *tenue,* respectively) and hence prepare the trill with either a long appoggiatura or a sustained main tone. He further illustrates ascending trill chains and expresses pleasure at having devised this term ("cadena di trilli" or "Trill-Kette"). His explanation that the individual links of the chain must connect so as to sound like one continuous trill (par. 37) that rises several degrees makes it clear that the trills have to start with their main tones because only then can the effect of a continuous trill be achieved. A *tenuta* on the main tone, as shown in example 14.3a, can be modified into the *ribattuta* of 14.3b, whose gradual acceleration leads into a long trill.

Example 14.3a.   J. Mattheson, *Der vollkommene Capellmeister,*
example of *tenuta*

Example 14.3b.   J. Mattheson, *Der vollkommene Capellmeister,*
example of *ribattuta*

Mattheson further lists the *groppo* and illustrates it in rising and falling form as shown in example 14.4, in (a) and (b). Some Italians called this grace a *circolo,* some Germans a *Kugel* (ball) because it could be made to roll like a ball. The *circolo mezzo* or *Halb-Circkel* shown in (c) is closely related, except that in Mattheson's models it moves two pitches up or down before turning around to form the half circle. This grace, he says, is best used on a cadence or phrase ending.

Example 14.4. J. Mattheson, *Der vollkommene Capellmeister,*
a = *groppo*, ascending; b = *groppo*, descending;
c = *groppo* with *circolo mezzo*

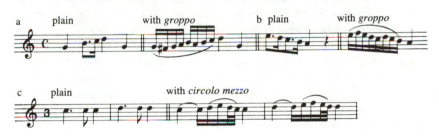

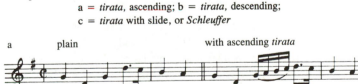

The *tirata* is a fast, scalewise—interbeat—connection between two pitches from a fifth to an octave apart. Mattheson stresses the need for speed and considers the term ill used by Brossard for a leisurely progression. Specimens are shown in example 14.5 (a) and (b). Furthermore, he shows the slide (*Schleuffer*) as a "small *tirata*" from the third above or below and illustrates it as in (c). In contrast to the interbeat *tirata* the grace is placed on the beat.

Example 14.5. J. Mattheson, *Der vollkommene Capellmeister,*
a = *tirata*, ascending; b = *tirata*, descending;
c = *tirata* with slide, or *Schleuffer*

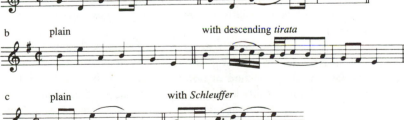

What he calls *Durchgänge* are *Nachschlag*-type pitches added as suffixes
to a note as shown in example 14.6.

Example 14.6.   J. Mattheson, *Der vollkommene Capellmeister,*
                example of *Durchgänge*

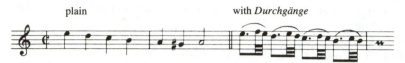

For the vocal mordent Mattheson explains and illustrates the single-alterna-
tion type and stresses the need for the utmost speed, which will give the impression of the three pitches merging into a single sound. The speed is the reason
why he makes no attempt to divide the two ornamental notes into the measure.
Example 14.7 shows two distinct types: one at the start of a note and the other
as a *Nachschlag*-type suffix to an ascending appoggiatura (a *port de voix*).
Again he stresses the inadequacy of notation for suggesting ornament execution.

Example 14.7.   J. Mattheson, *Der vollkommene Capellmeister,*
                examples of vocal mordent

Finally he mentions the *acciaccatura,* as explained by Gasparini and
Heinichen: the simultaneous striking but quick release of a pitch one step below
that of the principal tone. Mattheson has little use for it. It occurs, he says, only
on the keyboard, in thorough-bass accompaniment, and causes many an impu-
rity of harmony.

Mattheson passed in review most of the "small" ornaments that he felt had
more than temporary significance. He showed symbols only for the trill and the
Accent. For the other ornaments the printer may have lacked the necessary types
or, more likely, Mattheson expected them to be improvised. In a later (the
penultimate) chapter he touches briefly upon the arpeggio, *passaggi,* and diminutions (p. 477, par. 56–59).

The importance of Mattheson's writings on performance lies less in the
illumination of specific details, however enlightening some of these glimpses
are, but in his basic aesthetic posture of opposing the tyranny of rules. Much
stiffness and outright unmusicality in today's performances of early music is
due to a far too literal interpretation of rules found in old treatises. Most of their
authors probably never meant to be interpreted so literally and with so little

imagination, but they mostly failed to say so, and this failure opened the door to widespread modern misinterpretations. Mattheson did say so, and again and again he returned with the refrain that rules are relative, not absolute, that interpretation is a matter of taste and thus subject to change, and that models of ornaments are only very inadequate approximations. In thus articulating what others left unsaid, he made what may be his greatest contribution to our quest for historical correctness. It behooves all modern theorists and practitioners of historical performance to engrave in their consciousness Mattheson's words: "The rule of nature, in music, is nothing but the ear."

Notes

1. *Melotheta* (dated Hamburg, 1721; autograph MS, Deutsche Staatsbibliothek, East Berlin), part 4, sec. iii, par. 9.

2. Mattheson's criticism of Printz for defining *trillo* as tone repetition is unjustified; use of the term in this meaning was frequent among seventeenth-century theorists and was usually contrasted with *tremolo* for the regular trill.

15

Notes on the Violin Sonatas of Bach and Handel

The following essay was written for program notes. It is included here because it deals, however briefly, with an important problem of accompaniment and touches other performance questions as well.

Bach and Handel were born in the same year, 1685, within a short distance from each other in the German heartland. Their names are always paired as the two gigantic figures that represent the culmination of a style period now commonly called the Baroque. But their musical personalities are as different as their life stories, so well known to most music lovers. The two sets of six violin and harpsichord sonatas faithfully reflect the vast differences between the two masters.

Handel's sonatas have spirited fast movements often derived from the dance, slow movements of beguiling sensuous beauty straight out of Italian opera, and fugal movements written with virtuosic abandon that never smack of effort or learnedness. The harmonies are simple, the forms compact and easy to grasp and everything has a luminous sound. There are no problems for the listener.

Bach's sonatas make greater demands on the listener. Their harmony, melody, counterpoint, and even rhythm are more complex, and their forms, by virtue of their greater length alone, not always easily grasped. In part, but only in part, these differences stem from contrasting compositional techniques for the two sets of sonatas.

The Handel Sonatas

Handel's sonatas are written on two staves for violin and figured bass. This standard setting—often without figures—for countless "solo" sonatas of the

This article originally appeared in *American String Teacher* (Summer 1982): 26–27. Reprinted by permission of the publisher.

Baroque usually involved both a harpsichord that "realized" the bass, i.e., filled out the harmonies indicated or implied by the bass, and a bass melody instrument: a cello, gamba, or a bassoon that doubled the bass line. Such doubling was often indicated because the bass, as genuine melodic line, was a full-fledged counterpart to the melody "solo" instrument. But if the harpsichord has a strong, sonorous low register (or if a modern piano is used), such reinforcement can be dispensed with. For the D-Major Sonata, the only one for which an autograph survived, Handel wrote as title *Sonata a Violino solo e Cembalo* and this title alone would seem to vindicate performance without a reinforcing bass instrument.

We do not know when the sonatas were written. Three of the six were published in Amsterdam in 1724. These three and two more appeared interspersed in a collection of twelve sonatas for flute, recorder, violin, and oboe, published in 1732 by Walsh in London (Handel's chief publisher) as op. 1. The sixth, the above-mentioned Sonata in D Major, probably the finest of the set, was included only in the complete Handel edition from the end of the nineteenth century.

The six sonatas are all in the Italian style, modeled after Corelli and more specifically after the latter's "church sonatas" (*sonate da chiesa*) with their typical four-movement form of which the first and third are slow and songful, the second fast and in fugal style, the fourth usually in the character of a gigue or another fast dance. The slow-fast-slow-fast design is common to all six sonatas, but only two, the D-Major and the first A-Major (op. 1, no. 3), have a fugal second movement. Also thoroughly Italian is Handel's method of writing adagios in unfinished form. They were not meant to be played as written: performers of the time were jealous of their privilege of adding florid embellishment to the basic melodic line. Thus Handel's—like Corelli's or other Italian masters'—often austere lines of an adagio do not mirror noble simplicity, but are a melodic skeleton to be fleshed out by the performer, who thus becomes a partner in the creative process.

The Bach Sonatas

Bach's sonatas are an entirely different matter. They may have been composed during his years as court Capellmeister in Cöthen (1717–23), which saw the production of the greatest part of his chamber music, but recent research favors a later Leipzig origin. The sonatas were written for violin and harpsichord obbligato, meaning that the keyboard part was fully written out and the two instruments treated as equal partners. Bach's first five sonatas derived their slow-fast-slow-fast pattern also from the Italian *sonate da chiesa,* but characteristically, *all* of his fast movements (as well as some slow ones) are fugal. The typical texture is that of a trio of three independent and equivalent voices: the harpsichordist's left hand, the right hand, and the violin. There are exceptions which will be pointed out presently. Italian influence is evident, not in Corellian traits as in Handel, but in the driving rhythms of Vivaldi's concerto style that made a lasting impression on Bach ever since he was exposed to it. But Bach did not follow the Italian—and Handelian—procedure of providing only more or less detailed sketches of his adagio movements; he wrote out all the notes he wanted played and none need or ought to be added.

Sonata No. 1 in B Minor

The first movement with its lovely pastoral mood is, in spite of its five-voice writing (much of it moving in thirds or sixths), quite transparent and easily accessible. The sprightly second movement, a genuine trio, combines fugal writing with the ternary ABA form of the Italian da capo aria. Its first four measures offer a performance problem that recurs in other movements and deserves mention because it is widely misunderstood. The theme is announced by the violin, not alone as in a genuine fugue, but attended by the bass. Practically all editors and modern performers "realize" this bass part by filling in harmonies. This was quite certainly not intended. Bach wrote neither figures nor the abbreviation *accomp[agnando]*, which he would have done had he expected a harmonization. Also, by leaving the right hand idle, its entrance with the theme in the fifth measure gains considerably in plasticity. The two lines are self-sufficient, and if left alone they help again to clarify to the listener the onset of the da capo. The third movement is a duet between the violin and the right hand, with the left in the role of an accompanying but melodically moving bass. The fourth movement has the unmistakable imprint of the Vivaldian concerto style.

Sonata No. 2 in A Major

The tender first movement in moderate $\frac{6}{8}$ meter is in strict three-part writing with all three voices equally participating in thematic elaboration. The second movement integrates Italian concerto style, fugal treatment, and the da capo form (ABA). Its B part is climaxed by brilliant violin arpeggios set against the elaboration of the principal theme in the harpsichord. The third movement has the violin and the right hand of the harpsichordist engaged in an enchanting duet in strict canon over the lute-like plucking accompaniment of the left hand. The brilliant last movement is fugal in binary form. Again, the two-part writing at the start should not be thickened by harmonization.

Sonata No. 3 in E Major

Perhaps the most beautiful work of the set, this sonata starts with an Italian-style aria sung by the violin with all the coloraturas written out while the harpsichord is limited to accompaniment. The following jolly fugal movement echoes the spirit of French dance music. Here the theme is announced in the harpsichord and its strict two-part setting confirms that there should be no harmonization for all similar openings. The third movement in C♯ minor, in the form of a passacaglia, starts with the four-measure bass theme that is repeated fifteen times. Over it the violin announces a melody of exquisite tenderness with the right hand of the harpsichord providing a very simple chordal harmonization. Then the roles are reversed: the right hand takes over the melody and the violin harmonizes, whereupon both melody voices join in a duet. The exhilarating last movement in da capo form bears again the clear physiognomy of the concerto style. The B part offers a fascinating contrast in graceful triplet figurations set against binary accompanying figures of the bass. The ensuing rhythmic clashes add a delightful flavor to this section. The suggestion of some editors to eliminate the clashes by "adapting" the accompaniment are based on unconvincing modern theories. (On this subject, see chapter 3 of this volume.)

Sonata No. 4 in C Minor

The first movement is a siciliano lament whose kinship to the famous aria *Erbarme dich* from the St. Matthew Passion has been often noted. The harpsichord is limited to simple accompaniment. The second, fugal movement is very long, vigorous, and rich in invention, but may be somewhat academic. It is followed by an Adagio in E♭, an elegant, serene aria for violin with simple accompaniment. The last movement again shows clear traits of the Italian concerto style.

Sonata No. 5 in F Minor

The profound meditation of the first movement makes for a majestic start. The center of gravity lies in the harpsichord with its consistent writing in three eloquent parts to which the violin adds a fourth voice, first hesitatingly, later in full commitment. The second movement returns to strict three-part texture. The next adagio is unique in its absence of any distinct melody; its musical substance, as if in premonition of Chopinesque mood pieces, resides solely in shifting harmonies. The ever-recurring alternating thirty-second note figures of the harpsichord—scale-derived in the right hand, arpeggios in the left—were enlivened from original sixteenth notes in the earlier version of this piece. The last movement, Vivace in $\frac{3}{8}$ meter, concludes the sonata in a whirlwind of chromaticism, complex counterpoint, and rapidly shifting harmonies.

Sonata No. 6 in G Major

Bach has taken considerable pains over this work: three different versions of it exist. The first and the last have five movements, which is most unusual, yet the second version had even six! In its final form the sequence of movements is fast-slow-fast-slow-fast, whereby the center movement is an extended binary allegro for harpsichord solo. The first movement, with its impetuous rhythmic drive, is again indebted to the Italian concerto. The splendor of this movement is contrasted with the dark colors of the two elegiac slow movements and well balanced by a last one that, alone in the whole set, evokes the spirit of a gigue.

A reinforcement of the bass line by a gamba or cello, as recommended by an important editor, is not advisable. Considering the full equivalence of both hands in almost every movement, a reinforcement of the left would result in an unjustifiable imbalance of the parts.

Part Five

Book Reviews

16

Peter Brown: *Performing Haydn's "Creation"*

A review of A. Peter Brown's Performing Haydn's "Creation": Reconstructing the Earliest Renditions *(Bloomington: Indiana University Press, 1986).*

The early music movement is closely identified with the search for "authenticity" of performance. The concept of authenticity is obscure, almost impossible to define, and its very existence is questioned by a number of eminent musicians and scholars. Yet even without any reference to "authenticity," few will deny that the original performance conditions of any old masterwork are a matter of intense interest. These conditions varied from favorable to miserable depending on number and competence of the performers, the accuracy of the parts, the availability of rehearsal time, and the knowledge and ability of the director. But whenever the composer himself was at the helm or otherwise involved in the performance, an attempt to reconstruct what happened is a challenge of endless fascination. In most cases we know very few facts, and in attempting reconstruction must resort to much guesswork to fill the many voids that surround the few certainties.

Among great works of the eighteenth century, Haydn's *Creation* occupies a perhaps unique position in both the favorable performance conditions and in the relative wealth of information about first performances under Haydn's active direction. It is Professor Brown's great achievement to have unearthed and brought to light more facts about the earliest performances of this work than we may have about any other major composition of the era. The reason for the wealth of information is clear: Haydn was at the pinnacle of his international fame, and the eagerly awaited first performance in Vienna on 28 April 1798 was a musical and social event of the first magnitude. Its enormous success led to many repeats. In Vienna alone, forty-five performances took place through early 1810. In some of the most fascinating pages of his book, Brown records

This article originally appeared in *Historical Performance, the Journal of Early Music America* (Spring 1988): 30–32. Reprinted by permission of the publisher.

these performances and lists, along with the dates and places, the sponsors, the principals, the presumable number of performers, and the literature about each event. We learn that Haydn himself conducted the first fourteen of these public concerts and several of the later ones. For at least ten performances Salieri sat at the keyboard, and he was the conductor for many of the later events. For most of these we also know the concertmaster and the solo singers, and can gather from their prominent names that the finest artists available were involved. Whereas in the London concerts of his symphonies Haydn sat at the keyboard, and was at best on an equal footing with Salomon, who did the actual directing from his concertmaster post (Haydn's role was likely more ornamental than executive), for the *Creation* the functions of the leaders seemed to have undergone a mutation towards the modern system: Haydn, the conductor, with either stick or roll, assumed the musical leadership, while concertmaster and keyboard player were cast in the role of assistants, of subconductors.

Of great interest are contemporary reports on the number of participants and their seating arrangement. The reports on the numbers vary, but the figure of about 180 appears most often, and Brown calculates that 120 of this total referred to the orchestra and about 60 to the chorus. What seems today a lack of balance was probably largely rectified by the placement of the chorus in front of the orchestra. The large number of instrumentalists is a further indication that the obsession of our modern "authenticists" with chamber-orchestra sizes for the classical masters is unjustified. (Mozart was enchanted when he played symphonies with an orchestra of 40 violins, 10 violas, 8 celli, 10 basses, doubled woodwinds, and 6 bassoons, as related in a letter to his father of 11 April 1781.) Most orchestras were small, not by artistic choice of the composer, but by the force of circumstances: no larger forces were available. In a performance, under Haydn's direction, of the *Creation* at the Esterházy Palace in Eisenstadt in September 1800 there were, according to pay lists, no more than 8 singers and some 24 instrumentalists involved. Clearly this was by no means Haydn's preferred arrangement.

As to the placement of the large forces in Vienna, we have a report that is specific enough to ring true: Brown quotes (p. 29) Johan Berwald on a performance of 19 March 1799. The stage, he wrote, was in the form of an amphitheater. On the lowest level was the pianoforte player, surrounded by the vocal soloists, the chorus, a violoncello, and a double bass. On the next higher level "stood Haydn himself with his conductor's baton." On the next level were the violins: the first on the left, the second on the right (an arrangement that was still adhered to by Toscanini), the lower strings in the middle with more double basses in the wings. On the next level the woodwinds, and at the very top the trumpets, timpani and trombones. (H. C. Robbins Landon, in his *Haydn,* vol. 3, p. 53, reports a similar arrangement in London oratorio performances in the 1790s and believes it to have been the model for the premiere of the *Creation*.)

From the original sources we learn that the woodwinds and horns were organized in three groups as "Harmonie" 1, 2, and 3 respectively, of which the first group (of one pair each) was presumably the solo group, the other two groups joining for tutti passages, which in at least one of the original parts are carefully marked to this effect. Solo and tutti passages are distinguished even for the timpani, implying at least two players.

This brings us to the question of the sources. Haydn's autograph does not survive, but three copyists' scores are extant that Brown with good reason characterizes as "authentic" because one of them ("Tonkünstler") was Haydn's conducting score and contains autograph cues. This is the score with solo-tutti indications. A second score ("Estate") contains numerous corrections in Haydn's hand, and a third served as the engraver's copy for the first edition of the full score, published by Haydn himself in 1800. There are, in addition, three sets of parts, which Brown for similar reasons also considers to be authentic.

The original print served as the basis for the Mandyczewski edition, published by Breitkopf & Härtel (1920) and widely used in modern performances. I am in no position to judge how closely this edition agrees with the original print. However, in at least one instance—the articulation of a few passages in No. 3, where Brown (pp. 64–66) shows discrepant patterns in the first edition and in six other authentic sources—we see that Mandyczewski altered the bowing patterns of the original print in order, so it seems, to make them conform to Riemann's theories of upbeat phrasing. This one example makes one wonder in how many other instances the modern editor may have tried to "improve" on Haydn's text.

Interestingly, Haydn did not use the original print for his performances, but rather parts and scores that had undergone a number of emendations. These changes mostly involve refinements of orchestration, such as the addition of bass trombone and contrabassoon in certain passages (listed by Brown, p. 26) or the reorchestration of the famous sunrise passage in the accompanied recitative of No. 13. The listing of a few other such discrepancies is scattered within the chapter. It would have been helpful to have a complete tabulation of those instances where, as Brown puts it, Haydn "kept tinkering with the music" in the course of the early performances.

One of these discrepancies is found in an unusual notation in the parts written by Haydn's personal copyist (and servant) Elssler in measures 4–7 from the "Chaos," as shown below (ex. 16.1). According to Landon, these were the original performance parts, and Brown considers this notation of slur, dynamic *messa di voce* and an apparent staccato mark as "the most vexing interpretive question found in any of the authentic sources."

Example 16.1.   F. J. Haydn, *Creation*, "Chaos," mm. 4–7

Landon interprets this sign as an attempt to fix the exact middle point of the hairpin symbol for a crescendo-decrescendo combination. He speculates that Haydn did not include it in the first edition for fear it might be misunderstood. Brown thinks it might represent a kind of *Luftpause* before the beginning of the diminuendo (p. 32). Neither of these explanations is very convincing. A *Luftpause* within a legato slur is highly unlikely; and as to the middle point of a *messa de voce*, it is rarely a problem and its exactness hardly ever essential. I would like to suggest another answer: the vertical dash was used throughout the eighteenth century, from Bach to Haydn and Mozart, frequently in accentual meaning (to take the place of the > sign that was not yet available until Haydn used it in the last decade of the century). In our example it probably meant a short and sharp accent at the divide between the hairpins. A *sforzando* would have been too violent and too broad; the vertical dash stood for a quick accentuation, produced by a sudden increase of bow pressure followed by its immediate release.

Concerning ornamentation, Brown offers interesting testimonials about Haydn's aversion to unnecessary ornamental additions. Among them is a statement by Albert Christoph Dies (in his *Biographische Nachrichten von Joseph Haydn,* [Vienna, 1810]) relating Haydn's personal report that Mademoiselle Fischer "sang her part with the greatest delicacy and so accurately, that she did not permit herself the least unsuitable addition." And Therese Saal, who sang the soprano part of the *Creation* many times under Haydn's direction, was praised in a journal for her "simple, sincere, and appropriate delivery" and her judicious abstention from runs and embellishments so often interpolated by others.

Some additions are of course needed, such as cadential fermata embellishments. Two of the sets of parts include a few such embellishments penciled in, and they are appropriately brief. Their design is sometimes perfectly fine, but in at least two of the reproduced instances from the "Tonkünstler" parts, they are inelegant and un-Haydnish (in No. 30, mm. 115 and 218, reproduced in Brown, pp. 50 and 51). Brown cautions that these specific parts were used for performances throughout the nineteenth century; the interpolations could have been written at any time during that period. These two, whenever written, are quite certainly not exemplary.

Regarding bowing and articulation, our current concern with consistency and uniformity of bowing was unknown at the time. In fact, prior to World War

II few European orchestras practiced such uniformity until Toscanini enforced it at La Scala. Some conductors actively opposed it, among them Richard Strauss, who believed that better tonal results were achieved when the choice of bowing was left to individual preferences of players. With that in mind, we must not be surprised to hear that "careful editing of the bowings was of little concern to Haydn" (p. 62). Brown tabulates different bowing patterns in seven sources for two passages in No. 3 (referred to above). In view of this lack of uniformity we should realize that exactness of articulation can be important in certain cases and relatively unimportant in others. In a basic legato context, for instance, the exact disposition of the bowings can be a minor matter. Consequently we find in the *Creation,* as in many other classical works, inconsistencies where consistency is immaterial.

Brown's attempts to provide guidelines for such inconsistencies, however, seem neither clear nor convincing. In discussing the discrepant bowings of No. 3 he says, *inter alia:* "Articulatory irregularities with regard to large-dimension repetitions in the case of a more generalized articulation are usually parallel, and if the articulation is more detailed, it must be carefully considered." I have read this sentence several times and still do not understand it.

Another principle formulated, "The repetition of the same pitch in values of a quarter note or larger when occurring over a bar line is often meant to be tied," is questionable and dangerous. While composers, Haydn among them, may often have been nonchalant about the niceties of consistency regarding slurs, ties are another matter altogether: they affect not only melody but also rhythm and are an essential structural element. I cannot remember having seen a case in, say, Bach or Mozart, where a presumably intended tie was not so marked. Naturally, even a genius can stumble, but I would think that one would need telling evidence from either parallel spots or simultaneous parts before introducing an unmarked tie.

Regarding tempo, Brown holds that Haydn's preferences were overall on the fast side. This is perfectly possible, but the evidence Brown cites does not seem to be sufficiently substantive for such a generalized statement. Landon criticizes modern conductors for taking Haydn allegros too fast, and he may have a case. But then there is hardly an aspect of performance practice more difficult to pin down than tempo.

The tempo indications in the *Creation* are remarkably consistent—so Brown affirms—in all sources (a few exceptions are listed on p. 72). He makes a good point about the tempo of the "Representation of the Chaos." Marked Largo ¢, it is usually taken at an extremely dragging pace. Modern conductors are bewildered by the frequent combination in the Classical period of largo or adagio and ¢. It seems incongruous, since many of these adagios cannot reasonably be beaten in two (like, say, the introduction to Mozart's great E♭ Symphony), and consequently the sign is ignored as meaningless. The sign must not be ignored. It did not mean to beat in two, but rather that the piece should be rendered at the fast end of what is still within the character of an adagio or largo (which can be less slow than an adagio). The "Chaos" should be beaten in four, paced as in an andante con moto to give the triplet arpeggio figures a *leggiero* character. The *alla breve* sign thus finds a sensible interpretation.

Brown's monograph contains within its small size a wealth of often fascinating material. It vividly depicts the complexity of the source situation, given the intricate relationship between several sets of parts and several manuscript scores as well as the first printed score, all of which were closely linked to the early performances of the oratorio under Haydn's direction. Considering that some emendations by Haydn, and others of uncertain origin, were entered into certain but not other sources, some before, some after the publication of the first edition, we have the unusually confusing situation of several "authentic" sources that do not agree with one another. We cannot therefore speak of a definitive version. To have analyzed these intricate relationships and laid them out with insightful clarity is the considerable merit of this book, which should be studied by every conductor of this work and by every musicologist engaged in source studies of any kind.

17

Anthony Newman: *Bach and the Baroque*

A review of Anthony Newman's Bach and the Baroque: A Performing Guide to
Baroque Music with Special Emphasis on the Music of J. S. Bach *(New York,
1985)*.

Anthony Newman is well known as a splendid keyboard performer who can
dazzle his audiences with brilliant virtuosic feats. He can, and often does, play
faster than perhaps any of his colleagues, and shows occasionally other signs
of eccentricity. Yet he is a fine and sensitive musician who has unquestionably
a great deal to offer his students. Wishing to share his experience, knowledge
and insights with performers at large, he wrote a guidebook to Baroque, and
more specifically, Bach performance. As anybody knows, the subject is emi-
nently topical in this age where the search for "authenticity"—whatever that
may mean—has become an obsessive pursuit. The subject is also a thicket of
controversy and unanswered questions where any new reliable guide would
deserve to be enthusiastically welcomed. I regret to say that those who expect
this latest entry into the thorny field to provide such reliable guidance will be
disappointed.

Not that the book is without merit. A man with Newman's keen intellect
and rich performance experience can be expected to have some valuable observations to impart. He does live up to this expectation and we have reason to
applaud some helpful contributions. There is, however, a negative side to the
picture that, alas, seems to outweigh its positive counterpart. The negative side
has various aspects, many of which can be gathered under the label of careless
scholarship.

To start on a positive note: at the very outset of the book Newman has
some astute things to say about the danger of biases formed by hearing a work,

This article originally appeared in *The American Organist* (April 1987): 40–43. Reprinted by permission of the publisher.

or a passage, played in a certain manner and about the ensuing resistance to a performance that deviates from the familiar.

Valuable, too, is the reprint on pages 30–36 of an extended passage from Kirnberger, Bach's student, about the relationship of meter and tempo, including his discussion of circumstances where an alternation of heaviness and lightness applies not just to beats but to whole measures. Newman asks how strong and weak measures can be recognized. In a thought-provoking chapter he expounds a theory that makes some good points and illustrates them with Bach's *Italian Concerto*.

Interesting and valuable is the chapter on the dance, dance music and the suite, written "with Richard Troeger." The chapter deals with the actual steps and movements involved in the various dances. The information is interesting but only of relative pertinence to instrumental dances. Mattheson had already pointed to the considerable differences between actual dances, and "play-dances" and "song-dances." Still, though Bach's dance pieces were often highly stylized and removed from the actual dance, an awareness of the latter's origin is of help in grasping its basic character. The table of dance tempi (derived from metronome-like devices) was taken from the modern studies by Borrel and Sachs. Most of the tempi shown are surprisingly fast.

The chapter on symbolism, written "with Marion Shepp," gives a good summary of the findings of previous writers on both melodic symbolism and on Bach's fascinating, mysterious involvement with the medieval mysticism of number symbolism. Some new items were added to those previously discussed.

The chapter on organ, harpsichord, and clavichord, written with the help of Laurette Goldberg, pleads for tracker-action instruments, discusses specific problems of American organs, and, very interestingly, contrasts the two main types of German Baroque organs, the Schnitger and Silbermann types. It contains helpful remarks on the harpsichord and on lute playing.

Newman takes a very reasonable and courageous stance about playing Bach on the modern piano which, he says, "can bring out lines in a way that the harpsichord cannot" (p. 202). One could add in support of this thought that what matters for Bach is line and not tone color. Had he been concerned about tone color, he would have prescribed registrations for the organ which, as every organist knows, he hardly ever did.

When we turn to the main subject of the book, the problems of performance, there is, unhappily, hardly a chapter that does not invite criticism. So much is questionable that it is impossible to deal with all of it short of writing a whole book. Not that anybody has or will ever have all the answers; and whoever might claim to know how exactly Bach or any other master of the period intended to be interpreted is either touchingly naive or is a charlatan. But it is possible to look at theories on performance and recognize that they are wrongly argued or based on faulty assumptions. And that is where the many weaknesses of this book can be found. For reasons of space alone, I shall limit my comments to a few important subjects.

The chapter on "Tactus, Pulse, Beat and Time Signatures" that contains the mentioned extensive quote from Kirnberger is marred by a near-total confusion of terms and concepts. The introduction of the term "tactus" for Bach and his contemporaries is pointless. It referred, in mensural notation, to a basic beat, a "normal" beat of about M.M. = 70 that was presumably valid as a solid guide-post around 1500 but began to lose its solidity in the course of the sixteenth century, when directors chose and changed the beat according to their sense of the music. In the eighteenth century, the term was long since forgotten. Worse still, Newman first equates "tactus" with pulse and beat: "Tactus, sometimes called pulse or beat" (p. 24), when later in example 22 or 25 he clearly distinguishes between them by explaining the beat as "tactus and a half." Here he meant a faster beat than 70, namely 90–120 (p. 35); hence, I would think, a smaller (minus one-third), not a larger tactus. See also the tabulation of meters, beats and tactus on pages 40–41. It is all totally confusing. A $\frac{3}{4}$ signature with sixteenths as the fastest notes is not necessarily "fast, to very fast" (p. 40). Not to speak of those works where an adagio or largo is marked, there are many unmarked ones in $\frac{3}{4}$ that surely are not lively, such as the organ Passacaglia, the violin Chaconne, the E-Minor Prelude preceding the "Wedge Fugue," the Chorale Prelude *Wir danken dir, Herr Jesu Christ* (BWV 623) and many others.

The ideas expressed in the chapter on "Irregular Beat Alternations" are highly suspect. When Bach divides a virtuoso passage between the two hands and indicates the division by patterns of beaming, as for instance in measures 65–67 of the *Chromatic Fantasy* (see Newman's ex. 83) Newman sees in these beaming patterns a clue to phrasing and accentuation when in fact they were a sort of silent fingering that served to facilitate the execution, but were not meant to be heard. In fact, the suggested execution that phrases according to recurring melodic designs weakens the passages by making ordinary what is extraordinary: the power of passages like these lies in their very irregularity, in the very conflict of melodic design and rhythmic disposition that gives the repeated melodic figure each time a new physiognomy. This is true of example 82 from the D-Minor Concerto, and more so of example 83 from the *Chromatic Fantasy*. To melodically regularize such passages amounts to a triumph of pedantry over poetic imagination.

When we come to questions of inequality, of fingerings, of overdotting, the so-called French overture style and of ornamentation, I have to overcome my repugnance to tooting my own horn. I have written at length on these matters and have taken issue with the very authorities that Newman relies on. I believe that without undue arrogance I can say that an author dealing with these questions with a scholarly pretense ought to have acquainted himself with my pertinent writings on these subjects as well as with David Fuller's articles in the *The*

New Grove. In 1985 it was not sufficient any more to see in Sol Babitz, Michael Collins and John O'Donnell the ultimate authorities without being guilty of incomplete research. (For several years my main writings on matters of rhythm have been conveniently available in *Essays in Performance Practice.*)

In the chapter on "Inequality and Note Holding," Newman offers a variation on Babitz's theme song that the old keyboard fingerings produced an involuntary unevenness and that therefore such unevenness must have been intended by the composer. The argument is fallacious since any involuntary unevenness is due to technical defect, not to artistic intent. (I have dealt with this question in *Essays,* pages 42–48, and plan in the near future to return to the subject in greater detail.) Newman contends that fast playing of a string of notes on the piano produces dynamic, but not rhythmic inequality; on the harpsichord, by contrast, "rhythmic unevenness of adjacent notes . . . independent of the technical proficiency of the performer" (p. 104). This does not have to be so. Such unintended inequality is, here too, simply a matter of defective skill and Newman would be the first to be able to play fast notes with perfect equality. Also it makes little sense that a performer who can play fast notes on the piano with rhythmic equality should be unable to do so on the organ or harpsichord. The very idea that virtuoso passages like, say, the grandiose sweep of measures 3–8 in the G-Minor Fantasia and Fugue are to be rendered as a series of uneven pairs of notes is nothing short of grotesque.

Newman further confuses matters by mixing five different kinds of inequality under one heading. Apart from unevenness caused by technical incompetence (the would-be "Scotch snaps") he lists four more: as second type he presents Caccini's famous illustration of rubato singing (from 1602), whereby equally written notes are rhythmically manipulated in various manners, while remaining within the beat. There is neither any regularity nor any convention involved; the rhythmic freedoms are arbitrarily chosen by artistic judgment.

Third is the genuine convention of the French *notes inégales* which regularizes inequality according to meter—note-value relationships (e.g., eighth notes in 3-meter, sixteenth notes in C meter for passages that move predominantly stepwise). In such contexts the long-short, generally mild unevenness came close to a stylistic requirement. Incidentally, Newman's example 121 from "Dom Bedos" (the actual writer was Père Engramelle) is incorrect: the second pair of eighth notes is played like the first, not at half its duration. Incorrect too is his statement that sixteenths or eighths are uneven in C meter: after Nivers in 1665, all following writers insist that eighths in C are always strictly even. Moreover it is not true that "Bedos" and Couperin specifically state that dissonant pairs on a "good" beat should be played short-long (p. 107). Neither says anything to that effect. Couperin simply has a notational symbol: a dot over the second of two notes under a slur that indicates its emphasis. (He quit using it after the second book of clavecin pieces.) It does not apply to notes not so marked and Engramelle (including "Bedos") makes no mention of short-long inequality.

Fourth, Newman refers to several writers who suggest that the first note under a slur is to be slightly lengthened. He is mistaken in saying that Leopold Mozart excepted from this rule notes that are in a rhythmically weak position. On the contrary, among the illustrations of contexts for this rule Mozart shows (chap. 7, pt. 2, par. 5) no fewer than nine where the respective notes fall on a subdivision of the beat, the weakest possible placement in the measure.

Fifth, the author offers up a whole series of alleged proofs for inequality in Bach that have been presented by others several times before but are by now damaged goods: I am confident to have disposed of their evidence value many years ago. There is no point in repeating all the arguments, and I shall limit myself to declaring that the would-be evidence of example 123 from the B-Minor Mass (Domine Deus), example 125 from the *Trauerode*, example 134 from the Magnificat and example 135 from the D-Minor Clavier Concerto is strictly chimerical, while referring to my *Essays*, pages 48–53 and 61–64. Readers interested in the matter of uneven notes might wish to read my whole chapters 3, 4 and 5. My advice would be not to apply inequality to Bach, Handel, the German organists, nor to the Italians. Limit a mild long-short inequality in its proper context to French masters only.

The chapters on dotted notes and the overture style suffer from the same failure to keep abreast of scholarly developments. As main proof for what is commonly called the French overture style Newman adduces again a piece of shopworn evidence: the comparison of the two versions of Bach's French Overture in C Minor and in B Minor (Newman, exx. 140 and 143). Some fine scholars had fallen into the trap before by seeing in the later, rhythmically sharpened B-minor version an "orthographic variant" of the C-minor that is supposed to sound exactly the same. The theory is untenable. B minor is, after all, not an "orthographic variant" of C minor and Bach, who revised countless of his works, had a perfect right to choose another rhythm along with another key. A careful measure-by-measure analysis of the two versions reveals the utter absurdity of the theory of identity. The B-minor version is as little an "orthographic variant" of the C-minor one as the *Leonora* Overture No. 3 is of *Leonora* No. 2. With it this "proof" for the "overture style" vanishes into thin air. (For a thorough discussion of the overture style see in my *Essays*, chaps. 6–10 and especially 10.) *Do not overdot the E-flat Prelude of* Clavierübung *III!*

The chapter of triplets is perhaps the most misleading of all. It starts inauspiciously with a quote from a Mr. Banner, an obscure Paduan organist about whose musical competence nothing is known. Michael Collins discovered a manuscript treatise of his in which he delivers himself of the opinion that two notes against three is "one of the most forbidden musical situations." Like Collins before him, Newman accepts Banner as supreme arbiter of musical taste for his age, and his stern verdict as binding law. Thus Newman writes (p. 125) that "two against three ... did not belong to the musical vocabulary of the period." The statement is simply not true. Binary-ternary conflicts never ceased to occur, and to be intended, in the music of the last four or five hundred years. However, the question of both triplets and rhythmic conflicts is complicated and certainly not answerable with the help of Banner's Law. Triplets were always meant to be rendered literally, though at all times to the present performers, including some famous virtuosi, often squared them when it was easier to do so. As to rhythmic conflicts, they were often meant to be rendered as written, but in Bach's time, due mostly to notational deficiencies, there were instances where an assimilation was sometimes certainly, sometimes probably, intended. Such assimilation took place always from binary to ternary rhythms, not the other way around. In an attempt to sort out these complexities I have written an essay that by now has come out in the sixth volume of the *Music Forum* and is reprinted here as chapter 3. For cases of intended conflict I can refer here only to one irrefutable example, the Chorale from Bach's Cantata No. 105. Here no master juggler, no magician can resolve the magnificent clash of twos against threes. There are many more instances of such intended clashes; Bach clearly did not bow to the authority of Banner's Law.

Newman, leaning on Collins, affirms that under certain circumstances triplets, dactyls and anapests can be used interchangeably, meaning that Bach often wrote a triplet when he meant a dactyl or anapest and vice versa, even where no rhythmic clash might serve as pretext for such manipulation. Are we truly to assume that Bach played witless teasing games with his performers, expecting to get a good laugh at those who did not see through such masquerade? Newman does not limit such masquerades to three-note figures. In his examples 145 and 146 he demonstrates how Bach's binary gigues from the first French Suite and the fifth Partita and even the horn call at the opening of the first Brandenburg Concerto are to be ternarized. All these suggestions are misjudgments. Binary gigues are minorities in the eighteenth century, but they have a venerable ancestry, going back to English virginalists, French lutenists (the Gautiers among others), masters like Froberger, Schmelzer, Biber, Georg Muffat, Poglietti, and many others who used binary next to ternary designs. Why should not Bach do so, he who took great freedoms with dances, many of which are much more "in the spirit of ... " or "in the tempo of ..." than in conformance with the textbook types. There is no need to sanitize his binary gigues by pressing them with clumsy force into a ternary mold. Bach knew what he wanted and wrote it out accordingly.

Then in order, maybe, to compensate the binary realm for its losses to ternary aggression, Newman allows the reverse operation: in the fifth Brandenburg Concerto at the first entrance of the soloists (ex. 148), the triplets in the right hand of the clavier set in measure 10 against binary sixteenth notes in the left should be played as anapests, and so no doubt the analogous triplets in violin and flute in measures 14–16—all this in order to comply with Banner's Law! So far I have luckily been spared in concert such an all-binary treat.

There are many more statements and discussions in the book that invite critical comment but I think I have made my point; the book contains some valuable sections but those parts that deal with interpretation are severely flawed by incomplete research and careless documentation. It cannot be recommended as a guide to historical performance.

18

Raymond H. Haggh: Translation of Türk's *Klavierschule*

A review of the School of Clavier Playing (Klavierschule) *by Daniel Gottlob Türk. Translated and with introduction and notes by Raymond H. Haggh (Lincoln and London: University of Nebraska Press, 1982).*

One of the many manifestations of the current intense interest in historical performance is the growing list of old treatises that are available in English translation. Türk's voluminous (over 400 pages in the original) *Klavierschule* in its first edition of 1789 is a valuable addition to this list, but should be viewed from the perspective of what it is and what it is not. Basically, the book is a review of North German mid-eighteenth-century theoretical thought on performance and keyboard technique, extended to encyclopedic length by two factors: 1) Türk's compulsive urge to pursue every question to the last detail (even Professor Haggh admits to a pedantic streak in his author), and 2) his remarkable and quite innovative referral to, and discussion of, what previous writers have said on a subject. In this respect it is certainly the most scholarly of all the major eighteenth-century tracts on performance.

Concerning his own ideas, his indebtedness is greatest to C. P. E. Bach and Marpurg, but mostly to the former. Notably the chapters on fingering and the "essential ornaments" are by and large elaborations of what these two authors had to say. As to fingerings, he admits—as does C. P. E. Bach—besides the modern scale pattern, the older manner of crossing over of fingers other than the thumb. In matters of ornaments Türk is, if possible, more severe still about their regimentation than Philipp Emanuel (though he does follow Marpurg in admitting *Nachschläge*).

The most valuable, least derivative, and least dated chapters are the last

---

This article originally appeared in *The American Recorder* (November 1983). Reprinted by permission of the publisher.

two, on extemporaneous ornamentation and execution. There we find very fine discussions of fermata embellishments and cadenzas, and valuable remarks on the problems of phrasing. But for the rest, this is a retrospective work, a fact made apparent almost immediately by the focus not on the fortepiano, not even the harpsichord, but the *clavichord,* which at the time of publication was on the verge of extinction.

From all this we can gather what the book, its date notwithstanding, is emphatically not: it is not a guide to Mozart and Haydn performance (with the possible exception of the last two chapters). If we accept this limitation, its availability in English is to be warmly welcomed.

The translation was a true labor of love. It was done over a period of twelve years, during which Professor Haggh, besides grappling with an old-fashioned vocabulary, did a huge amount of research to provide the text with a thorough underpinning of references to both old and new writers. Embodied in back notes that are intermingled with—but clearly distinguished from—Türk's own, these annotations offer helpful amplifications as well as frequent résumés of theoretical thought on various problems discussed in the text. They greatly enhance the value and usefulness of the publication.

The prose translation is, on the whole, very satisfactory and reads well. I do not claim to have made a word-by-word comparison; I limited myself to some spot checks whenever a passage seemed questionable. In a few of these cases I found minor lapses, where the translator tripped over a hurdle of antiquated German. A single example will have to do. At the beginning of chapter 3, Türk explains why he devotes a whole chapter to the appoggiatura. He writes: "Da es aber Vorschläge von sehr verschiedener Dauer etc. giebt, so dass eine etwas ausführliche Anzeige erfordert wird," which is rendered: "But since appoggiaturas are of very differing durations and require a very detailed notation. . . ." I checked this sentence because I found it confusing. A more precise rendition would be: "But since appoggiaturas are of very differing durations, etc. [the 'etc.' implying additional problems], they call for a somewhat detailed explanation . . ." (hence the devotion of a whole chapter).

Such are minor flaws within a frame of overall competence. What I found more disturbing are infelicitous translations of certain terms. One that bothered me (and maybe should not have) is the unorthodox subdivision of chapters into "parts" (Türk's *Abschnitte*), when traditionally parts are the larger, chapters the smaller units of a book. "Section" would have been a better, and more literal, rendition.

"Termination" for *Nachschlag* is not a happy choice, because the term so pointedly implies an ending, whereas in the overwhelming majority of cases a *Nachschlag* is a connective grace that does not end a phrase but leads into another melody note. Haggh derived the term from Edward Reilly's splendid translation of Quantz, where it is used to denote the suffix of a trill. In that case it is not an ideal choice either, but it is less confusing because the focus is on the way a trill is ended; such focus is absent in all other applications, as shown, for instance, in every example in chapter 3, part 4 of Türk. The reader is advised to substitute mentally the term *Nachschlag* for all occurrences of "termination." (Walter Emery, in his book on Bach's ornaments, naturalized the term, using "nachschlags" as plural, because he found no proper equivalent for it.)

Infelicitous, too, is the rendition of *Vorhalt* as "suspension." Following the example of other theorists (among them Petri), Türk uses this term to designate the long appoggiatura (*veränderliche Vorschlag*). Now a long appoggiatura *that is prepared* and resolves stepwise has the harmonic function of a suspension (though a suspension in the narrower sense is tied over the beat), hence the term would be acceptable in such contexts. But often the appoggiatura enters unprepared (see the start of the example on p. 205 in chap. 15), in which case the term is improper and misleading. "Long appoggiatura" or, to stay with Türk's (and C. P. E. Bach's) terminology, "variable appoggiatura," would have been the better choice.

In another instance, what would seem to be the obvious translation is not an advisable one. Following the example of Kirnberger and his student Schulz, Türk, in his discussion of phrasing, uses the term "Rhythmus" to designate a not clearly specified subdivision of a melody (see on this Haggh's notes 19 and 21 on pp. 506ff.). Understandably, Haggh renders "Rhythmus" as "rhythm." But the concept of rhythm, as it is commonly applied today, is complicated enough that it is ill-advised to introduce a new meaning foreign to its present usage. "Melodic unit" or "phrase subdivision" might have been preferable.

Professor Haggh gives good reasons why he used the first edition, and not the enlarged second one of 1802, for his translation. Still, those who value Türk as theorist would have welcomed an appendix containing some of the more important additions of the later version, in which he makes a number of new references to Haydn and Mozart.

The index, like Türk's, is limited to terms and common expressions. In view of the many theorists mentioned in the notes of both Türk and Professor Haggh, an index of names would have been useful.

The book is well produced (though, surprisingly, with a ragged right margin), and the music examples are well printed. Of the few misprints I found, I want to mention only one because it is misleading. In music example (e) on page 275 the turn is printed with four equal, small thirty-second notes, when the first three should have four, and the fourth note only two, beams.

I do not wish the reservations expressed in this review to obscure the undeniable fact that this translation represents a major scholarly achievement, and that the book belongs in the libraries of all graduate schools.

Index

Academy of Ancient Music, 12

Academy of St.-Martin-in-the Fields, 12

Accent, 215, 218. *See also* Grace note; *Nachschlag; Port de voix; Vorschlag*

Acciaccatura, 218

Accompaniment, interpretation of, 19, 222–23

Adlung, Jacob: on the history of music, 4

Agogic accents, and *notes inégales,* 66, 69, 74, 75

Agricola, Johann Friedrich: and *galant* style, 20; and J. S. Bach's obituary, 196; on parallels in ornaments, 132; on synchronizing triplets with dotted notes, 45; theoretical writings applied to other composers, 20

Agricola, Martin: on sesquialtera, 40

Aldrich, Putnam: and J. S. Bach's keyboard ornaments, 125; and ornament tables, 127; and performance practice, 22

American Society of Ancient Instruments, 14

Amsterdam Baroque Orchestra, 13

Anglebert, Jean Henri d': Dolmetsch on, 20; keyboard works of, 27; ornamentation, 130, 131, 137; ornament tables, 129, 134

Appoggiatura, 127, 132–33, 139, 151, 202, 204, 244, 245; beat placement, 126–27, 130; improvisation of, 178; in Mozart, 150–51, 166, 184–91; in Vivaldi, 180–81, 183; length of, 139–43, 147–50, 180–81, 184–86, 244; symbolized, 140, 181; written out, 140, 166, 183. *See also Vorschlag*

Appoggiatura trill, 114, 127, 179–81, 183, 184–86, 188–90, 216

Aria, history of the term, 205

Arpeggio: and articulation, 107, 108–9; beat placement, 95, 107, 108–9, 114, 118, 127, 163–64; and harmony, 127; and neighbor note principle, 126; symbolized, 130, 164; written out, 107, 164

Articulation: and dotted rhythms, 74; and historical performance techniques, 29; idiomatic considerations, 80; in early music, 23–24, 26, 29, 170, 233; and *notes inégales,* 74; and ornamentation, 105–10, 126, 127–28, 136–37; and phrasing, 112–13; relative importance of, 26, 78, 79, 232–33

Aston Magna Foundtion, 15

Authenticity (in architecture), 8–9

Authenticity (in musical performance): 3–4, 5, 7–16, 25–26, 169–70; and historical vs. musical factors, 28–30; nature of, 17–24, 169–70, 229; and numbers of performers, 170, 230–31; and ornamentation, 123–25; and scholarship, 17–18, 19–24, 170–71, 229, 235–36, 243; and seating arrangements of performers, 239–31; and use of vibrato, 169–170, 171–73. *See also* Articulation; Early music; Expression; Historical instruments; Ornamentation; Performance practice; Phrasing; Rhythm; Tempo

Azaïs, Pierre-Hyacinthe: and slide notation, 138

Babitz, Sol: on *notes inégales,* 65, 68; on uneven notes and keyboard fingerings, 238

Bach, Anna Magdalena, notebook for, 205–6, 208n.6

Bach, C. P. E.: appoggiatura, 133, 139, 141, 245; and *galant* style, 20, 133 and J. S. Bach's obituary, 196; and ornamentation, 94–95, 98–99, 104, 132, 184; and parallels, 132; slide, 138; theoretical writings applied to other composers, 20–21, 94–95, 141, 151, 184–85; trill, 134; turn, 110

Bach, Johann Sebastian: and Agricola, 20; appoggiatura, 130–31, 132–33, 137, 202, 204; articulation, 23–24, 79, 80, 83n.4,